PROSODY
MANAGEMENT
of
COMMUNICATION
DISORDERS

Clinical Competence Series

Series Editor
Robert T. Wertz, Ph.D.

Prosody Management of Communication Disorders
Patricia M. Hargrove, Ph.D., and Nancy S. McGarr, Ph.D.

Clinical Manual of Laryngectomy and Head and Neck
Cancer Rehabilitation
Janina K. Casper, Ph.D., and Raymond H. Colton, Ph.D.

Sourcebook for Medical Speech Pathology
Lee Ann C. Golper, Ph.D., CCC-SLP

PROSODY
MANAGEMENT
of
COMMUNICATION
DISORDERS

Patricia M. Hargrove, Ph.D.
Mankato State University
Mankato, Minnesota

Nancy S. McGarr, Ph.D.
St. John's University
Jamaica, New York
and
Haskins Laboratories
New Haven, Connecticut

WHURR PUBLISHERS

Singular Publishing Group, Inc.
4284 41st Street
San Diego, California 92105-1197

© **1994 by Singular Publishing Group, Inc.**

Typeset in 10/12 Times by CFW Graphics
Printed in the United States of America by BookCrafters

This book is sold and distributed exclusively throughout the world outside North America by Whurr Publishers, Ltd., 19B Compton Terrace, London, N1 2UN England.

British Library Cataloguing in Publishing Data Available

Library of Congress Cataloging-in-Publication Data

Hargrove, Patricia M.
    Prosody management of communication disorders / Patricia M. Hargrove and Nancy S. McGarr.
       p.   cm. — (Clinical competence series)
    Includes bibliographical references and index.
    ISBN 1-879105-88-8
    1. Speech disorders. I. McGarr, Nancy S. II. Title.
III. Series
    [DNLM: 1. Speech Disorders — diagnosis. 2. Speech Disorders — therapy. WM 475 H279p 1993]
    RC429.H375   1993
    616.85′5 — dc20
    DNLM/DLC
    for Library of Congress   93-11904
                                                      CIP
                                                      Rev

CONTENTS

FOREWORD

com·pe·tence (kom′pə təns) n. The state or quality of being properly or well qualified; capable.

Clinicians crave competence. They pursue it through education and experience, through emulation and innovation. Some are more successful than others in attaining what they seek. This book, Prosody Management of Communication Disorders, is one of several selected for the Singular Clinical Competence Series. It is designed to move each of us further along the path that leads to clinical competence. It covers a disorder — disrupted prosody. If we master its content, we will increase what we know and improve what we do. Its purpose is to create competent clinicians who know the profession's current body of knowledge; have the ability to add continuously to that knowledge; and can apply it in their appraisal, diagnosis, and treatment. These clinicians will know that no principal or technique is true or useful until it has been tested; that tests do not diagnose, and treatment programs do not treat — clinicians do. Drs. Hargrove and McGarr have developed these traits. Their book conveys what makes them that way. Your attention to what they provide indicates your competence and your effort to improve it, because competent clinicians seek competence as much for what it demands as for what it promises.

Robert T. Wertz, Ph.D.
Series Editor

PREFACE

This book is written for undergraduate students, graduate students, and professionals who are interested in theoretical and clinical aspects of prosody. The foundations for this text are from many disciplines. There is an extensive literature of acoustic and physiological studies of prosody in normal speaking persons and, on first blush, there is a surprisingly large treatment literature. This includes the areas of articulation, phonology, fluency, neurogenics, developmental delay, voice disorders, child language impairment, hearing impairment, and music therapy.

This review of the prosodic literature across disciplines and disorders results in a global perspective concerning the nature of prosody and disturbances in prosody. Moreover, this literature reveals that the extent and depth of the extant treatment literature varies and is marked by parochialism. Thus, while studies of prosody treatment for some speakers with impaired communication skills (e.g., persons with hearing impairment) are extensive, there may be little or no cross-reference to the literature on prosodic disturbances in persons with other forms of communication impairment (e.g., individuals with neurological impairments). While one might correctly argue that these groups are distinguished, and indeed would be marked as different from each other, as well as from many other groups with communication disorders, we argue that there is great insight to be gained by looking cross-discipline and cross-disorder. Such a vantage encourages the adoption of pedagogical techniques that have proven helpful in facilitating correction of prosodic disturbances.

This same review of the literature also establishes, with rare exception, the lack of empirical data base regarding therapeutic effectiveness of treatment plans. This book recommends that we begin the process of evaluating treatment efficacy and attempts to motivate others to apply some measure of self-scrutiny.

A third observation that may be made when one views prosody from a global perspective is that clinicians often consider the prosodic features of pitch, duration, pause, and loudness to be part of the problem, as well as part of the solution. Prosodic features are combined to realize the prosodic components of tempo, intonation, stress, and rhythm which are used to send a linguistic message. One problem evidenced by many persons with communication disorders is difficulty or inability to execute consistently one or more prosodic features which ultimately interferes with the client's ability to send a linguistic message. Fortunately, these features co-exist and may even be redundant so that attenuation on one feature may not result in failure to realize the prosodic components, but which features or groups of features are critical? How does the clinician prioritize the order of treatment? What information can be obtained from studies of speech science or from different groups of speakers with disordered communication? How can the client use prosodic features compensatorily to convey the prosodic components? A major premise in this book is that these, and other important issues, are obscured by a failure to look at prosody from a global perspective.

Fourth, when one examines the treatment literature, a central theme emerges. There is a dichotomy between direct and indirect prosody treatment methods. On the one hand, direct treatment methods have as their purpose modification of prosody per se. On the other hand, indirect methods are ones in which prosody is used to change other aspects of communication such as overall intelligibility or fluency. In the literature, the number of indirect approaches far exceeds the direct approaches, suggesting that those working in this area have made certain a priori assumptions about the impact of prosody on other aspects of communication. Again, with little exception, there is a paucity of evidence to argue conclusively for either direct or indirect therapeutic approaches.

A view across disciplines and disorders may well motivate the reader to consider and test assumptions in his or her own area of expertise, to explore new paradigms adopted from other theoretical or treatment studies, or to question the validity of current practice. We submit that the Prosodic Teaching Model provides an excellent organizational framework for doing so. By gathering the theoretical and research literature and by focusing on teachability issues, the Prosodic Teaching Model attempts to acquaint the clinician with critical information concerning prosody and provides a framework to operationalize this information thereby increasing clinical effectiveness. The use of a model to organize treatment and to set priorities for treatment objectives is especially critical given the lack of empirical data regarding treatment effectiveness. The information which follows might best be considered to represent "current" practice rather than "proven" practice. We hope it will provoke thought and motivate research into this crucial aspect of communication.

ACKNOWLEDGMENTS

The impetus for this collaborative project was begun many years ago and is derived from personal and professional paths that intertwine. Like all interesting paths in life, it is filled with adventure near and far, by anticipation and anxiety, by exhalation and exhaustion, by belief and disbelief, but, most of all, by fun. Along the path to this particular collaborative effort, there have been many people who have assisted us and deserve our thanks.

Our editors from Singular Publishing Group encouraged us in our ideas and in bringing them to reality. Marie Linvill helped us identify a writing "voice" that was neither too clinical nor too theoretical, and thereby saved the collaboration. Her calm, clear support and guidance was appreciated as was R. Terry Wertz for his careful editing and humane (and humorous!) comments.

We thank too our colleagues and graduate students who provided us with innumerable measures of help through the evolution of this book. Dr. Richard Schiming (double cast as colleague and family member) provided important feedback, guidance, and editing by reading an early draft of the book. Graduate students at Mankato State University, Carol Larson and Chris Carr, and at St. John's University, Diane Elliot and Donna Coloprisco, carefully proofed drafts and tracked down references. Thanks are also extended to Bonnie Lund of the University of North Dakota for developing the sample procedures presented in Appendixes A and B. Judy Kuster, Dr. Bob Brooks, and Dr. Cindy Busch of Mankato State University, who will be happy to have their books and journals back, are thanked for their patience (and for not calling campus security when they noticed missing materials). The preparation of this manuscript was graciously supported in part by NIH Grant DC-00121 to Haskins Laboratories to the second author. Also, thanks are extended to the McDonald's restaurant on Highway

169 in Mankato. McDonald's provided a quiet haven for one of us to proof drafts of the book during "off" hours.

We thank especially our families. Richard Shiming and John McGarr combined their talents in academic and corporate economics and graciously provided support for this project even though we have never fit their economic forecasts. Our children, Rachel and Lawrence Schiming, and Katherine and Eileen McGarr, have been tolerant and amused by our work. They have come to realize that one must carefully choose schoolmates because one can never predict good future collaboration. Finally, we thank the "Blue and the Gold" which brought us together in our first joint project decades ago.

CHAPTER

1

Orientation

I. DEFINING PROSODY

A. Definition of Prosody

Prosody represents the linguistic use of the vocal aspects of speech
without consideration of the segmental aspects (speech sounds or
phonemes). The rules of prosody are systematic, bound by con-
ventions, and convey important information to listeners. Other
terms used to represent prosody include nonsegmental phonology or suprasegmental aspects of speech. However, Couper-
Kuhlen (1986) suggests that these labels have somewhat different meanings.

This problem with terminology is not limited to the definition of
words such as "prosody," "nonsegmental phonology," and "suprasegmentals." Various authors give different labels to the same,
or similar, prosodic concepts or assign similar labels to different
concepts. Additionally, various prosodic models have different
subdivisions. The different terminologies and different subdivisions, although important for model building and for the ad-
vancement of knowledge, can confuse clinicians charged with de-

veloping intervention programs. Readers who choose to explore the literature are cautioned that the terminology varies and, in applied work, may even be misused.

To understand prosody fully, one needs a historical and theoretical perspective on prosodic models and terminology which is beyond the scope of this book. Rather, the following sections contain definitions and descriptions of prosody and its subdivisions without specific reference to historical or current linguistic models.

B. The Complexity of Prosody

Prosody is complex (Abe, 1980; Crystal, 1969, 1975, 1978); several factors contribute to this notion.

1. **Prosody is multifaceted** and is not a single homogeneous entity (Crystal, 1981). Many features (pitch, loudness, duration, pause) and components (intonation, tempo, stress, rhythm) comprise prosody. Using a single aspect of prosody to represent all of prosody is analogous to using a door handle to represent a car — it may be an integral part of the car but it is not the whole car. Additionally, prosody is not a simple, additive combination of these features or components. Rather, it is the product of the interaction among the different features and components, exceeding the sum of its parts (Crystal, 1975).

   CLINICAL NOTES: (1) Understanding that prosody is multifaceted is critical for clinicians working on prosody with persons who have communication disorders. The different aspects of prosody interact, and this interaction plays a part in the difficulty speakers experience when attempting to alter a single aspect of prosody. (2) Clinicians need to achieve a balance between oversimplifying and over specifying prosody. Oversimplification results in distorted information, and in over specification one risks being swamped in a sea of uninterpretable data.

2. **There is no one-to-one correspondence between prosody and specific linguistic meaning.** Many linguists (e.g., Couper-Kuhlen, 1986; Crystal, 1978, 1980, 1981; Wode, 1980) note that the interaction between prosody and other dimensions of communication (e.g., linguistic structure, kinetics, gestures, facial movements) precludes the establishment of a

direct correspondence between prosody and specific linguistic meaning.

The influence of context on prosody illustrates the difficulties in directly associating prosodic patterns with specific linguistic meaning (Allen & Hawkins, 1980; Crystal, 1980). Hadding-Koch and Studdert-Kennedy (1964), for example, report that listeners interpret identical prosodic patterns differently depending on verbal and situational environments. In selected contexts, a rising pitch direction (i.e., a rise in the pitch level) at the end of a phrase may be identified as a tag question (to verify meaning), as a request for information, or as conveying irony.

CLINICAL NOTE: Subtle differences in the use and interpretation of prosody are difficult to assess and to treat in clinical populations because prosodic behaviors have shifting, not static, meanings.

3. **Prosody can be redundant.** The information conveyed by prosody may be present in other parts of the communicative act. Characteristics of prosodic redundancy involve productive and linguistic components.

   a. **Productive redundancy** results when prosodic elements combine to produce a single meaning. For example, several different prosodic features and/or components typically combine to signal utterance boundaries. Speakers typically pause and lower pitch at the end of utterances as well as "reset" pitch level at the beginning of new utterances. Productive redundancy complicates research attempts to link prosody and specific linguistic meaning because interpretation can be accurate, even if all the prosodic elements typically used are not present (Wingfield, Lombardi, & Sokol, 1984).

   CLINICAL NOTE: To be understood, clients need not use all the prosodic characteristics typical for a specific meaning. For example, when pausing is minimal (as in rapid speech), productive redundancy permits listeners to perceive the ends of utterances because of the cues of pitch direction (see Chapter 4) and reset onset pitch level (see Chapter 8).

   b. **Linguistic redundancy** results when a single meaning is expressed through the use of several different aspects of language such as syntax, morphology, semantics, pragmatics, and/or prosody (Couper-Kuhlen, 1986; Lieberman, 1967). For example, expression of anger may be conveyed not only prosodically but also semantically by word selection.

CLINICAL NOTE: Because it is not necessary that all parameters associated with a particular meaning be present for interpretation, the loss or addition of a given prosodic skill may not co-occur with communication failure or even with improvement in communication skills. Thus, both productive and linguistic forms of redundancy contribute to prosody's complexity, and both impede or impel the study of prosody and treatment of prosodic disorders.

4. **There is not a one-to-one correspondence between perceptual judgments of prosody and instrumental measures of prosody** (Crystal, 1981). Instrumental measures include acoustic parameters such as fundamental frequency (F_0), amplitude, vocalization time, intervals between vocalized items, and articulatory parameters such as subglottal air pressure. Each of these measures may reflect one aspect of prosody, but as individual measures they may not directly reflect listeners' perception of prosody. In connected speech, one may "hear" a rising pitch direction but "see" it on an instrument, such as a Visipitch, as a *decrease* in frequency, an *increase* in amplitude, and an *increase* in duration (Rubin-Spitz & McGarr, 1990).

CLINICAL NOTE: The lack of a direct correspondence between listener judgment and a single instrumental measure warrants caution among users of sensory aids.

II. WHY TREAT PROSODY?

The ratonale for treating prosody is two-fold: (a) prosody serves several communicative roles and (b) prosody facilitates or constrains other dimensions of communication.

A. The Communicative Roles of Prosody

Although a prime reason for treating prosody is that it serves communicative roles, it is important to realize that this view is not without criticism. Despite speakers' ability to convey meaning prosodically, they also use nonprosodic methods. Thus prosody plays a part in, but may not be necessary for, communication. Neverthe-less, knowledge of the roles prosody *can* play helps to define and to highlight its significance.

1. Pragmatic roles

a. Prosody allows the speaker to **focus attention** on the important information in the utterance, thereby freeing the listener from the task of continuously monitoring ongoing speech (Allen & Hawkins, 1980; Martin, 1972).

b. Speakers **differentiate given or old information from new information** (Couper-Kuhlen, 1986) with prosody. Contrast:

- *Bill* was born in June⌐

- Bill was born in *June*⌐

In the first example, the speaker believes that the commonly known information is that June is the birth month of someone, but the listener does not know who was born in June. In the second example, the speaker thinks that the listener does not know Bill's birth month. Many persons with communicative impairments have difficulty in producing prosody to effect this differentiation.

c. Prosody can **signal turns in discourse** (Silliman & Leslie, 1983). Speakers employ distinctive prosodic patterns such as pausing and/or producing a falling pitch level at the end of an utterance (this is referred to as a terminal contour). These cues are so clear that listeners rarely mistake within-turn hesitations for the end of a speaking turn.

d. **Speech acts** can be differentiated prosodically. For example, during the early stages of language learning, children produce questions by altering the terminal contour of the utterance. The first example below is typically categorized as a statement because of its fall in pitch. The second example, with a rise in pitch, is usually categorized as a question.

- cat (\ )⌐

- cat (/)⌐

Likewise, for more advanced speakers, asking and telling speech acts are represented prosodically (Crystal, 1981):

- It's a nice dress (\ )| isn't (/) it|
- It's a nice dress (\ )| isn't (\ ) it|

The first of the two utterances is an "asking" tag question in which the speaker asks the listener to verify information with a "yes" or a "no." The second example is a "telling" tag question; the speaker expects the listener to comply with the statement. Other prosodically signaled speech acts include vocatives (Abe, 1980), suggestions (Couper-Kuhlen, 1986), and indirect speech acts (Crystal, 1981). Many persons with communication impairments such as hearing impairment, voice disorders, or neurological impairment have difficulty producing these changes in pitch.

e. Couper-Kuhlen (1986) describes prosody's **textural role** in which speakers use prosody to link together sentences. For example, speakers apparently use selected prosodic patterns to add information to a topic and other prosodic patterns to initiate new topics. This provides listeners with cues as to whether consecutive sentences are topically related or independent. Speakers also may use specific prosodic patterns to increase the cohesiveness of sustained monologues.

2. **Syntactic roles**

a. Prosody **marks different syntactic structures** (Crystal, 1981) such as the difference between restrictive and nonrestrictive clauses as in

- My sister| who lives in Oregon | has enrolled in school |
- My sister who lives in Oregon | has enrolled in school |

The first utterance contains a nonrestrictive clause indicating the speaker has one sister. The second is a restrictive clause that indicates the speaker has more than one sister. Prosody also can be used to mark coordination, ellipsis, direct/indirect objects, and positive and negative contrasts (Couper-Kuhlen, 1986; Crystal, 1981).

b. The underlying syntactic organization of utterances can be cued by prosody. Without prosody, it is difficult to identify the boundaries of the syntactic units within an utterance. As Lieberman (1980) notes, the simple task of trying to read a passage with the punctuation moved over one place highlights our dependence on prosody. For example, attempt to read aloud the following passage from a previous paragraph in this chapter:

> This problem with terminology is not limited to the definition of words such as, "prosody," "nonsegmental, phonology" and. "Suprasegmentals" various authors give different labels to the, same or, similar concepts or may assign similar labels to different. Concepts, additionally various prosodic models have different. Subdivisions the different terminologies and the different, subdivisions although important for model building and for the advancement of, knowledge can confuse clinicians charged with developing intervention. Programs readers who choose to explore the literature are cautioned that the terminology varies, and in applied, work may even be. Misused.

3. **Lexical roles.** Although some languages extensively use prosody to distinguish between different words, English makes only limited lexical use of prosody. Nevertheless, there are instances when only prosodic cues differentiate sets of words or phrases (Fry, 1955). For example:

- *ob*ject versus ob*ject*

- *di*gest versus di*gest*

Many speakers with communicative impairments (e.g., individuals with hearing impairment) have great difficulty producing these lexical changes.

4. **Intelligibility roles.** The impact of modifications in prosody on speech intelligibility has been demonstrated by studies that indicate that (a) the degrading of prosodic information negatively influences performance on comprehension tasks; (b) segmentally degraded speech remains quite intelligible as long as the prosodic information is retained; and (c) as segmental information becomes progressively degraded, prosody becomes increasingly important (Allen & Hawkins, 1980; Lieberman, 1967; Wingfield et al., 1984). Moreover, apparently minor errors in prosody may impede intelligibility because

the speech is rendered unnatural and may attract undue attention to the prosodic patterns, thereby reducing attention to content.

CLINICAL NOTE: The interrelationships between prosody and intelligibility may be particularly important to speakers with speech-language disorders because communicatively impaired speech may be considered analogous to degraded speech. For an individual with disordered speech, the effect of prosodic errors on intelligibility may be additive or even multiplicative.

5. **Language acquisition role.** Prosody plays a role in child directed speech (CDS) as reflected in the following summaries.

   a. The following are **typical characteristics of pitch or intonation** that English-speaking, white, middle-class adults use when speaking to children: falsetto voice (Blount & Padgug, 1977), high pitch on single words (Blount & Padgug, 1977), increased mean or fundamental frequency (F_0) (Jacobson, Boersma, Fields, & Olson, 1983; Remick, 1976; Shute & Wheldall, 1989), greater F_0 variability (Fernald et al., 1989; Garnica, 1977; Jacobson et al., 1983), more rising terminal contours (Garnica, 1977; Remick, 1976; Stern, Spieker, Barnett, & MacKain, 1983), exaggerated overall intonation (Blount & Padgug, 1977), and less pitch compatibility between the end of one utterance and the initiation of the next utterance (Stern et al., 1983).

   b. Research also indicates that modifications in several aspects of **tempo, duration, and pausing** occur during CDS. These include increased overall duration of utterances (Stern et al., 1983), less overall talking time (Remick, 1976), fewer words per minute (Ringler, 1978; Sacks, Brown, & Salerno, 1976), increased duration of vowels (Blount & Padgug, 1977), increased duration of vowels in the final position of clauses relative to vowels in the medial positions of clauses (Bernstein Ratner, 1985), increased duration of selected key words (Garnica, 1977), and increased likelihood of pauses between utterances (Broen, 1972; Remick, 1976).

   c. There is little empirical information about how adults use **loudness, rhythm, and stress** during CDS. For example,

Blount and Padgug (1977) report that parents tend to reduce loudness during CDS, but we know little more. Moreover, although the probability of more than one primary stress marker in certain directives increases (Garnica, 1977) and stresses occur with increased respiratory regularity (Stern et al., 1983), little other documentation of rhythm and stress changes in CDS exists.

   d. Despite the widespread use of prosody in CDS, its **function** is not clear. Prosody is described as an "attention getter" and also as a teaching device (Clark & Clark, 1977; Colmar & Wheldall, 1985). Other claims suggest the prosody serves as a facilitator by promoting the segmentation of units (Peters, 1983), permitting the mapping of meaning (Crystal, 1978), anchoring perception (Klein, 1981), encouraging the selective imitation of various aspects of language (du Preez, 1974), and/or inducing socialization (Furrow, 1984).

6. **Attitudinal role.** Although the role of prosody in the expression of attitude may not be linguistic, it is most assuredly communicative. Prosody is used to express personal emotions such as joy, sadness, sorrow, anger, concern, surprise, and puzzlement (Abe, 1980; Baltaxe, 1981; Crystal, 1980; du Preez, 1974; Lieberman, 1967).

7. **Indexical role.** Despite individual variation evident in speakers' use of prosody, listeners can identify patterns common to various groups. Couper-Kuhlen (1986) labels this as the indexical role of prosody which occurs when listeners categorize speakers' gender, age, racial or ethnic background, geographical region, intellectual capacity, professional status, social class, and/or personality on the basis of prosody (Abe, 1980; Crystal, 1975). The indexical role permits categorizations relative to perceived social status which, in turn, may influence interactions (Warren & McCloskey, 1993).

8. **Psychometric role.** Performance on recall, imitation, comprehension, and discrimination tasks is influenced by prosodic modification (Berry & Erickson, 1973; Blasdell & Jensen, 1970; Bonvillian, Raeburn, & Horan, 1979; Crystal, 1981; du Preez, 1974; Goodglass, Fodor, & Schulhoff, 1967; Stark, Poppen, & May, 1967). For example, Stark and colleagues

report that alteration of the stress patterns in strings of single syllable words influences the ability of language-impaired children to imitate strings of words. Additionally, the rate of speech influences performance on receptive tasks (Berry & Erickson, 1973) and children imitate sentences consisting of normal intonation patterns better than flat intonation patterns (Bonvillian et al., 1979).

B. Facilitation/Constraints

Some literature suggests prosody plays facilitating and constraining roles in communication. Listeners and speakers apparently have a bias to produce or perceive certain prosodic patterns. Speech that conforms to these patterns is easier to produce and/or perceive than speech that violates these biases. A facilitating effect occurs because the listener or speaker requires less effort to monitor or produce utterances that conform to biases and can devote more attention to the nonprosodic dimensions of communication (Allen, 1975). The converse also affects communication; prosodic patterns that violate biases impede or constrain communication. The facilitating or constraining effects of prosody can be seen in (1) segmental phonology and (2) syntax/morphology.

CLINICAL NOTE: When prosody plays a constraining role, clinicians may use prosody to increase task complexity by employing prosodic features or components that make the task more difficult. For example, a clinician may present a targeted speech sound in unstressed syllables of multisyllabic words (e.g., production of /m/ in "hippopotamus") once a client regularly produces the speech sound in stressed syllables (e.g., /m/ in "more" or "monkey"). Conversely, clinicians may use facilitating prosodic patterns to elicit target behaviors. Thus, a clinician may introduce singing or chanting (with its slowed rate, limited range of pitches, and predictable rhythms) to induce fluency in a stutterer.

1. **Segmental phonology.** The speech/language pathology literature suggests that prosody has an effect on segmental phonology and vice versa. For example, certain prosodic patterns and speech sound errors tend to co-occur (Chiat, 1989; Kelin, 1981; Klein & Spector, 1985). Moreover, Kollman (1991) notes that a subject's intelligibility and speech sound accuracy improved following prosody therapy. Additionally, Grube, Spiegel, Buchhop, and Lloyd (1986) and Edwards, Strattman,

Cuda, and Anderson (1990) report that prosody therapy may have more benefits than phonological/articulation therapy for children with phonological impairment and for accent reduction.

Moskowitz (1973) indirectly describes a facilitating effect of prosody in a 2-year-old child who had been labeled as having outstanding (segmental) phonological skills. Analysis revealed that the child functioned within normal limits with respect to segmental phonology but that she had an advanced prosodic system. Moskowitz suggests that prosody rather than segmental phonology was the source of the child's perceived exceptionality.

Prosody also can constrain or interfere with segmental phonology. Allen and Hawkins (1978, 1979) report that children have problems producing unstressed syllables and that when they do begin to produce their first unstressed syllables, the unstressed syllables are not likely to occur in the initial position of words. Thus young children are likely to say /*da da*/ or /*da* da/ but rarely do they say /da *da*/. Likewise "banana" is produced as /*na* na/ or /*ba* na/ but not /ba *na*/. This apparent bias against unstressed syllables can have a negative effect on the production of segmental phonology. Klein (1981, p. 541), for example, notes that when children attempt to produce multisyllabic words, sounds from the stressed syllables are more likely to be retained than sounds from unstressed syllables. For example:

ADULT PATTERN	pi*no*cchio
CHILD PRODUCTION	/*no*go/
ADULT PATTERN	*car*rot
CHILD PRODUCTION	/*kæ*/
ADULT PATTERN	spa*ghe*tti
CHILD PRODUCTION	/*ge^l*/

2. **Syntax/Morphology.** There are some hints that prosody facilitates or constrains syntax and/or morphology; however, confirmation of such effects awaits experimental verification.

The constraining effects of prosody may be present in the acquisition of articles. Articles, which are usually unstressed, emerge earlier in object noun phrase positions than they do in subject noun phrase positions. For example, at Brown's Stage II (Brown, 1973), children tend to produce "lookie at the box" and "baby crying" but not "the baby crying." This pattern corresponds with a reported rhythmic constraint that biases against initiating utterances with unstressed syllables (Allen & Hawkins, 1980). The emergence of suffixes before prefixes also supports such a prosodic constraint (Allen & Hawkins, 1978, 1979) because prefixes require beginning a word with an unstressed syllable.

Prosody also may have an impact on syntactic or morphological structures of individuals with communicative impairments. Oliva and Duchan (1976) note that their subjects produced function words in sentences when using a certain rhythmic pattern. (See Chapter 11 for a more complete description of this case.) Likewise, Goodglass, Fodor, and Schulhoff (1967) report that subjects with aphasia are more likely to produce function words in the initial position of sentences when using a certain rhythmic pattern.

C. Summary

Prosody is an integral part of communication. Thus, speech-language pathologists must evaluate and treat prosody in individuals with communication impairments despite prosody's complexity and the difficulty inherent in its analysis. Prosody's role in communication, its facilitating effects, and its constraining effects continue to warrant research.

CHAPTER

2

Treating Prosody: An Overview

I. A MODEL FOR TEACHING PROSODY

A. Background Information

This book espouses an applied model of prosody and a discrete approach to structuring information about prosody. Although the Prosodic Teaching Model is referred to frequently, we caution that it has not been empirically tested.

1. The Prosodic Teaching Model is an **applied model** derived from the theoretical literature, from existing treatment strategies or techniques, and from clinical experience. Integrating these three sources provides information that may be new to some clinicians.

2. In the Prosodic Teaching Model, the **information is discretely organized**. Aspects of speech behavior included in the model, when viewed together, provide a valid and under-

standable representation of prosody. By adopting a discrete approach, prosody, which is a complex and multifaceted entity, is subdivided into simple and conceptually manageable units called prosodic features and prosodic components.

In many ways, a discrete approach to describing prosody is comparable to describing art using labels such as "form, shading, line, color," and so on. The discrete approach is convenient and provides a basis for discussion, but there are pitfalls, because the very act of division distorts the concept under discussion (i.e., art or prosody). For example, dividing prosody into categories fails to capture its holistic essence, just as by referring to shape, form, line or color fails to capture the essence of a work of art. Nevertheless, a discrete approach is a necessary convenience for our current level of knowledge about prosody. By studying the various prosodic categories, we hope learners will appreciate prosody holistically.

B. Prosodic Teaching Model

The Prosodic Teaching Model consists of two major divisions — prosodic features and prosodic components (Figure 2-1). For the prosodic features there are four subdivisions—pitch, loudness, duration, and pause. For the prosodic components there are also four subdivisions — tempo, intonation, stress, and rhythm. Each prosodic feature or prosodic component is further divided into categories which are presented in Chapters 4 through 11.

1. **Prosodic features** (pitch, loudness, duration, and pause) are building blocks of the prosodic components. Prosodic features can be described in terms of their productive and perceptual characteristics. These features usually are excluded from linguistically based models of prosody but are included in the Prosodic Teaching Model because speakers use prosodic features to produce and to perceive prosodic components. Thus, the ability to perceive and produce prosodic features may be viewed as a prerequisite to perceiving and producing prosodic components. An example of the relationship between prosodic features and prosodic components can be seen in the production of intonation—intonation (a prosodic component) is produced, in part, by manipulating pitch (a prosodic feature).

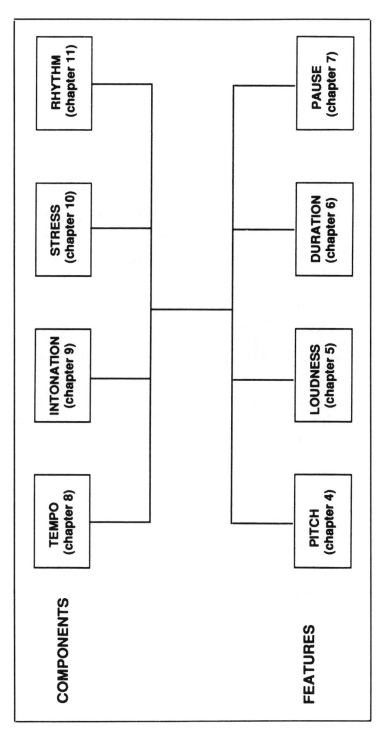

Figure 2-1. A representation of the prosodic features and the prosodic components. (The information within the parentheses directs readers to the chapter which details the specific feature or component.)

CLINICAL NOTE: Although control of prosodic features may seem a rather simple task for normal speakers, one cannot assume that it is easy for speakers who are communicatively impaired. Clinicians must ensure that their clients can produce prosodic features acceptably before work begins on prosodic components.

The four prosodic features are described below to facilitate understanding of the Prosodic Teaching Model. A discussion of each of the prosodic features and its subdivisions (categories) is presented in detail in Chapters 4 through 7.

  a. **Pitch** is the auditory perception primarily associated with the acoustic dimension of frequency.

  b. **Loudness** is the auditory perception primarily associated with the acoustic dimension of amplitude or intensity.

  c. **Duration** is the auditory perception primarily associated with the acoustic dimension of time.

  d. **Pause** is the auditory perception primarily associated with silence.

2. **Prosodic components** are the elements that constitute prosody. They are described briefly below and are delineated more fully in Chapters 8 through 11.

  a. **Tempo** involves use of timing elements, such as rate of speech, to impart meaning.

  b. **Intonation** is the communicative use of pitch.

  c. **Stress** is the use of prominence for purposes of communication.

  d. **Rhythm** is concerned with the use of sequences of stresses and the flow of speech during communication.

II. EXISTING TREATMENT LITERATURE ON PROSODY

A. The Nature of the Existing Literature

1. Range of prosodic treatment approaches.

    a. Prosodic treatment suggestions are available for individuals who display a variety of **disorders** including aphasia, apraxia of speech, stuttering, phonological or articulation impairment, specific language impairment, and abnormal voice. Prosodic treatment ideas also are available for those wishing to reduce foreign accents and those with hearing impairment, learning disability, or developmental delay. In addition, treatment suggestions exist for normal speakers wishing to improve their overall communication skills (speech improvement).

    b. Treatment approaches span the range of **prosodic features and prosodic components**.

    c. Individuals from a variety of **professions** (e.g., learning disability, music therapy, speech-language pathology, English as a second language, special education, and hearing impairment) have designed approaches to treat prosody.

2. A review of the prosodic treatment literature reveals that there are two distinct **purposes for working with prosody**.

    a. Direct purposes are used when the aim of treatment is to improve a specific aspect of prosody. These approaches have improved prosody as the primary treatment objective.

    b. Indirect purposes are employed when aspects of prosody serve as intermediate objectives, as facilitators, or as constrainers. That is, prosody is used to improve other dimensions of communication such as intelligibility, semantics, or fluency.

3. The **distribution of direct and indirect treatment purposes** is decidedly in favor of indirect purposes. Clinicians are more likely to use prosody as a means of achieving some other communicative goal than to work directly on prosody itself. Clinicians interested in treating prosody directly should not be discouraged because many of the indirect approaches have potential applications for direct treatment. Moreover, the dichotomy between direct and indirect treatment may be somewhat artificial. For example, one reason for classifying treatment approaches as indirect is that the terminal behavior is not prosody per se. However, in some cases, approaches are listed as indirect when the means of improvement is one as-

pect of prosody and the target of therapy is another aspect of prosody (e.g., working on duration to improve phrasal stress). Indirect approaches such as these often are structurally similar to direct treatment approaches and have potential to be used in direct treatment. Accordingly, clinicians interested in modifying prosody directly will want to become familiar with both the direct and indirect treatment sections in Chapters 4 through 11 to gain the maximum amount of information.

B. Criticisms

1. **Parochialism.** The number and range of published prosodic treatment programs is quite extensive. This surprises many clinicians. Apparently, there is a lack of awareness of available resources rather than a lack of resources. This appears to result from parochialism among and within the professions treating prosody. For example, speech-language pathologists rarely refer to the work of music therapists, and teachers of English as a second language rarely refer to the work of speech-language pathologists. Moreover, within a diverse profession such as speech-language pathology, there is little reference to work across disorder categories. Clinicians working with individuals who stutter do not refer to the voice disorders literature, those who work with children with specific language impairment do not refer to the literature on hearing impairment, those who work with people with voice problems do not refer to the articulation disorders literature, and so forth.

   Because of this parochialism, the richness and the breadth of the prosodic treatment literature is underestimated. More importantly, parochialism results in restricted notions about what should be treated, how it should be treated, and what has proved effective. This book provides references from a cross section of professions, disorder groups, and etiologies in an effort to remedy this problem.

2. **Treatment effectiveness** usually is unsubstantiated. The lack of empirical support for prosody treatment approaches cannot be overstated. Presentation of effectiveness data, even in the form of case history information, is the exception rather than the rule. The result of this dearth of verification is that clinicians have no way of determining if treatment ap-

proaches are effective or appropriate for their clients. There is an obvious need for extensive research in this area.

Not only is the lack of verification evident for claims of overall effectiveness, but also it is evident for assumptions about indirect treatment programs. Authors assume that change in a selected aspect of prosody will change other dimensions of communication without ascertaining if these assumptions are correct. For example, an author may recommend the modification of rate to improve intelligibility without determining if rate changes result in changes in intelligibility *for the specific client.*

3. Treatment approaches tend to be **model-free**. The summaries which are presented in Chapters 4 throughly 11 reveal that treatment approaches tend to be problem oriented rather than model driven. Clinicians usually select goals by isolating something that is "different" about their clients' prosody without reference to prosody as a whole. This can fragment prosodic treatment and result in treating the proverbial "trees" without attending to the "forest."

The use of a model, such as the Prosodic Teaching Model, can provide guidance in identifying which aspects of prosody should be treated and in ordering treatment objectives. The use of a model to organize treatment and to set priorities for treatment objectives is especially critical given the lack of empirical data regarding therapy effectiveness.

III. USING THIS BOOK

A. Organization of the Book

Chapters 1 through 3 provide background information about prosody and the use of this book. Chapter 1 briefly describes prosody and why it should be considered in treatment. Chapter 2 details the extant treatment literature and the organization of this book, and Chapter 3 describes the assessment of prosody for treatment purposes. Chapters 4 through 11 are the "treatment chapters." Chapters 4 through 7 are concerned with the prosodic features: pitch, loudness, duration, and pause, respectively. Chapters 8 through 11 convey information about the prosodic components of tempo, intonation, stress, and rhythm. Each treatment chapter is organized into two subdivisions — background information and treatment information.

1. **Background information** is provided in each treatment chapter to assist clinicians in understanding the Prosodic Teaching Model and to facilitate understanding of terms used in the chapters. The following describes typical background information found in Chapters 4 through 11.

    a. The **normal use** of the prosodic feature or component is explored by providing a perceptual description of the feature or component, delineating the categories (subdivisions) which make up the feature or component, providing normative information, and/or describing the role that the prosodic feature or component plays in communication.

    b. Descriptions of the acoustic correlates of the various prosodic features and prosodic components provide explanations about the **perception** of prosody.

    c. The articulatory correlates of the different prosodic features and prosodic components are provided to explain the **production** of prosody.

2. The **treatment sections** are organized to facilitate access to clinical information. A typical treatment section contains:

    a. A division of treatment approaches grouped on the basis of treatment purpose and focus (**purpose/focus combinations** or PFCs).
       (1) The **purpose** of a treatment approach may be either direct or indirect.
          (a) The purpose of **direct treatment** approaches is to change a particular aspect of the client's prosody.
          (b) The purpose of **indirect treatment** approaches is to use one or several aspects of prosody to change another aspect of prosody or to change another dimension of speech and/or language.
       (2) Treatment approaches also have a **focus** which is derived from the categories (i.e., subdivisions) of the prosodic feature or prosodic component in question.

For example, there are three focuses for the direct treatment of stress: lexical stress, phrasal stress, and emphatic stress. Identical focuses are provided for indirect treatments of stress.

(3) After the treatment approaches are grouped according to purpose and focus, several **intervention characteristics** of the PFC (purpose/focus combination) in question are described.

(a) **Population** represents the disorder group(s) or the etiological group(s) for which the treatment approach is designed.

(b) **Terminal objectives** are the exit behaviors or the behaviors desired at the end of treatment; they are relevant only for indirect treatment approaches. (Prosodic exit behaviors are presented as "target behaviors.")

(c) **Target behaviors** are the prosodic behaviors that are being modified or used during treatment.

(d) The **hierarchy** of procedures is the ordering of the treatment steps. There are six, nonexclusive hierarchies.

- **Combination** hierarchies use two or more of the hierarchies listed below to order treatment steps.

- **Disorder** hierarchies involve monitoring clients' progress throughout the treatment process, evaluating changes that occur (presumably as the result of treatment), and altering treatment procedures and objectives in response to the changes in the clients' speech.

- **Empirical** hierarchies are developed by verifying that the ordering of the treatment steps does, in fact, progress from easy to difficult or by instructing clinicians to determine which tasks are relatively easy and/or difficult for *the specific client.*

- **Horizontal** hierarchies consist of the simultaneous treatment of two or more objectives.

- **Linear** hierarchies consist of only a single step or objective without increases or decreases in task complexity.

- **Logical** hierarchies are the most commonly used ordering of treatment procedures. These arrange treatment steps in an *assumed* order of difficulty.

(e) **Productive characteristics** are the means by which speakers realize or produce the targeted prosodic feature and/or prosodic component.

(f) **Techniques** are methods used to achieve objectives. Throughout the treatment sections, the techniques are highlighted in bold italics. All techniques are defined in the Glossary.

b. A **sample treatment program** is presented to provide a general overview of treatment. The sample treatment programs are presented to discourage a fragmented approach to therapy which could result from strict adherence to the discrete organizational system in this book.

B. Guidelines for Clinical Decision Making

These guidelines are provided to assist clinicians in developing the content and form of therapy.

1. The clinician **determines the purpose** for working with prosody. That is, the clinician determines whether the reason for therapy is to improve prosody (direct purpose) or to use prosody to improve another aspect of communication (indirect purpose).

2. The clinician **determines the focus** of treatment. If the purpose of treatment is indirect, the clinician identifies which prosodic feature or prosodic component has an impact on the targeted (nonprosodic) terminal behavior. If the purpose of treatment is direct, the clinician identifies the prosodic feature or prosodic component in need of change and then determines the specific category to be treated. When the focus of treatment is a category (i.e., subdivision) of one of the four prosodic components, the clinician also determines if the client has sufficient control of prosodic features to produce the component acceptably.

3. The clinician becomes familiar with the **sample programs** and the text pertaining to the selected PFC (purpose/focus

combinations involve identifying the purpose from Guideline #1 and the focus from Guideline #2). This information can be found by referring to the appropriate cross-reference chart provided in the Treatment Index. Because of limitations in the existing literature, attention should not be restricted to the information for a specific PCF. Rather, clinicians are encouraged to be familiar with the treatment summaries from related PFCs.

4. The clinician identifies specific **treatment objectives** for the targeted PFC. This can be accomplished by referring to the tables and text that are relevant to the purpose and focus of therapy which can be found in the "Terminal Behavior" and "Target Behavior" sections of the Treatment Index. Again, it is recommended that clinicians become familiar not only with information that is pertinent to their targeted PFC but also with related PFCs.

5. The clinician identifies potential **treatment techniques**. The location of treatment techniques used for each PFC can be ascertained by referring to the Treatment Index. Clinicians should be familiar with the treatment techniques for their targeted PFC and related PFCs to maximize information.

6. For additional treatment ideas, the clinician identifies treatment approaches used for **clients with similar disorders** by referring to 'Population' sections of the Treatment Index.

7. When there are a variety of ways that a client may produce a target behavior, the clinician **identifies the means by which the client will produce that targeted behavior**. If the client has control of the typical productive mechanisms for a given prosodic behavior, it is recommended that the prosodic feature or component be produced in that manner. However, if a client's productive control is lacking, the clinician has two options: (a) teach the client to produce the correct productive behavior(s) or (b) encourage the client to use an alternate strategy. This decision should be tempered by consideration of time/effort constraints and naturalness/normalcy issues.

C. Guidelines for Treatment Ordering Decisions

The current level of knowledge prevents providing specific directions about which prosodic features or prosodic components should be treated first. Nevertheless, the Prosodic Teaching Model provides some guidelines for selecting initial features or components for treatment. These guidelines have not been verified empirically.

1. Because prosodic features are the cornerstones of prosodic components, some **control of prosodic features is necessary before initiating treatment on prosodic components**. Clients, however, need not use an "idealized" pattern of prosodic features to produce a particular meaning. If control of "typical" prosodic feature(s) is beyond their capabilities, clients may use only one of the several prosodic features usually used to produce a particular prosodic component, or they may develop compensatory patterns to produce the targeted prosodic component.

2. Prosodic categories that have a positive impact on **intelligibility** have the highest priority for treatment. Because speakers' prosody varies and because of the current level of knowledge about prosody, the influence of the different prosodic categories on intelligibility must be determined on an individual basis. Thus, for one subject, phrasing (part of tempo) may be the first focus of treatment, and for another subject, stress sequencing (part of rhythm) may be the first treatment focus.

3. Prosodic categories that have **high communicative value** also have high priority for treatment. Clinicians need to include their clients' views on the utility of treatment targets as well as considering their own academic and clinical experience when determining which behaviors have high communicative value.

4. If the client produces a certain **prosodic category correctly approximately 50%** of the time, this category may be a candidate for early treatment focus, because it has potential for providing the client with a successful treatment experience and a sense of accomplishment.

5. Clinicians should pay attention to the prosodic and non-prosodic **changes that co-occur** with changes in the targeted aspect of prosody. Targets that result in positive co-occuring changes should have priority over those that have negative or no co-occuring changes.

6. Changes that increase speech naturalness should have priority over those that disrupt it unless the purpose of treating

prosody is to improve another aspect of communication, for example, intelligibility.

7. When using prosody indirectly (as an intermediate objective, as a facilitator, or as a constrainer), clinicians should give priority to aspects of prosody that **cause change** in the targeted dimension of communication before treatment begins. For example, when treating dysfluencies, clinicians should determine if, for the *specific client,* changes in rate, rhythm, and/or loudness affect the frequency of dysfluencies. Prosodic features or prosodic components that result in change should be given preference over those that do not.

8. Extensive attention should not be devoted to **improving prosody comprehension and discrimination**. Except for incidental steps in various treatment approaches, this book devotes little attention to the comprehension or discrimination of prosody. Although some may argue with this approach (e.g., Dworkin, 1991), comprehension and discrimination are viewed as separate from and not necessarily prerequisites for the production of prosody. Many normal speakers experience a great deal of difficulty making even the most simple prosodic discriminations. This suggests that one can produce accurate prosody without being able to judge or discriminate it. An exception to this are methods that employ auditory stimulation techniques in which clients listen to but are not required to demonstrate comprehension of discrimination (e.g., Appendix A).

D. Cautions in Using the Treatment Sections

1. **Representativeness of references.** The methods described in the treatment sections were selected as representations of current practice. Although the intent was to include as many prosody treatment approaches as possible, doubtless some excellent approaches have been excluded. Exclusion should not be viewed as judgmental.

2. For several reasons, there is **redundancy** in the treatment section.

   a. Some **approaches target several behaviors** for treatment (e.g., Fairbanks, 1960, pp. 167–168 treats intelligibility and stress; Orion, 1988, pp. 45–52 treats pausing, terminal contour, and stress). Thus, the same reference may be cited in several different chapters.

b. Some **approaches use several different prosody categories**. For example, Ling (1976, pp. 206–211) indirectly uses pitch slope, pitch variation, pitch height, pitch direction, and loudness level to ensure that speakers with impaired hearing have sufficient control of pitch for speaking. Accordingly, Ling (1976, pp. 206–211) is listed in several sections.

c. Because it is anticipated that some clinicians will use this as a source book and refer only to selected chapters, redundancy has been intentionally introduced to **facilitate accessibility to treatment information**.

3. The original **terminology** used by authors of treatment methods has been converted to Prosodic Teaching Model terminology. In some instances, authors of the treatment approaches described in Chapters 4 through 11 did not employ the terminology used in this book (e.g., Pindzola, 1987a). In other instances, authors of treatment approaches described in Chapters 4 through 11 did not identify their approach as a means to treat prosody (e.g., Boone, 1971, pp. 130–132; Wilson, 1972, pp. 107–111). Nonetheless, such approaches are included in this book because of their apparent usefulness for treating prosody using the Prosodic Teaching Model.

4. In some cases, **procedures and contents of treatment have been simplified**. For example, several indirect treatment approaches use both prosodic and nonprosodic procedures to achieve the terminal objective (e.g., Swift & Rosin, 1990). Because of space limitations, the nonprosodic objectives, procedures, or steps were excluded.

5. There is considerable variation in the **clarity of instructions** provided in the sample programs, because of the lucidity of the original descriptions. Some authors clearly delineated objectives and procedures, others vaguely alluded to treatment ideas, and others presented information in a manner that is neither of the two extremes. Obviously, these qualitative differences affected the clarity of the instructions found in Chapters 4 through 11.

6. Seemingly **contradictory information** is presented within and among the chapters. In many instances, this is the result of multiple citations from a single source. For example, at one point, Moncur and Brackett (1974) are described as using pitch to produce stress, and, at another point, they are described as using duration. The reason for such apparent contradictions is that in the first citation (pp. 80–81), Moncur and Brackett use pitch, and in the second (pp. 86–89), they use duration to produce the targeted prosodic component (stress). Thus, although in both instances Moncur and Brackett ultimately target stress, the contexts of treatment differ; therefore, quite logically, the methods differ.

7. Finally, readers are reminded that the **discrete organization of the Prosodic Teaching Model is an oversimplification**. Speakers typically do not isolate single prosodic categories when they talk, and current practice often treats multiple aspects of prosody. Clinicians should be sensitive to the integrative nature of prosody and consider the Prosodic Teaching Model organizational framework as a convenience. To encourage the viewing of prosody as an integrative entity, each chapter cites and/or presents several exemplar programs which treat more than one aspect of prosody. Moreover, Appendixes A and B present sample programs for the treatment of prosody from a naturalistic or holistic viewpoint.

CHAPTER

3

The Assessment of Prosody

I. WHAT TO ASSESS

This chapter focuses on the assessment of prosody as it relates to treatment. Two types of questions are addressed: questions that need to be asked before therapy and questions that need to be asked during or after therapy.

A. Pretreatment Questions

Questions asked before treatment differ based on whether the clinician chooses to treat prosody directly or indirectly. In *direct approaches,* treatment attempts to change a prosodic behavior. That is, the primary goal of treatment is to improve prosody. In *indirect approaches,* treatment manipulates a prosodic behavior which, in turn, changes other dimensions of communication. Thus, the prosodic behavior is a secondary goal or a procedure used to achieve the primary goal.

1. **Questions for direct approaches.**

    a. **Is there a prosodic problem?** Whether or not the client has a prosodic problem may be difficult to determine because of the lack of normative information about and specific evaluation techniques for prosody. Unlike other aspects of speech and language, there are few standardized tests or even clinical guidelines to determine if a prosodic problem is present. In most cases, clinicians rely on intuition and general knowledge of overall communication to determine if speakers have prosodic problems.

    b. **What is the nature of the prosodic problem?** To answer questions of this type, clinicians explore clients' strengths and weaknesses regarding the use of prosody and its major subdivisions (i.e., the features — pitch, loudness, duration, pause, and the components — tempo, intonation, stress, and rhythm). Usually, clinicians place special emphasis on identifying the area(s) of breakdown or deficit by determining clients' abilities to produce or comprehend the different prosodic features and components. However, in cases in which component problems are noted, it is important to determine the intactness of prosodic features which function as prerequisites to the normal production of prosodic components. Thus, for example, clinicians should determine if clients with intonation problems have adequate pitch control. Additionally, clinicians should identify aspects of the prosodic system that are intact and that may be available for compensatory intervention strategies.

    c. **Are there causal factors that can eliminate or reduce the prosodic problem?** Although causal factors are not always easily identifiable, it is critical that clinicians determine if respiratory, laryngeal (phonatory), structural, and/or auditory factors exist that cause or contribute to the prosodic problems. Some of these factors may require working with a team of professionals such as otolaryngologists, neurologists, or audiologists to determine if there is an underlying physiological problem. Linguistic competency also should be considered.

2. Questions for indirect approaches.

Do changes in prosody result in changes in the speech or language behavior that is the primary target of therapy? To answer this question, clinicians systematically explore the effect of changes in a specified prosodic feature or component on another dimension of communication. If prosody is to be a facilitator (i.e., make the task easier or simpler), the data need to indicate improvement of the nonprosodic target behavior. If prosody is to be a constrainer (i.e., make the task more difficult or complex), the data should indicate deterioration of the nonprosodic target behavior.

CLINICAL NOTES: The use of facilitators and constrainers also can be seen in the following examples. (1) Initially, the clinician designs a series of tasks in which the client speaks or reads aloud at different speaking rates. Then, the clinician calculates intelligibility for each speaking rate. Finally, the clinician analyzes the effect of rate on intelligibility. The rate that results in the highest intelligibility is the most facilitative rate and may be used to improve intelligibility (a facilitator). The rate that results in the lowest intelligibility rating is the constraining rate and may be used to increase task complexity (a constrainer). Thus, once the client is able to produce acceptably intelligible speech under ideal conditions, the clinician can increase speaking rate to automate or habituate the intelligibility. (2) A clinician determines that a slowed rate of speaking (part of tempo) improves intelligibility in a neurologically impaired client. Therefore, treatment focuses on slowing the speaking rate of the client, and rate serves as a facilitator. (3) A clinician determines that certain loudness levels result in decreased levels of phoneme accuracy for a specific client. Therefore, after the client has achieved production of a target speech sound in optimal conditions, he or she will be encouraged to produce that speech sound in sentences using troublesome loudness levels. Thus, loudness is serving as a constrainer.

B. Treatment Effectiveness Question

Does prosody therapy make a difference? To determine the benefits of prosodic treatment, two issues need to be considered:

(1) how to define effectiveness and (2) how to collect effectiveness data.

1. Often, **definitions of effectiveness** are limited to measures of success in meeting task performance criteria (e.g., the percentage of correct taps to the beat of a metronome). Although task performance data are important to researchers and to program designers because they provide information about task complexity or the ability to learn specific behaviors, task performance data frequently fail to reveal significant information about clients' ability to function communicatively or to use targeted behaviors in contexts outside of therapy. For clinicians, effectiveness should be defined operationally using behaviors that are important and representative of improvement in daily communication.

   CLINICAL NOTE: Clinicians should be wary of claims of treatment effectiveness in which the reported changes in prosody, although numerically impressive, do not influence communicatively based activities of daily living.

2. **Evidence for treatment effectiveness may be collected** using group or individual data. Group studies document clients' improvement following prosody therapy by comparing a treatment group to a control group. Based on group studies, we know that prosody can be altered in certain types of disorders (e.g., deafness) and that these changes affect overall communication skills. However, compared to other forms of speech and language therapy, the amount of group effectiveness data for prosody is qualitatively and quantitatively limited.

   For clinicians, prosody's dearth of large group treatment data is not devastating because group data do not establish effectiveness for the individual clients. Single subject experimental designs (SSED) provide the best evidence of treatment effectiveness for specific clients. (See McReynolds and Kearns [1983] for information about SSED designs.) Unfortunately, the development and application of SSED evaluations can be time-consuming and cumbersome, some treatment objectives are difficult to quantify sufficiently for the SSED, and therapy administered during SSED treatment evaluations tends to be rigid.

A popular alternative to SSEDs is the collection of data before and after treatment (pre- or post-evaluations) for the client in question. Because pre- or post-evaluations do not control extraneous factors, they fail to *prove* treatment effectiveness. Nevertheless, pre- or post-evaluations do provide some evidence about change and are used regularly to support effectiveness claims for individual clients in clinical contexts.

II. EVALUATING PROSODY

Prosody can be evaluated instrumentally and perceptually.

A. Instrumentation

Clinical measures of speech and voice have a long and interesting history in experimental phonetics; speech science; and in studies of individuals with speech, language, or hearing disorders. Measures may be either acoustic or physiological. The adaptation of some of these measurement devices as sensory aids, particularly for persons with hearing impairment, is well documented (McGarr, 1989).

For the purposes of augmenting perceptual evaluations, instrumentation can be used to obtain measures of prosody. Traditionally, this has not been part of the assessment protocol; however, the advent of computer-based programs permits access to such information. Examples of commercially available computer-based systems are the Visipitch or the IBM SpeechViewer, among others. Instrumentation permits clinicians to measure intensity; vocal fundamental frequency (F_0); laryngeal function; air pressure; air flow and volume; sound spectrography; or in more experimental cases, speech movements. The types of measures depend on whether the clinician is interested in acoustic or in articulatory measures; the clinician's own comfort and understanding of these measures; and, of course, the instrumentation available. These issues are discussed in great detail by Baken (1987). Obviously, because prosody is multifaceted and many acoustic cues are redundant, clinicians should not expect a direct relationship between the one or two instrumental measures and listeners' judgments. This is especially true when measuring the productions of persons with speech disorders.

B. Perceptual Measures

Perceptual assessment measures involve the use of established procedures in the administration and/or the scoring of behaviors that are judged auditorily. Examples of perceptual assessment measures include employing a uniform set of stimuli to elicit prosodic behaviors and analyzing the prosody of spontaneous speech samples using a uniform set of procedures. Perceptual strategies for assessing prosody may be divided into two categories: evaluative tests and informal guidelines. No one perceptual assessment measure covers all aspects of prosody nor does one measure answer all the clinical questions presented above in Sections I.A and I.B. The following points highlight trends in the current status of perceptual assessment of prosody. Summaries of prosodic assessment measures are presented in Appendix C.

1. **Methods.** The most common form of prosody assessment is the analysis of spontaneous speech; although, there are some exceptions. For example, the *Tennessee Test of Rhythm and Intonational Patterns* (T-TRIP) (Koike & Asp, 1981; Shadden, Asp, Tonkovich, & Mason, 1980) consists of an imitative task, and Yorkston's (1988) and Kent's (1988) guidelines employ a variety of tasks.

2. **Content.** The *Prosody-Voice Screening Profile* (PVSP) (Shriberg, Kwiatkowski, & Rasmussen, 1990), Kent's (1988) guidelines, and Yorkston's (1988) guidelines assess an extensive array of categories. The other assessment measures presented in Appendix C usually focus on only one or two prosodic components and some of the prosodic features used to produce them. With the exception of parts of the *Profile of Prosody* (PROP, Crystal, 1982) and Yorkston's guidelines (1988), assessment of prosody does not extend beyond the sentence level. Quite naturally, the Prosodic Teaching Model Checklist (Appendix D), which was developed for this book, focuses on all the categories described in Chapter 2.

3. **Supporting data.** Normative, reliability, and validity data are rare. Only the PVSP offers extensive standardization data.

4. **Questions answered**

   a. **Problem/no problem.** Most of the assessments attempt to answer questions regarding the presence or absence of a problem by relying on clinical judgment. An exception is the PVSP which provides specific guidelines for judging if a category warrants additional evaluation.

b. Nature. Most of the assessments permit judgments of prosodic strengths and weaknesses. However, the extent of the analysis of strengths and weaknesses is limited by number of categories each assessment explores and the lack of empirical data.

c. Causes. Only two measures (Kent, 1988; Yorkston, 1988) explore causality.

d. Facilitating/constraining effects. Only Kent (1988) and Yorkston (1988) assess the constraining or facilitating effects of prosody on other aspects of communication or the effects of other domains of communication on prosody.

e. Therapy effectiveness. None of the perceptual assessments described in Appendix C was developed to evaluate treatment success. Several of the measures have potential for evaluating treatment effectiveness, if the proper methodology is employed.

CLINICAL NOTE: Judging prosody may be a daunting task for clinicians with poor to fair discrimination skills. Until, or unless, prosodic discrimination training is available as part of preprofessional or continuing education classes, clinicians might employ one of the following strategies. First, they may listen to training tapes such as those developed by Darley, Aronson, and Brown (1975); Shriberg, Kwiatkowski, and Rasmussen, (1990); or Subtelny, Orlando, and Whitehead (1981). Second, they may compare their judgments to the judgments of peers. For example, a clinician may independently analyze a client's prosody and, then, consult with a colleague who has excellent prosodic discrimination. The colleague should listen to the speech samples and describe his or her impressions of the client's prosody. Then, the clinician should attempt to reconcile his or her original judgments to the colleague's impressions. Obviously, most colleagues will not be familiar with every analysis system. Thus, the clinician will need to "translate" the colleague's impressions into his or her own system. (Sometimes this requires rather extensive questioning of the colleague.) Although this second strategy may not be as rigorous as the use of training tapes (the first strategy), it allows clinicians to use the prosodic model of their choice.

CHAPTER

4

Treating Prosodic Features: Pitch

I. NORMAL USE OF THE PROSODIC FEATURE OF PITCH

A. Description

Vocal pitch is one of the four prosodic features that form the cornerstone for the prosodic components of tempo, intonation, stress, and rhythm. Pitch also is a property of nonspeech sounds such as animal noises, music, mechanical sounds, and pure tones, but only vocal pitch of speech is explored in this book. For the sake of simplicity, vocal pitch is referred to as "pitch."

Pitch is an auditory percept associated with the vibration of the vocal folds or fundamental frequency (F_0). The physical attribute of pitch, F_0, is dependent on the number of times the vocal folds open and close per second. When the vocal folds vibrate rapidly, a high pitch sound is heard. When the vocal folds vibrate slowly, a low pitched sound is heard. F_0 can be displayed and measured by commercially available instruments such as the Visipitch, IBM SpeechViewer, or Spectrograph.

Pitch is included in the Prosodic Teaching Model because control of pitch is essential to produce certain aspects of prosody (e.g., stress and intonation). However, only aspects of pitch that affect prosody and the teaching of prosody are presented in this chapter. A more extensive discussion of pitch and pitch disorders can be obtained in speech science texts (e.g., Baken, 1987; Borden & Harris, 1984) or in voice disorders texts (e.g., Boone, 1971; Colton & Casper, 1990; Prater & Swift, 1984).

B. Categories

The prosodic feature pitch is composed of four categories (pitch height, pitch slope/declination, pitch direction, and pitch variation) which are graphically represented in Figure 4–1.

1. **Pitch height.** Pitch height or average vocal pitch is based on the number of times the vocal folds vibrate per second (i.e., fundamental frequency). Perceptually, this is referred to as the average height or level of pitch and is described subjectively as "low," "mid," or "high." Acoustic measures of F_0 are reported in terms of Hertz (e.g., 125 Hz, 200 Hz, or 400 Hz).

2. **Pitch slope and declination.** Pitch slope involves the time element associated with increases and decreases in F_0 at the syllable, word, phrase, or sentence level. Declination refers to one type of decreasing pitch slope — the pitch slope from the onset of an utterance to the end of the utterance. In American English, most utterances are declarative sentences and have a pitch slope (F_0) that gradually decreases throughout the course of the utterance (i.e., declination). Exceptions include tag-questions and intonation questions that require an increase in F_0 at the end of the utterance.

Irrespective of the linguistic unit that is considered (e.g., a syllable, word, or sentence), the time in which the pitch slope occurs is an important component in perception. Pitch changes that occur rapidly and in a short time have "steep" slopes. Pitch changes that occur slowly and over a relatively long time have "gradual" slopes. Pitch slope may be measured by calculating the F_0 at the onset and at the end of the linguistic

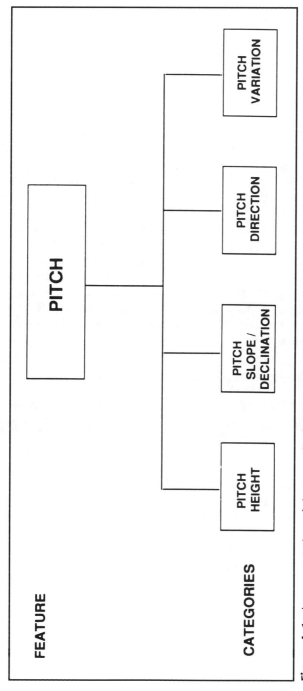

Figure 4-1. A representation of the prosodic feature pitch and its categories

element (e.g., a word, a phrase, or an utterance) and then subtracting the higher F_0 from the lower F_0 while noting the time in milliseconds (msec).

CLINICAL NOTE: Time may be as important a factor as the change in Hz in perceiving the pitch of some disordered speakers such as hearing-impaired persons (Rubin-Spitz & McGarr, 1990).

3. **Pitch direction.** Pitch direction represents the perception of change in pitch. There are three major types of pitch direction: rising, falling, and level. All of the other types are permutations of the three major types (e.g., rising-falling and falling-rising).

4. **Pitch variation.** Pitch variation is the vocal range from the highest pitch height to the lowest pitch height. Pitch variation is influenced by changes in pitch height, direction, and slope. Pitch variation that is "narrow" traverses through a small range of pitches, whereas "wide" pitch variation signifies movement through a large range of pitches. The terms pitch range and pitch width may be used in place of pitch variation.

C. Normative Information

1. Normal **pitch height** (i.e., average pitch level) varies with the speaker's age and gender. For example, men are described as having relatively low-pitched voices with respect to women and their average pitch is reported to be about 125 Hz with ranges from 120–175 Hz. Women are described as having higher pitched voices than men, and their average pitch is reported to be about 200 Hz with ranges from 175–250 Hz. The pitch of young children is perceived to be considerably higher than either adult males or females. The average pitch of pre-pubescent children is 300 Hz with a range of 170–400 Hz (Boone, 1980; Colton & Casper, 1990; Ohde & Sharf, 1992). Before puberty, the range of F_0 for young males and young females is similar. With the onset of puberty, there is overall physical growth in both males and females and, in particular, growth and change in the larynx. This laryngeal growth is more dramatic and occurs over a shorter period of time in males than in females. Reference tables for determining the appropriateness of a speaker's average pitch can be obtained from a variety of sources (cf. Baken, 1987).

2. **Pitch slope and declination** (i.e., perceived change in F_0 over time) varies as a function of the individual speaker.

3. **Pitch direction** (i.e., perceived pitch change) is used in the production of different intonation categories. Thus, normative data about pitch direction are closely tied to intonation and vary as a function of its use in intonation.

   a. Crystal (1981) reports that, for speakers of British English, the pitch direction of the sentence **nucleus** (i.e., the most prominent word in an utterance) most frequently is a falling pitch direction. Other common pitch directions on sentence nuclei include rising pitch directions and complex pitch directions such as falling-rising and rising-falling. Information about American English, although not as specific as Crystal's, can be derived from Pike (1945).

   b. The most common **terminal contour** (i.e., the final pitch direction at the end of an utterance) is the falling or downward pitch direction. The rising pitch direction is the next most common terminal contour.

   c. Ohde and Sharf (1992) report that for speakers of American English, the three main types of **overall intonation contour** (i.e., the pitch configuration from the initiation to the end of the utterance) consist of falling, rising, and level pitch directions.

4. For most speakers, **pitch variation** (i.e., pitch range) extends approximately two or three octaves (Nicolosi, Harryman & Kresheck, 1989), but the pitch variation of trained singers may be even greater. Pitch variation also can be described by using measures of standard deviation. The standard deviation in F_0 is expressed in semitones and is called pitch sigma. Normal speakers exhibit a frequency standard deviation between two and four semitones (cf. Baken, 1987). Speakers who lack normal variability in frequency may be perceived as monotonous.

D. Communicative Roles

The following communicative roles are attributed to pitch:

1. Speakers use pitch features to **produce the different categories of intonation** (see Chapter 9).

2. Pitch combines with other prosodic features to play a **role in the production of the other components of tempo, stress, and rhythm** (see Chapters 8, 10, and 11).

3. Pitch or, more specifically, differences in F_0 contribute to the **production of speech sounds.** Thus, the intrinsic pitch of vowels and differences in pitch following voiced and voiceless speech sounds are segmental in nature.

II. PERCEIVING THE PROSODIC FEATURE OF PITCH

Pitch is the perceptual correlate of F_0. When the vocal folds vibrate rapidly, the F_0 increases, and a high pitch sound is perceived. When the vocal folds vibrate slowly, the F_0 decreases, and a low pitch sound is heard. Changes in loudness (the perceptual aspect) or amplitude (the acoustic measure) also enter into the perception of pitch. For example, a stable frequency may be perceived as a rising pitch in contexts in which loudness increases. Alternatively, in certain voice disorders, it is possible to perceive a low pitch without an excessively low F_0 because of changes in voice quality (e.g., breathiness) or other resonant characteristics.

Several factors are important in the perception of pitch. First, pitch measures are constrained by length of the speech sample, the phonetic context, and the task (e.g., reading versus speaking). Thus, in one context, speakers may use certain pitch patterns, and in other contexts, they may use other patterns. A second factor to consider is the amount of pitch perturbation. This refers to the regularity of the vibratory cycle of the vocal folds both in terms of the time of vibration and also the amplitude of the vibrations. The acoustic representation of this phenomenon is called vocal jitter (cf. Baken, 1987). Normal speakers show little variation in pitch perturbation and little vocal jitter. Measures of vocal jitter may signal problems in the mass of the vocal folds, in the degree of tension, muscular activity, or in the integrity of the nervous system.

III. PRODUCING THE PROSODIC FEATURE OF PITCH

Differences in F_0 (and its perceptual correlate, pitch) in males, females, and children can be attributed to differences in the size of the vocal folds. The larger the vibrating mass of the vocal folds, the lower the F_0. Typically, males have larger, more massive vocal folds than women and children. Thus, the vocal folds of males vibrate more slowly, and the pitch of male voices is perceived as relatively low compared to the voices of females and children.

Changes in F_0 and pitch in a given speaker are caused by additional factors. Lengthening and tensing the vocal folds as a result of muscular contraction decreases the size of the vibrating mass and effectively increases the rate of vibration. This results in an increased F_0 and the perception of increased pitch.

Vocal F_0 is also affected by the position of the tongue in the mouth, particularly when producing vowels. This is because "strap" muscles which connect the tongue, jaw, and larynx at the hyoid bone influence the relative position of the larynx and may exert different tensions on the vocal folds. For example, high vowels such as /i/ and /u/ are articulated with the tongue positioned high in the mouth. This articulatory posture indirectly exerts an upward pull on the larynx thereby increasing the tension on the vocal folds. Consequently, when subjected to aerodynamic forces, the vocal folds vibrate more rapidly. These vowels are said to have a high intrinsic pitch. Low vowels such as /a/, articulated with the tongue positioned low in the mouth and with the jaw opened, cause the larynx to be fixed in a relatively low anatomical position. The vocal folds are less tense and when subjected to aerodynamic forces, vibrate at a slower rate. Thus, the intrinsic pitch of these vowels is lower. Normal talkers are able to vary the discrete differences between vowels and consonants while maintaining an appropriate overall average pitch level.

IV. A MODEL FOR TREATING PITCH

A. A Teaching Model for Pitch

The teaching model for pitch is composed of the four pitch categories (height, slope or declination, direction, and variation).

B. Treatment Decisions: Pitch

Readers are referred to Chapter 2 (Section III.B) for a more extensive explanation of the guidelines in the Clinical Note. Additionally, readers may consult the Treatment Index to facilitate locating of purposes, focuses, objectives, hierarchies, treatment techniques, and examples of pitch-related treatment programs referred to in the guidelines.

CLINICAL NOTE: GUIDELINES FOR DECISION MAKING

1. **Determine the purpose** (direct, indirect) for working with pitch.
2. **Identify the categories** of pitch (height, slope/declination, direction, variation) that will serve as the focus of therapy.
3. **Identify** specific **treatment objectives** for the targeted purpose/focus combination (PFC) (i.e., the purpose from Guideline #1 and the focus from Guideline #2 above).
4. **Decide how to order objectives.**
5. **Select treatment techniques** appropriate for the client and the PFC.
6. Identify sources in which **clients with similar disorders** have similar PFCs.

V. SUMMARY OF PUBLISHED LITERATURE ON TREATING PITCH

A. Direct Purpose Treatment Strategies

1. **Approaches that focus directly on pitch height** (i.e., direct pitch height PFC). (**Pitch Height** = Average pitch level.)

   a. **Population.** Individuals with the following disorders may benefit from the direct treatment of pitch height: hearing impairment, motor speech disorders, and voice disorders. Pitch height also has been the direct purpose of treatment programs for normal speakers wishing to improve their voice or overall speaking skills (speech improvement).

   b. **Intervention**
      (1) **Content**
         (a) The **target behaviors** include

            • auditory discrimination of pitch heights;

            • production of vowels as specified pitch heights with low vowels being treated before high vowels or diphthongs;

- production of optimum pitch for sustained vowels, syllables, words, sentences, phrases, monologues, and/or dialogues;

- reading of passages using specified pitch heights; and

- using of specified pitch height during conversation.

   (b) Typically, a logical **hierarchy** is used in methods directly treating pitch height. Table 4–1 shows a sample program containing a logical hierarchy.
   (2) Many different **techniques** are used to treat pitch height problems directly as evidenced in Table 4–2 (which lists the techniques used with the different pitch PFCs). The most commonly used techniques for direct height PFCs are **metalinguistics, feedback,** and **reading aloud**.

2. **Approaches that focus directly on pitch slope (or pitch declination)** (i.e., direct pitch slope PFC). (**Pitch slope** = Change in fundamental frequency over time.) No treatment approaches have been identified that directly treat pitch slope. For treatment ideas, clinicians are referred to indirect pitch slope PFCs (section V.B. #2) and to Appendixes A, B, and E.

3. **Approaches that directly focus on pitch direction** (i.e., direct pitch direction PFC). (**Pitch direction** = Perceived pitch change.) Because the literature pertaining to treating direct pitch direction PFCs is limited, no summary information is presented. Rather, Table 4–3 presents one method that directly uses pitch direction.

4. **Approaches that directly focus on pitch variation** (i.e., direct pitch variaton PFC). (**Pitch variation** = Pitch range.)

   a. **Population.** Pitch variation has been targeted directly in persons with the following problems: dysarthria, hearing impairment, and voice disorders. Moreover, several methods have been developed for normal speakers wishing to improve their overall vocal and/or speaking skills (speech improvement).

Table 4–1. Program for direct pitch height PFC

POPULATION:	Voice disorders, speech improvement.
TECHNIQUES:	Metalinguistic tasks; imagery; feedback (auditory, tactile/kinesthetic, verbal); reading aloud; conversation; posturing. (The Glossary contains definitions of the techniques.)
OBJECTIVES:	1. To identify optimum pitch height. 2. To establish habitual production of optimum pitch height.
PROCEDURES:	1a. The client says "Uhhuh" with closed lips and a rising terminal contour while attempting to sound spontaneous.
	b. The client vocalizes while placing a finger of one hand lightly on the bridge and sides of his or her nose.
	c. Alternative techniques for identifying optimum pitch height: • saying "Hello" with a rising terminal contour; • producing natural, spontaneous laughter; and • employing supraoptimal pitch height for those who use "too low" pitch height.
	2a. The clinician employs a tape recorder or a Language Master during treatment activities to provide the client with feedback. The clinician notes that some transitory symptoms may occur while the pitch height is being habituated. These transitory symptoms may include tension under the mandible, in the soft palate, in the sternocleidomastoid muscle, or in the oronasopharyngeal region. The clinician explains that these symptoms are not negative, that they should not persist, and that the client should resist reverting to the old, comfortable pitch heights.
	b. The clinician directs the client to form a mental picture of himself or herself using the appropriate pitch height and encourages the client to imagine that he or she is producing the pitch at a high point in his or her head. The client then attempts to produce the targeted pitch with the clinician providing verbal feedback. Additionally, the clinician may use posturing to help the client identify the means by which the targeted pitch height may be produced.

PROCEDURES
(continued)

c. The client practices using the optimum pitch height in "key word plus number" contexts. This involves producing a key word, such as "meme" or "nim-nim" and a one digit number. The client uses the optimum pitch height on the "key word" and on the number.

d. The client produces the optimum pitch height in phrases and in short sentences using the following hierarchy:
   • The client combines a "key word" and a number with a short phrase such as "Me-me, one, how are you?"
   • The client pairs a "key word" with a short phrase, for example, "Me-me, I feel fine."
   • The client repeats the above pattern but alters the "key word."

e. The client reads sentences aloud from lists such as those provided by Fairbanks (1960), using one "key word" for the first set of sentences and a different "key word" for a second set of sentences.

f. The client spontaneously talks in sentences but produces a "key word" before, during, or after each sentence.

g. The client reads aloud selected passages from a magazine. The clinician provides verbal feedback regarding pitch height.

h. The client and the clinician converse. The clinician verbally provides feedback regarding the appropriateness of pitch height.

Source: The above program was derived from information provided in Cooper, M. (1973). *Modern techniques of vocal rehabilitation* (pp. 76–86). Springfield, IL: C. C. Thomas.

b. **Intervention**
   (1) **Content**
      (a) The **target behaviors** include producing appropriate pitch ranges in the following contexts:
         • reading sentences or paragraphs aloud and
         • conversing

Table 4–2. Treatment techniques for the various pitch PFCs. (Definitions of all treatment techniques are provided in the Glossary.)

Technique	Purpose/Focus Combinations
Backups	indirect pitch variation
Breathing Activities	indirect pitch height
Compensatory Strategies	direct pitch variation
Contrastive Sets/Minimal Pairs	direct pitch height, direct pitch direction, direct pitch variation, indirect pitch height, indirect pitch slope, indirect pitch direction, indirect pitch variation
Conversation	direct pitch height, direct pitch variation, indirect pitch height
Cues	
Auditory	indirect pitch height, indirect pitch variation
Tactile/Kinesthetic	indirect pitch height, indirect pitch slope, indirect pitch variation
Visual	direct pitch height, direct pitch direction, direct pitch variation, indirect pitch height, indirect pitch slope, indirect pitch direction
Discrimination	direct pitch height, direct pitch variation, indirect pitch height, indirect pitch slope, indirect pitch variation
Dramatics	direct pitch height, direct pitch variation
Drill	direct pitch height, direct pitch direction, indirect pitch direction, indirect pitch variation
Exaggeration	direct pitch direction, indirect pitch height, indirect pitch slope, indirect pitch variation
Fading	indirect pitch height, indirect pitch variation
Feedback	
Auditory	direct pitch height, direct pitch variation, indirect pitch height, indirect pitch direction, indirect pitch variation
Tactile/Kinesthetic	direct pitch height, direct pitch variation, indirect pitch height, indirect pitch slope, indirect pitch variation

Technique	Purpose/Focus Combinations
Feedback (continued)	
Verbal	direct pitch height, direct pitch variation, indirect pitch height, indirect pitch slope, indirect pitch variation
Visual	direct pitch height, direct pitch variation, indirect pitch height, indirect pitch slope, indirect pitch direction, indirect pitch variation
Games	direct pitch height, indirect pitch height
Imagery	direct pitch height
Imitation	direct pitch height, direct pitch variation, indirect pitch height, indirect pitch slope, indirect pitch direction, indirect pitch variation
Latency	indirect pitch variation
Metalinguistics	direct pitch height, direct pitch variation, indirect pitch height, indirect pitch slope, indirect pitch direction, indirect pitch variation
Modeling	direct pitch height, direct pitch variation, indirect pitch height, indirect pitch slope, indirect pitch direction, indirect pitch variation
Motor Movement	direct pitch height, direct pitch variation, indirect pitch height, indirect pitch variation
Musical Instruments	direct pitch height, direct pitch variation, indirect pitch height
Narratives	direct pitch height, direct pitch variation
Negative Practice	direct pitch height, direct pitch variation
Play	indirect pitch height, indirect pitch slope, indirect pitch direction, indirect pitch variation
Posturing	direct pitch height
Production on Demand	direct pitch height, indirect pitch height
Query Responding	indirect pitch variation

(continued)

Table 4-2 *(continued)*

Technique	*Purpose/Focus Combinations*
Reading Aloud	direct pitch height, direct pitch direction, direct pitch variation, indirect pitch height, indirect pitch slope, indirect pitch direction, indirect pitch variation
Rituals	indirect pitch height
Self-Monitoring	direct pitch height, indirect pitch height, indirect pitch variation
Sequencing	direct pitch height, indirect pitch height, indirect pitch slope, indirect pitch direction, indirect pitch variation
Shaping	indirect pitch variation
Signing	indirect pitch variation
Singing/Chanting	direct pitch height, direct pitch variation, indirect pitch height, indirect pitch variation
Stimulation	
Auditory	indirect pitch height, indirect pitch slope, indirect pitch direction, indirect pitch variation
Visual	indirect pitch variation
Unison Reading	direct pitch height, direct pitch variation
Whispering	indirect pitch height

(b) The typical **hierarchy** used to treat pitch variation directly is logical as exemplified in Table 4–4.

(2) The most common **techniques** used to treat pitch variation directly are *metalinguistics* and *cues*. A listing of the techniques for direct pitch variation PFCs is shown in Table 4–2 which presents techniques used in all pitch PFCs.

Table 4-3. Program for direct pitch direction PFC

POPULATION:	Voice disorders, speech improvement.
TECHNIQUES:	Drills, contrastive sets, reading aloud, modeling, exaggeration, cues (visual). (The Glossary contains definitions of the techniques.)
OBJECTIVES:	To produce the following pitch directions using selected pitch heights: falling (\), rising (/), and rising-falling (/\).
PROCEDURES:	1. The client reads aloud a list of words with a falling pitch direction (\) (loudness level also decreases). The client then reads other word lists in which the \ is produced using progressively greater pitch variation. This continues until the client produces a one octave drop over a single word.
	2. Step #1 is repeated, but a rising (/) pitch direction is used with the loudness level decreasing during the reading task.
	3. Step #1 is repeated using a rising-falling (/\) pitch direction. The clinician may have to simplify the task for the production of /\. For example, the /\ may be introduced on isolated vowels and later modeled in words.
	4. The clinician creates sentences with visual cues using the words from Step #1 and, then, directs the client to read aloud each sentence three times first using /, then \, and finally /\ pitch directions on target words. For example: • Bryan is *happy* (\)| • Bryan is *happy* (/)| • Bryan is *happy* (/\)|
	5. The clinician presents a set of sentences without visual cues for the client to read aloud. The client is directed to use one of the three pitch directions (/, \, /\) on the specified word, but the pitch direction is not specified.

Note: The legend for symbols used in this table are entered under "Symbols" in the Glossary.

Source: The above program was derived from information provided in Moncur, J. P. & Brackett, I. P. (1974). *Modifying vocal behavior* (pp. 75-77). New York: Harper & Row.

Table 4-4. Program for direct pitch variation PFC

POPULATION:	Hearing impairment.
TECHNIQUES:	Discrimination; modeling; singing; musical instruments; physical gestures; narratives; imitation; feedback (auditory, tactile/kinesthetic, verbal, visual); negative practice; dramatics; metalinguistics; cues (tactile/kinesthetic, visual); unison reading; self-monitoring. (The Glossary contains definitions of the techniques.)
OBJECTIVES:	1. To discriminate among pitch heights. 2. To produce speech using an acceptable variety of pitch heights (pitch variation).
PROCEDURES:	1a. The clinician presents two prerecorded pitches of differing heights. One pitch represents an acceptable pitch height for the client; the other represents an unacceptable pitch height. The client discriminates between the two pitches. In this and in subsequent steps, the clinician provides verbal feedback to the client.
	b. The clinician prerecords high and very low pitch heights and directs the client to discriminate between the two.
	c. The clinician presents three pitch heights (high, middle, low) to the client (the middle pitch height represents the client's habitual level). The client discriminates among the three pitch heights.
	d. The clinician continues to present three pitches for the client to discriminate; the differences among the pitch heights gradually decrease.
	e. The clinician presents two samples of the client's voice for the client to discriminate—one sample is acceptable and the other is unacceptable. The comparisons between the examples gradually move from gross to fine and from two (high, low) to four variants (very high, high, normal, low).
	f. If necessary, the clinician employs singing and musical instruments to facilitate discrimination. (However, the discrimination of vocal pitch is the ultimate objective.)
	g. Other variations include • lights may flash for certain pitch heights; • different toys may be activated by designated pitch heights; and

• discrimination of pitch heights may be required in natural contexts, such as in story telling activities.

2a. The client imitates the clinician as he or she hums the scale upward and downward.

b. The clinician hums middle C, B, or B flat while directing the client to place his or her hand on the clinician's face or throat. The client attempts to imitate the clinician's humming.

c. The clinician produces specific notes, and the client imitates. Tactile and/or kinesthetic cues may be used.

d. The clinician hums /m/ at the client's optimum pitch. The client attempts to produce the following pairs of sounds at the same pitch:
/m/—/a/; /m/-/a/; /ma/
/m/—/o/; /m/-/o/; /mo/
/m/—/i/; /m/-/i/; /mi/

e. The client repeats Step #2d increasing the pitch height one octave.

f. The client utters short sentences at optimum pitch and attempts to keep pitch height constant (i.e., a monotone).

g. The client produces the same sentences as in Step #2f but varies acceptable pitch (pitch variation).

h. The client tells stories and engages in dramatic play using his optimum pitch and with pitch variation.

i. If necessary, the clinician and the client read aloud in unison. The clinician may provide the client with a binaural trainer and gradually increase the loudness level until the client cannot hear his or her own voice. The clinician models appropriate pitch variation, pitch height, and rhythm.

j. If necessary, the clinician uses a pitch meter to provide visual feedback for the client. The clinician also encourages the client to attend to the tactile/kinesthetic differences among pitch heights.

k. The clinician provides the client with a Speech Chart that has metalinguistic objectives, such as "I know the rule about the pitch height of my voice," and production objectives, such as "I can use the correct pitch height all the time."

Source: The above program was derived from information provided in Wilson, D. K. (1972). *Voice problems of children* (pp. 172–175). Baltimore: Williams & Wilkins.

B. Indirect Purpose Treatment Strategies

1. **Approaches that focus indirectly on pitch height** (i.e., indirect pitch height PFC). (**Pitch height** = Average pitch level.)

   a. **Population.** Pitch height has been the indirect target of treatment methods for individuals with the following problems: apraxia of speech, hearing impairment, learning disability, specific language impairment, and voice disorders. Additionally, approaches have been developed for normal speakers to improve overall speaking skills or to reduce foreign accent.

   b. **Intervention**
      (1) **Content**
         (a) **Terminal objectives** for the indirect treatment of pitch height include

         • improved intelligibility,
         • improved articulation skills,
         • improved overall pitch skills,
         • elimination of vocal abuse,
         • improved intonation skills,
         • improved overall vocal skills,
         • improved preverbal communication skills, and
         • improved social skills.

         (b) For indirect treatment, the **target behaviors** of the pitch height phase of treatment include

         • discrimination of pitch heights and
         • production of selected pitch heights in a variety of vocalizations, syllables, words, and in connected speech.

         Table 4–5 provides an example of a program that uses an indirect pitch height approach.
         (c) When pitch height is an intermediate objective or a facilitator/constrainer (i.e., is used indirectly), the **hierarchy** tends to be logical.
      (2) **Techniques** employed in pitch PFCs are presented in Table 4–2. The most commonly used techniques for indirect pitch height PFCs include *metalinguistics, reading aloud, cues, discrimination,* and *contrastive sets*.

Table 4-5. Program for indirect pitch height PFC. (Steps related to pitch height are preceded by an asterisk [*].)

POPULATION:	Learning disability.
GOALS:	To improve social skills.
TECHNIQUES:	Minimal pairs; feedback (verbal, visual); discrimination; imitation; metalinguistics; modeling. (The Glossary contains definitions of the techniques.)
OBJECTIVES:	1. To discriminate pairs of prosodic stimuli.
	2. To associate attitude with selected aspects of prosody.
	3. To produce utterances using prosody to signal different attitudes or emotions.
	4. To produce prosodic patterns that are appropriate for the context.
PROCEDURES:	*1. The clinician presents pairs of speech stimuli that may vary in one aspect of prosody. (Because this table focuses on pitch height, the examples relate to pitch height. However, treatment may also involve rate, loudness, pausing, etc.) Although the client's task is to judge the pairs as same or different, the client is also encouraged to imitate the pairs. The clinician provides verbal and visual feedback (e.g., a pitch meter) to the client, as needed. The complexity of the task gradually increases using the following hierarchy:
	• live stimuli produced by clinician and
	• audiotaped stimuli produced by the clinician and others.
	2a. The clinician models utterances with various prosodic patterns to depict a range of emotions or attitudes and describes situations in which they would be used appropriately.
	b. The client judges the appropriateness of particular prosodic patterns for designated meaning. (For example, the clinician says sadly, "It's Monday," and asks, "Did I sound happy?")
	3a. The client attempts to convey selected emotional meanings of neutral statements, such as "That's my homework," using different prosodic patterns.
	b. The client names the emotion conveyed by prosodic patterns paired with neutral statements.

(continued)

Table 4–5 *(continued)*

PROCEDURES: *(continued)*	4a. While observing role-playing or a movie, the client identifies communication breakdowns caused by inappropriate prosody by noting the misuse or misinterpretation of prosody. For example, the client views a scene involving a teacher and a student in which the teacher repeats "Now" at increasingly high pitch heights, but the student is not reponsive to the message.
	b. The clinician presents examples of sarcasm and teasing which are conveyed by prosody. She or he explains that the client should rely on the information conveyed by prosody when the prosody and the message do not match.
	COMMENT: Virtually any aspect of prosody can be used indirectly in this approach. Minskoff's approach also includes other nonverbal communication skills.

Source: The above program was derived from information provided in Minskoff, E. H. (1980). Teaching approach for developing nonverbal communication skills in students with social perceptual deficits. Part II. Proximic, vocalic, and artifactual cues. *Journal of Learning Disabilities, 13,* 34–39.

2. **Approaches that focus indirectly on pitch slope (or pitch declination)** (i.e., indirect pitch slope PFC). (**Pitch slope** = Perceived change in fundamental frequency over time.) Because the literature pertaining to treating indirect pitch slope PFCs is limited, no summary information is presented. Rather, Table 4–6 presents one method that indirectly uses pitch slope. Another example of an indirect slope method can be found in Chapter 9, Table 9–1.

3. **Approaches that focus indirectly in pitch direction** (i.e., indirect pitch direction PFC). (**Pitch direction** = Perceived pitch change.) Readers are referred to Table 4–7 which is a sample program for indirect focus on pitch direction that was designed to reduce inappropriate accent in speakers of English as a second language (Brazil, Coulthard, & Johns, 1980). The sample program in the previous section (Table 4–6) can also be used to work indirectly with pitch direction.

   a. **Population.** Pitch direction is used indirectly for speakers with hearing impairment and voice disorders. In addition, pitch direction is used in attempts to improve the overall speaking skills of normal speakers (speech improvement).

Table 4-6. Exemplar program for indirect pitch slope PFC. (Steps related to pitch slope are preceded by an asterisk [*].)

POPULATION:	Hearing-impairment (children).
GOAL:	To establish vocalization skills with pitch sufficient to serve as a basis for speech.
TECHNIQUES:	Modeling; discrimination; imitation; cues (tactile/kinesthetic, visual); sequencing; play; feedback (tactile/kinesthetic, visual); fading; physical manipulation; motor movement. (The Glossary contains definitions of the techniques.)
OBJECTIVES:	**INFORMAL**
	To produce vocalizations spontaneously with a variety of pitches that are appropriate to the context.
	FORMAL (The author recommends that the Formal Objectives be used only as supplements to the Informal Objective.)
	1. To vocalize, on separate breaths, pitches that approach the highest and the lowest extremes of the pitch range.
	2. To vocalize while varying between two extremes in pitch height.
	3. To vocalize, on separate breaths, high, low, and midpoint pitch heights.
	4. Within a single vocalization, to vary between different pitch heights (e.g., high to mid, mid to low, low to mid, etc.).
	5. Using separate vocalizations, to produce contrasts from objective #4 accompanied by variations in loudness.
PROCEDURES:	**INFORMAL**
	The clinician provides an active, exciting environment and encourages the client to produce vocalizations spontaneously that vary in pitch height. The clinician reinforces pitches that match the child's emotional state.
	FORMAL
	1a. The clinician requires the client to discriminate between high and low pitch heights that differ by at least eight semitones, using the clinician's live voice. At first, the clinician may use visual cues (e.g., for high pitch, a hand is held above the head; for low pitch, a hand is held below the waist). These cues are faded gradually.

(continued)

Table 4–7 *(continued)*

PROCEDURES *(continued)*	b. To encourage voluntary modification of pitch patterns, the clinician encourages the client to imitate different pitch heights. The clinician demonstrates the vocal fold tension and subglottal tension associated with changes in pitch height. Example:

- The client lowers his or her chin and relaxes his or her arms and shoulders. (This increases mass and lowers pitch.) The client then vocalizes and alternates between low and normal pitch heights. The clinician gradually fades cues.

- The clinician assists (a) in lowering pitch height by manipulating the client's thyroid cartilage, (b) in varying the client's pitch by alternately applying and removing pressure on the thyroid cartilage, or (c) in causing pitch variations by alternately applying and removing pressure on the thyroid cartilage.

- The client places his or her hand on the clinician's larynx while the clinician models high and low pitch heights. The client imitates the clincian's vocalizations while placing a hand on his or her own larynx. The clinician fades this tactile feedback as soon as possible.

- The client practices changing pitch patterns. Once the client volitionally changes his or her pitch height, visual pitch indicators (e.g., the VisiPitch) may be employed to provide the client with feedback about the accuracy of his or her attempts to match a target pitch. Feedback that provides moment-to-moment information is not recommended.

* 2a. The clinician models smooth, continuous pitch movement from low to high pitch height (or vice versa) both steeply (in 1 second) and gradually (in over 3 seconds). Visual and/or tactile cues may be employed.

    b. If the client displays voice breaks, the clinician models pitch changes in only one direction (lowering or raising).

  3a. The clinician directs the client to discriminate among three pitch heights (high, middle, and low) that have been produced on three separate breaths. Visual cues may be employed.

b. The clinician presents a model of three different pitch heights, on three different breaths, for the client to imitate.

*4. The clinician presents a smooth, continuous vocalization for the client to imitate using mid to high, low to mid, high to low, and so forth pitch heights with both steep (1 second) and gradual slopes (3 seconds). If necessary, the clinician facilitates imitation with tactile or visual cues. For example, a touch on the hand may be for low pitch heights, a touch on the elbow may signify middle pitch heights, and a touch on the head may indicate high pitch heights. If the clinician uses tactile cues, the client may close his or her eyes to avoid visual cues.

5a. The clinician models loud and soft loudness levels of low, middle, and high pitch heights for the client to imitate.

*b. The clinician models combinations of pitch and loudness levels (e.g., soft loudness + high pitch + steep slope, loud loudness + mid pitch + gradual slope, etc.) for the client to imitate. To encourage the client's participation, the clinician plays with the client or introduces a game such as "Wake up the clinician" in which the clinician's participation is contingent upon the client's appropriate vocalization.

COMMENTS: This approach also can indirectly use the following prosodic categories: pitch variation, pitch height, pitch direction, loudness level.

Source: The above program was derived from information provided in Ling, D. C. (1976). *Speech and the hearing impaired child: Theory and practice* (pp. 206–211). Washington, DC: Alexander Graham Bell Association for the Deaf.

b. Intervention
(1) Content
(a) The **terminal objectives** for indirect pitch direction include

- improved intonation,
- improved stress,
- increased pitch variation,
- decreased vocal monotony, and
- improved preverbal communication skills.

Table 4-7. Program for indirect pitch direction PFC. (Steps related to pitch direction are preceded by an asterisk [*].)

POPULATION:	Foreign accent.
TECHNIQUES:	Metalinguistics, drill, discrimination, transcribing, imitation, auditory stimulation, reading aloud, feedback (verbal), cues (visual), motor movement, modeling scripts. (The Glossary contains definitions of the techniques.)
GOAL:	To improve overall intonation skills.

OBJECTIVES:

1. To recognize utterances and utterance boundaries.

2. To recognize the nucleus in
   - simple utterances and
   - utterances with two prominent syllables.

3. To produce an utterance with
   - one prominent syllable and
   - two prominent syllables.

*4. To discriminate pitch directions
   - \ and \/
   - \ and /\; \/ and /

*5. To produce utterances using nuclei with acceptable pitch directions.

6. To identify pitch sequences in monologues and to recognize their communicative significance. For example, a speaker's switch to high pitch at the beginning of an utterance following an utterance that ends with a low pitch may signal the speaker is changing the conversational topic.

7. To discriminate pitch height at the end of utterances (high, mid, low).

8. To discriminate pitch height at the beginning of utterances (low, mid, high).

*9. To produce utterances with acceptable
   - location of nuclei (most prominently stressed word),
   - pitch direction of nuclei,
   - initial pitch height (onset level), and
   - pitch height at the end of the utterance.

PROCEDURES: (Treatment proceeds in steps that are applied recursively to each of the objectives. Readers are reminded that any of the behaviors noted in the Objectives or the

60

PROCEDURES:
(continued)

Comments can be used with this approach. For illustrative purposes, this table focuses on indirect pitch direction.)

1. The clinician presents the target stimuli (different pitch directions) to the client. At first, the clinician controls the stimuli for complexity, rate, and number of speakers.

2. The clinician focuses the client's attention on the targeted stimuli. He or she provides cues (visual and gestural) to highlight the phonetic nature of the stimuli. For example, the clinician may present productions of the vowel /o/ using different pitch directions paired with different motor movements. The clinician may accompany a rising pitch direction by the raising of his or her hand or a falling pitch direction by the lowering of the hand.

3. The clinician explains the meaning of the targeted stimuli. For example, the clinician explains that a rising direction often signifies questioning.

4. The client practices the targeted behavior.

    (a) The client imitates the target behavior (i.e., the different pitch directions). At first, the stimuli are presented in short, simple utterances. Later, stimuli consist of monologues.

    (b) The client transcribes samples of speech containing the target structure. For example, the client marks a text for pitch direction while listening to speech samples. The clinician provides timely verbal feedback and increases task complexity as the client improves.

    (c) The client discriminates which of two pitch directions is appropriate for the context. For example, the client identifies the appropriate context for the reply "You've looked in the garage (/)"

    Question #1: "Why not have a look in the garage?"

    Question #2: "I've looked in the gara . . . (the rest is unintelligible)."

(continued)

Table 4-7 *(continued)*

PROCEDURES *(continued)*	(d) The client matches sentences that should be produced consecutively. For example:

COLUMN A   COLUMN B

x I heard you went   1 |I went to Cleveland|
  to Cleveland.   (\)

y Where did you go
  for your vacation?   2 |I went to Cleveland| (/)

key: x = 2; y = 1

(e) The client repetitively produces meaningful, routine patterns.

(f) The client reads aloud from transcripts.

COMMENT: Other categories used indirectly in this approach include intonation (onset, nucleus, terminal contour, pitch agreement); tempo (phrasing); and stress (lexical).

Note: The legend for symbols used in this table are entered under "Symbols" in the Glossary.

Source: The above program was derived from information provided in Brazil, D., Coulthard, M., & Johns, C. (1980). *Discourse intonation and language teaching.* Essex, England: Longman.

    (b) The target behaviors of the pitch direction phase of training include

- reading and
- conversing using selected pitch directions.

    (c) Usually, the **hierarchy** of indirect pitch direction methods is logical.

  (2) **Techniques** used with indirect purpose and pitch direction focus are listed in Table 4-2, which presents the techniques for the different pitch related PFCs. Commonly used techniques for indirect pitch direction PFCs include ***metalinguistics, cues,*** and ***reading aloud.***

  4. Approaches that focus indirectly on pitch variation (i.e., indirect pitch variation PFC). (**Pitch variation** = Pitch range.)

    a. Population. Pitch variation is used indirectly for speakers with developmental apraxia of speech, developmental delay, hearing impairment, motor speech disorders, and voice disorders. In addition, pitch variation is used to improve the overall speaking skills of normal speakers (speech improvement).

b. Intervention
(1) Content
(a) The **terminal objectives** for methods using indirect pitch variation include

- improved articulatory/phonological skills,
- increased fluency,
- increased intelligibility,
- establishment of pre-speech vocalization skills,
- improved overall pitch,
- improved overall vocal skills, and
- improved overall intonation or prosody.

(b) The **target behaviors** of the pitch variation phase of training include

- reading aloud passages of varying lengths;
- conversing;
- vocalizing;
- judging acceptability;
- imitating a series of changes in pitch;
- producing appropriate pitch variations in strings of syllables, single utterances, or conversation; and
- producing monotone speech (i.e., restricted pitch variation).

Table 4–8 presents an example of an approach that indirectly focuses on pitch variation.

(c) **Usually, the hierarchy** of indirect pitch variation methods is logical. That is, the clinician exposes clients to stimuli that are believed to increase in difficulty.

(2) The **techniques** used with indirect purpose and pitch variation PFCs are listed in Table 4–2, which presents techniques used with the different pitch PFCs. Two commonly used techniques for indirect pitch variation are ***metalinguistics*** and ***cues.***

Table 4–8. Program for indirect pitch variation PFC. (Steps related to pitch variation are preceded by an asterisk [*].)

POPULATION:	Developmental delay.
TECHNIQUES:	Exaggeration, singing, motor movement, play, stimulation (auditory), modeling. (The Glossary contains definitions of the techniques.)
GOAL:	To improve overall intelligibility.
OBJECTIVES:	1. To increase production of speech sounds during structured play. (Prosodic modifications are used to attract and maintain attention.)
	2. To increase production of language during structured play. (Prosodic modifications are used to attract and maintain attention.)
	3. To employ repair strategies to increase overall intelligibility.
PROCEDURES:	*1. The clinician employs exaggerated pitch variation during sound stimulation tasks.
	2. The clinician uses exaggerated overall (intonation) contours during language stimulation tasks. This may include singing, rhythms, and finger plays.
	3. The clinician models and reinforces the client's use of strategies to improve intelligibility following a communication breakdown. The client is exposed to a variety of repair strategies. The ones relevant to prosody are
	• slow rate,
	• modification of phrasing, and
	• modified overall (intonation) contour
COMMENTS:	Swift and Rosin detail a comprehensive approach for treating speech intelligibility for people with Down syndrome. They focus on deficits in processing sequential information and include discussions of hearing aids, singing, motor skill, parent training, structured play, augmentative communication, computers, tongue surgery, palatal lifts, repair strategies, and graphic symbols. The suggestions presented above relate only to prosody and are only a small part of the overall program.
	In addition to pitch variation, this approach also uses the following other categories indirectly: tempo (phrasing, rate) and intonation (overall contour).

Source: The above program was derived from information provided in Swift, E. & Rosin, D. (1990). A remediation sequence to improve speech intelligibility for students with Down syndrome. *Language, Speech, And Hearing Services in Schools, 21,* 140–146.

C. Summary Points

1. Treatment methods are available for all of the PFCs with the exception of the **direct slope (or declination) focus** PFC.

2. Treatment methods for pitch have been developed for individuals from a number of different **disorder and etiological groups**.

3. Many methods exist for teaching pitch in the **voice disorders literature**. The number of voice related pitch methods presented here was limited to increase the diversity of programs in this chapter.

4. Most methods for treating pitch order treatment steps using a **logical hierarchy**. Because few pitch treatment programs have been subjected to empirical validation, clinicians should feel free to use other types of hierarchies.

5. Many of the treatment methods use **reading aloud** as a treatment technique. This appears to ignore the evidence that prosody in reading and spontaneous speech are not always equivalent. Baken (1987), however, reports that the F_0 for read samples is only slightly higher than the F_0 in spontaneous speech. Thus, in the case of pitch, it may be efficient to use reading in place of spontaneous speech for clients who have adequate reading skills.

6. Other popular treatment techniques include **metalinguistic tasks** and **self-monitoring**. Both techniques are fairly complex and do not seem to be appropriate for young children (Healey & Scott, 1991) or cognitively impaired individuals.

7. Control of pitch is important in the production of other aspects of prosody. Clinicians working with clients who have **sufficient pitch control**, may use pitch to elicit other communicative behaviors (indirect purposes). For clients experiencing difficulty controlling the different pitch categories, clinicians should consider treating pitch directly prior to working on a prosodic component (i.e., tempo, intonation, stress, rhythm). Unfortunately, there are no criteria delineating the pitch skills required for the production of acceptable prosodic components. Therefore, clinicians must determine what is appropriate for their own clients.

8. Few pitch-based treatment approaches have been **verified empirically**. Accordingly, clinicians should confirm treatment effectiveness on an individual basis and should not be hesitant to alter undocumented treatment approaches to suit their views about intervention and their client's needs.

9. One infrequently used treatment strategy is to approach pitch treatment using an **integrated and/or holistic perspective** rather than using the categorical approach that currently predominates the intervention literature. Those wishing to use a holistic approach are referred to the references cited in section VI.H.

10. Most pitch treatment approaches are designed for adults. Section VI.I provides citations for approaches designed for **children**.

11. Readers will note that Table 4–2 contains an extensive array of **treatment techniques**. Because of the lack of effectiveness data, clinicians may view Table 4–2 as a preliminary listing of preferred practices rather than a listing of proven techniques. Researchers, on the other hand, may consider Table 4–2 as a listing of treatment techniques to investigate.

VI. PURPOSE/FOCUS TREATMENT CITATIONS

A. Citations for Approaches Directly Focusing on Pitch Height

Boone (1971, pp. 121–124, 127–130, 157–159); Cooper (1973, pp.76–86); Dworkin (1991, pp. 306–308, 321); Glenn, Glenn, & Forman (1989, pp. 80–84); Ling (1976, p. 252); McGarr, Youdelman, & Head (1992); Waling & Harrison (1987); Wilson (1972, pp. 128–136, 172–175).

B. Citations for Approaches Directly Focusing on Pitch Detection

Moncur & Brackett (1974, pp. 75–77).

C. Citations for Approaches Directly Focusing on Pitch Variation

Boone (1971, pp. 140–141); Glenn et al. (1989, pp. 90–91); Moncur & Brackett (1974, pp. 77–78, 86–98); Rosenbek & LaPointe (1978, pp. 282–286, 300); Wilson (1972, pp. 172–175).

D. Citations for Approaches Indirectly Focusing on Pitch Height

Andrews (1973); Boone (1971, pp. 114–115, 121–124, 127–130); Fairbanks (1960, pp. 132–134); Freedman & Garstecki (1973); Gilbert (1984 , pp. 15–16); King & DiMichael (1991); Ling (1976, pp. 206–211); Minskoff (1980); Rosenbek (1978, p. 214); Schomburg, Lippert, Johnson, Muss, & Tittnich (1989); Sikorski (1988, pp. 2–23, 47–50, 86–96).

E. Citations for Approaches Indirectly Focusing on Pitch Slope/Declination

Fairbanks (1960, pp. 132–134); Ling (1976, pp. 206–211); Moncur & Brackett (1974, pp. 78, 80–81, 82–84); Sikorski (1988, pp. 45–46, 51–53, 51–69).

F. Citations for Approaches Indirectly Focusing on Pitch Direction

Brazil, Coulthard, & Johns (1980); Ling (1976, pp. 206–211); Moncur & Brackett (1974, pp. 75–77; 78–80; 78, 80–81; 81–82; 86–89); Sikorski (1988, pp. 2–23, 47–50, 70–77, 86–96).

G. Citations for Approaches Indirectly Focusing on Pitch Variation

Freedman & Garstecki (1973); Glenn et al. (1989, pp. 90–91); Ham (1986, pp. 334–335); Helfrich-Miller (1984); King & DiMichael (1991); Ling (1976, pp. 206–211, 295–387); Moncur & Brackett (1974, pp. 75–77); Rosenbek (1978, pp. 191–241); Simmons (1983); Swift & Rosin (1990).

H. Citations for Integrative and/or Holistic Treatment Approaches

Berry (1980); Bergendal (1976); Ham (1986, pp. 333–334); Helfrich-Miller (1984); Krauss & Galloway (1982); Ling (1976, pp. 206–211, 295–387); Minskoff (1980); Moncur & Brackett (1974, pp. 78–80; 78, 80–81; 78, 81–82; 82–84; 84–86; 86–89); Schomburg, Lippert, Johnson, Muss, & Tittnich (1989); Simmons (1983); Sparks (1981); Stern (1987, Course #1, #2); Swift & Rosin (1990); Appendixes A & B.

I. Citations for Approaches Developed for Children

Andrews (1973); Berry (1980); Freedman & Garstecki (1973); Ham (1986); Helfrich-Miller (1984); Hoskins (1988); Krauss & Galloway (1982); Ling (1976, pp. 206–211, 252, 295–387); Minskoff (1980); Schomburg, Lippert, Johnson, Muss, & Tittnich (1989); Swift & Rosin (1990); Waling & Harrison (1987); Wilson (1972, pp. 103–105, 105–106, 106–107, 107–111, 128–136, 172–175); Appendix B.

CHAPTER

5

Treating Prosodic Features: Loudness

I. NORMAL USE OF THE PROSODIC FEATURE LOUDNESS

A. Description

Loudness is a prosodic feature that serves as one of the building blocks for the four components of prosody (tempo, intonation, stress, and rhythm). Loudness is the perception of changes in sound pressure level. Its physical correlates, intensity and sound pressure level, may be measured although the scaling of loudness, per se, is not simple.

B. Categories

Figure 5–1 presents the two loudness categories (loudness level and loudness variation).

70

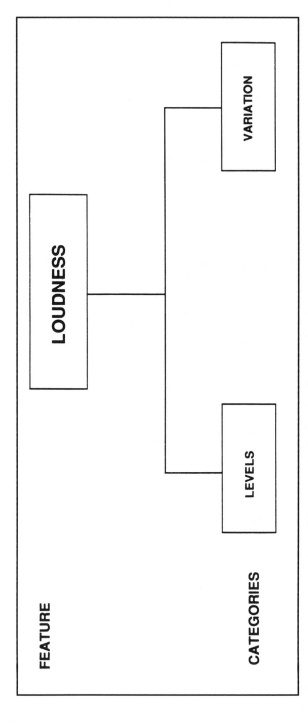

Figure 5–1. A representation of the prosodic feature loudness and its categories

1. The **loudness level** is labeled perceptually as "loud" or "soft" and is represented as the magnitude of the excursion from an arbitrary reference point. Measures such as decibels (dB) quantify the loudness level.

2. **Loudness variation** is the range of change in loudness levels from the greatest (loudest) to the least (softest) for any linguistic unit (e.g., a syllable, word, phrase, speaking turn). As with loudness level, loudness variation can be represented perceptually or instrumentally.

C. Normative Information

Although the normal loudness level of conversational speech is about 60–65 dB, loudness level is context dependent. The size of the audience, the ambient noise level, and the speaker's affective state are examples of factors that influence loudness level.

D. Communicative Roles

Loudness plays several roles in communication:

1. Loudness contributes to the **production of the prosodic components** of tempo, intonation, stress, and rhythm (Chapters 8, 9, 10, and 11, respectively).

2. Loudness **attracts and maintains listener attention**.

3. Loudness provides **segmentation** cues.

4. Loudness communicates **attitude or emotion**.

5. Loudness conveys different degrees of **politeness**.

II. PERCEIVING THE PROSODIC FEATURE OF LOUDNESS

At the acoustic level, the perception of loudness is related to intensity or amplitude. For the most part, as intensity increases, listeners perceive that loudness increases, and as intensity decreases, the perception of loudness decreases. However, there is not a direct correspondence between loudness and intensity. The perception of loudness can be influenced by extraneous factors. For example, changes in pitch height may result in the perception of increased loudness despite a fairly stable intensity signal (Borden & Harris, 1984). Additionally, listeners selectively attend to intensity changes when making judgments of overall loudness and apparently do not attend to intrinsic phonemic intensity fluctuations when making judgments of overall loudness (Couper-Kuhlen, 1986). For example, the intrinsic intensity of vowels varies with high vowels (e.g., /i/) having relatively low intensity levels and low vowels (e.g., /a/) having a relatively high intensity levels.

III. PRODUCING THE PROSODIC FEATURE OF LOUDNESS

The intensity of speech varies considerably over relatively short time intervals because of periods of silence, syllabic and word stress, and the inherent intensity of different phonemes. Variations in voice quality will also be reflected in differences in loudness. Baken (1987) provides considerable detail on the measured intensity levels of phonemes and instrumentation for evaluation.

The physiological correlates of loudness are closely related to those of frequency. Subglottal air pressure, which is a necessary condition for voicing, in the range of 7 to 10 cm of H_2O pressure is sufficient to produce an intensity of approximately 60 dB (conversational speech). Obviously, variations in subglottal air pressure will affect the percept loudness, but the relationship between intensity and frequency is complex. For example, increased vocal resistance due to muscular forces at the level of the vocal folds will cause increased vocal intensity. The greater subglottal air pressure forces the vocal folds to be abducted wider, allowing a greater release of air, which sets up a sound pressure wave of greater amplitude. The sound is perceived as louder. Certainly muscular adjustment in the larynx and management of respiration are also critical factors in loudness. Any factors that upset this balance between respiratory effort, laryngeal valving, and pressure will affect loudness. Moreover, even the added forces of intraoral pressure, that is, how the air stream is directed at the upper articulators, contribute to the complex phenomena. Obviously, speakers with numerous types of speech disorders may show difficulty in producing appropriate loudness levels and varying loudness when any of these physiological factors cannot be marshaled normally.

IV. A MODEL FOR TREATING LOUDNESS

A. A Teaching Model for Loudness

As noted in section I.B, the categories of loudness are loudness level and loudness variation.

B. Treatment Decisions: Loudness

Clinicians should consider the guidelines presented in the accompanying Clinical Note when planning to work on this feature. Explanations of these guidelines are elaborated in Chapter 2, Section III.B. In addition, the Treatment Index identifies the location of all the purposes, focuses, objectives, hierarchies, treatment techniques, and sample programs for the treatment of loudness in the Clinical Note and its explanation.

CLINICAL NOTE: GUIDELINES FOR DECISION MAKING

1. **Determine the purpose** (direct, indirect) for working with loudness.
2. **Identify the categories** of loudness (level, variation) that will serve as the focus of therapy.
3. **Identify** specific **treatment objectives** for the targeted purpose/focus combination (PFC) (i.e., the purpose from Guideline #1 and the focus from Guideline #2 above).
4. **Decide how to order objectives**.
5. **Select treatment techniques** appropriate for the client and the PFC.
6. Identify sources in which **clients with similar disorders** have similar PFCs.

V. SUMMARY OF PUBLISHED LITERATURE ON TREATING LOUDNESS

A. Direct Purpose Treatment Strategies

1. **Approaches that focus directly on loudness level** (i.e., direct loudness level PFC). (**Loudness level** = Magnitude of the excursion from an arbitrary reference point.)

a. Population. Direct treatment of loudness level has been attempted with persons with developmental delay, hearing impairment, motor speech disorders, and voice disorders. In addition, the improvement of loudness level has been the focus of programs that are designed to improve the oral communication skills of normal speakers (speech improvement).

b. Intervention
(1) Content
(a) The **target behaviors** most commonly used for this PFC involve increasing loudness level, although the decrease of loudness level also has been a target of therapy. Contexts for production include

- nonverbal vocalizations,
- ritual or routine phrases,
- conversations,
- labeling pictures,
- sentences or paragraphs to be read aloud, and
- responses to questions.

Additionally, some methods focus on discriminating and/or labeling loudness levels of one's own speech or the speech of others.
(b) The **hierarchy** of steps for the direct treatment of loudness level tends to be logical. The sample program presented in Table 5–1, however, is linear.
(2) The **techniques** for treating loudness PFCs are presented in Table 5–2. Commonly used techniques for direct loudness level PFCs include *metalinguistics, discrimination, reading aloud, feedback*, and *breathing activities*.

2. Approaches that focus directly on loudness variation (i.e., direct loudness variation PFC. (**Loudness variation** = Change in the range of loudness from loudest to softest for any linguistic unit.)

a. Population. Methods that directly treat loudness variation have been designed for individuals with the following problems: hearing impairment, motor speech disor-

Table 5-1. Program for direct loudness PFC

POPULATION:	Developmental delay (adult).
TECHNIQUES:	Feedback (visual, verbal); cues (visual, verbal); query responding; fading; coaching. (The Glossary contains definitions of the techniques.)
OBJECTIVE:	To answer questions about activities of daily living using an intensity level below 65 dB.
PROCEDURES:	1. The clinician plans an activity of daily living (e.g., making popcorn, cooking a meal, washing clothes, putting on make-up, etc.)
	2. The clinician asks the client 50 questions about ongoing activities, and the client attempts to answer each question using a loudness level of less than 65 dB. If the client's response is below 65 dB, the clinician verbally praises the client and provides a tangible response. If the client's loudness level exceeds 65 dB, a "Whisperlite" is activated. (The Whisperlite is an instrument that flashes a light when a designated sound pressure level is reached.)
	3. The clinician employs visual cues (e.g., placing hands over ears) and verbal cues (e.g., saying, "Remember to use your quiet voice") prior to the client's response to assist in the reduction of the client's loudness level.
	4. The client gradually fades the cues and the reinforcement.
COMMENTS:	Although generalization to conversation was not a step in the training procedures, follow-up data revealed that the loudness level of the client's conversational speech was reduced without direct treatment.

Source: The above program was derived from information provided in Lodge, J. M., & Yarnell, G. D. (1981). A case study of vocal volume reduction. *Journal of Speedh and Hearing Disorders, 46,* 317–320.

ders, and voice disorders. Additionally, several programs exist that attempt to improve the vocal skills of normal speakers (speech improvement).

b. Intervention
(1) Content
(a) The **target behaviors** of direct loudness variation methods involve the production of a variety of different loudness levels:

Table 5–2. Treatment techniques for the various loudness PFCs. (Definitions of all treatment techniques are provided in the Glossary.)

Technique	Purpose/Focus Combinations
Activities of Daily Living	direct loudness level
Amplification	direct loudness level, indirect loudness level
Auditory Masking	indirect loudness level
Breathing Activities	direct loudness level
Coaching	direct loudness level, direct loudness variation
Contrastive Sets/Minimal Pairs	direct loudness level, direct loudness variation, indirect loudness level, indirect loudness variation
Conversation	direct loudness variation, indirect loudness level
Cues	
Auditory	direct loudness variation, indirect loudness variation
Tactile/Kinesthetic	direct loudness level, direct loudness variation, indirect loudness level, indirect loudness variation
Verbal	direct loudness level
Visual	direct loudness level, direct loudness variation, indirect loudness level, indirect loudness variation
Discrimination	direct loudness level, direct loudness variation, indirect loudness level, indirect loudness variation
Exaggeration	direct loudness level, direct loudness variation, indirect loudness level
Fading	indirect loudness level
Feedback	
Acoustic	direct loudness level
Auditory	direct loudness level, indirect loudness level, indirect loudness variation
Tactile/Kinesthetic	direct loudness level, direct loudness variation, indirect loudness level
Verbal	direct loudness level, direct loudness variation, indirect loudness level, indirect loudness variation

Technique	Purpose/Focus
Feedback (continued)	
Visual	direct loudness level, direct loudness variation, indirect loudness level, indirect loudness variation
Games	direct loudness variation, indirect loudness level
Humming	direct loudness variation, indirect loudness level
Imitation	direct loudness variation, indirect loudness level, indirect loudness variation
Metalinguistics	direct loudness level, direct loudness variation, indirect loudness level, indirect loudness variation
Modeling	direct loudness level, direct loudness variation, indirect loudness level, indirect loudness variation
Motor Movement	direct loudness variation
Music	direct loudness variation
Musical Instruments	direct loudness variation
Negative Practice	direct loudness variation, indirect loudness level
Physical Adjustments	indirect loudness level
Picture Description	direct loudness variation
Play	indirect loudness variation
Production on Demand	direct loudness level
Query Responding	direct loudness level
Reading Aloud	direct loudness level, direct loudness variation, indirect loudness level, indirect loudness variation
Relaxation	direct loudness level, indirect loudness level
Review	indirect loudness level

(continued)

Table 5-2 (continued)

Technique	Purpose/Focus
Rituals	direct loudness level, direct loudness variation
Role Playing	direct loudness variation
Scripts	direct loudness variation
Self-Monitoring	direct loudness level, indirect loudness level
Sequencing	indirect loudness variation
Shadowing	indirect loudness level
Singing	direct loudness level, direct loudness variation
Stimulation	
Auditory	indirect loudness variation
Unison Speech	indirect loudness level

- during singing or humming
- during conversation, and
- while reading paragraphs or selected passages aloud.

Tables 5-3 and 5-4 contain examples of programs that directly treat loudness variation in children and adults, respectively.

(b) The **hierarchy** of objectives for the direct treatment of loudness variation usually is logical.

(2) Techniques used in loudness PFCs are presented in Table 5-2. Commonly used techniques for direct loudness variation include *metalinguistics* and *contrastive sets*.

B. Indirect Purpose Treatment Strategies

1. Approaches that focus indirectly on loudness level (i.e., indirect loudness level PFC). (**Loudness level** = Magnitude of the excursion from an arbitrary reference point.)

Table 5-3. Program for direct loudness variation PFC (children)

POPULATION:	Hearing impairment (children).
TECHNIQUES:	Cues (visual); discrimination; motor movements; games; music; singing; contrastive sets; metalinguistics; feedback (auditory, tactile/kinesthetic, verbal, visual); modeling, self-monitoring; imitation. (The Glossary contains definitions of the techniques.)
OBJECTIVES:	1. To discriminate among various loudness levels. 2. To produce loudness at a variety of acceptable levels in connected speech.
PROCEDURES:	(NOTE: Within each step, the procedures need not be presented in the order listed.)

1a. The clinician places pictures in the client's notebook that represent different loudness levels (very loud, loud, appropriate, too soft).
Examples:
- a child speaking at different loudness levels,
- vehicles or animals producing differing loudness levels, and
- children engaging in activities that may be associated with different loudness levels.

b. The clinician models appropriate loudness levels and explains that reduced rate may result in reduced loudness, and increased rate may result in increased loudness.

c. The clinician introduces a chart for use during self-monitoring and explains the different loudness levels and identifies
- the ideal loudness level,
- correct and incorrect loudness levels in others,
- correct and incorrect loudness levels for the client, and
- contexts in which loudness level should change.

d. The clinician assists the client in discriminating his or her own loudness level by tape recording the client's speech and demonstrating how the loudness level can be monitored using a VU meter.

e. The clinician and the client play "Hide and Seek" with a toy. The clinician hides a toy and plays music of various loudness levels. The further the toy is from the client, the softer the music is played.

(continued)

Table 5-3 *(continued)*

PROCEDURES *(continued)*	2a. The clinician pairs the following: • loud stomping and soft tiptoeing, • loud clapping and soft clapping, and/or • loud music and soft music. b. The clinician models loud and then soft humming or singing. The clinician also hums (or sings) softly and loudly to develop the loud/soft contrast. c. The clinician may use an amplifier to facilitate the production of reduced or increased loudness levels. If reduced loudness is desired, the clinician plays low intensity white noise through earphones as the client is speaking. If increased loudness is desired, the clinician plays high intensity white noise through the client's earphones. d. The client and the clinician play games using different loudness levels. For example, they play "Old Man" in which the client whispers when the clinician (the "Old Man") pretends to sleep. Production should be loud to awaken the "Old Man" and even louder to anger the "Old Man." Alternately, the clinician and the client may play with toys that are activated at certain loudness levels. e. The clinician instructs the client to use different loudness levels in different contexts. Examples: • loud in noisy contexts or • soft in quiet contexts As the client practices using the appropriate loudness level for the context, the clinician directs him or her to attend to auditory and tactile/kinesthetic feedback during production of the different loudness levels. The clinician provides frequent verbal feedback regarding the appropriateness of the client's loudness level for the context. f. If necessary, the clinician directs the client's attention to the intensity meter (VU) on a tape recorder to use as visual feedback. The client monitors the meter, and the clinician provides feedback about the appropriateness of the loudness level. The clinician also directs the client's attention to auditory and tactile/kinesthetic feedback.

Source: The above program was derived from information provided in Wilson, D. K. (1979). *Voice problems of children* (2nd ed., pp. 136–138, 175–176). Baltimore: Williams & Wilkins.

Table 5-4. Program for direct loudness variation PFC (adults)

POPULATION:	Motor speech disorders.
TECHNIQUES:	Conversation; monologues (picture description); modeling; feedback (verbal, visual); metalinguistics. (The Glossary contains definitions of the techniques.)
OBJECTIVES:	To use the upper two-thirds of the loudness range for at least 75% of the time spent talking (talking time).
PROCEDURES:	1a. The clinician determines the client's ability to modulate loudness by conversing with the client and/or by having him or her describe a picture.
	b. The clinician calculates the amount of time the client uses a low or soft loudness level. If more than 25% of the talking time employs a low or soft loudness level, treatment is recommended.
	2a. The clinician marks off three equal zones (within the client's loudness repertoire) on the VU meter of a tape recorder. The first zone represents the "soft" loudness level, the second zone is the "normal" loudness level, and the last zone is the "loudest" level.
	b. The clinician models natural conversation in which the loudness level varies between the second and third zones approximately 75% of the time. In appropriate contexts, the clinician models movement into the first level during production of the ends of utterances.
	c. The clinician describes the loudness variation indicated by the VU meter and the role that context plays in loudness variation.
	3a. The client converses with the clinician for 10 minutes. The clinician calculates the percentage of time the client uses zone one (the soft level) and provides feedback regarding the client's success.
	b. The client and the clinician continue the task until the client achieves 75% improvement over baseline (Step #1) or is without error for 10 consecutive minutes of discourse.
COMMENT:	The author notes that this objective may not be obtainable for all clients with motor speech disorders.

Source: The above program was derived from information provided in Dworkin, J. P. (1991). *Motor speech disorders* (pp. 315–316). St. Louis, MO: Mosby.

a. **Population.** Treatment methods for indirect loudness level PFCs have been designed for individuals with the following problems: hearing impairment, learning disability, motor speech disorders, specific language impairment, stuttering, and voice disorders. Programs also are available for normal speakers seeking to improve their speaking skills (speech improvement).

b. **Intervention**
   (1) **Content**
      (a) The **terminal objectives** of indirect loudness level methods vary considerably. Examples of common terminal objectives are

      • to promote fluency,
      • to promote preverbal vocalization skills,
      • to improve pitch variation,
      • to improve social skills,
      • to improve articulation skills,
      • to improve lexical stress,
      • to increase normalcy judgments,
      • to improve articulation,
      • to improve overall voice quality,
      • to increase intelligibility, and
      • to reduce vocal abuse.

      (b) The **target behaviors** for loudness level phases of treatment include

      • using normal loudness while listening to auditory masking,
      • reading aloud with auditory masking to produce the Lombard effect,
      • imitating phrases matching the clinician's loudness level,
      • whispering,
      • matching loudness level to context,
      • increasing loudness when attempting to produce troublesome structures,
      • producing specified loudness levels on a single breath,
      • producing utterances of varying lengths and complexities using specified loudness levels,
      • reading aloud selected passages using specified loudness levels,

- reading aloud sentences in which stressed words are produced by increasing loudness, and
- reducing loudness level.

Table 5–5 provides an example program for indirect loudness level PFC.

(c) When the appropriate production of the loudness level is an intermediate objective or a facilitator/constrainer, the **hierarchy** tends to be logical.

(2) The **techniques** used with the different loudness PFCs are presented in Table 5–2. Cognitively complex techniques such as *metalinguistics, reading aloud,* and the provision of *feedback* commonly occur in indirect loudness level PFCs.

2. **Approaches that focus indirectly on loudness variation** (i.e., indirect loudness variation PFC). (**Loudness variation** = Change in loudness from greatest (loudest) to least (softest) level for any linguistic unit.)

   a. **Population.** Methods with an indirect purpose and a focus on loudness variation have been designed for individuals from the following disorder or etiological groups: dysarthria, hearing impairment, and voice impairment. Methods also are available for normal speakers seeking to improve their speaking skills (speech improvement).

   b. **Intervention**
   (1) **Content**
      (a) The **terminal objectives** for the indirect use of loudness variation include

      - improving overall prosody,
      - improving overall pitch,
      - establishing preverbal vocal skills,
      - improving overall vocal quality, and
      - improving articulation skills.

      (b) The **target behaviors** for the loudness variation phases of treatment include

      - vocalizing at differing loudness levels,

Table 5–5. Program for indirect loudness level PFC. (Steps related to loudness level are preceded by an asterisk [*].)

POPULATION:	Dysarthria.
TECHNIQUES:	Reading aloud, feedback (visual), imitation, modeling, metalinguistics, self-monitoring. (The Glossary contains definitions of the techniques.)
GOAL:	To improve intelligibility.
OBJECTIVE:	To use specified rate and loudness.
PROCEDURES:	1. The clinician establishes the client's baseline performance by having the client read aloud 40 randomly presented sentences.
	2. The clinician models and stores target sentences lists in a storage oscilloscope.
	*3. Prior to reading aloud or imitating sentences, the client is directed to
	*a. keep the loudness level below a designated line on the oscilloscope (to reduce loudness) and
	b. make sure that the sentence extends over half the screen (to increase overall duration).
	*4. The client reads or imitates sentences from sentence lists. Simultaneous with the reading or imitating, each sentence is acoustically analyzed on the storage oscilloscope which permits the monitoring of rate and loudness.
	*5. The client monitors the oscilloscope and makes judgments about the adequacy of his or her productions.
	*6. When the client produces an acceptable sentence, the oscilloscope stores that sentence for later use as a model.
COMMENT:	Data elicited immediately following the completion of the program from one client indicated that the program was successful. The results also indicated that decreases in rate and increases in duration occurred primarily because of increased pause time. Unfortunately, the client's performance regressed at the 2-week post-treatment sampling. It should be noted, however, that the client experienced a TIA (transient ischemic attack) before the 2-week evaluation.
	Tempo (rate) also is used indirectly in this approach.

Source: The above program was derived from information provided in Berry, W. R., & Goshorn, E. L. (1983). Immediate visual feedback in the treatment of ataxic dysarthria: A case study. In W. R. Berry (Ed.), *Clinical dysarthria* (pp. 253–265). San Diego: College-Hill Press.

- reading aloud selected passages while varying loudness levels, and
- producing targeted speech sounds using a variety of loudness levels.

Table 5–6 presents an example of a treatment method which uses indirect loudness variation.

(c) When the appropriate production of the loudness variation is an intermediate objective or a facilitator/constrainer, the **hierarchy** tends to be logical.

(2) The **techniques** used in loudness methods are presented in Table 5–2. *Feedback* and *reading* aloud occur with relative frequency with indirect loudness variation PFCs.

C. Summary Points

1. Treatment methods have been identified for all the **loudness-based PFCs**.

2. Treatment methods for loudness are available for individuals from several different **etiological and disorder groups**. The most commonly targeted group for treatment of loudness problems is voice disorders and/or voice impairment. If the examples in the treatment sections were to represent accurately the distribution relative to disorder groups, this chapter would be dominated by examples of voice-related treatment methods. To increase the diversity of the represented disorder groups, the number of voice-related loudness treatment methods was restricted. Those wishing additional information about the treatment of loudness problems from the perspective of voice disorders and/or improvement are referred to Colton and Casper (1990).

3. The summaries in the preceding sections indicate that logical **hierarchies** are the most frequently used hierarchies. Recalling that empirical data are not used to establish logical hierarchies, clinicians may consider horizontal or disorder hierarchies when planning treatment.

4. There is a heavy emphasis on **metalinguistic tasks** such as describing, making judgments, and attending to symbolic feedback (i.e., verbal or visual feedback). Even methods de-

Table 5–6. Program for the indirect loudness variation PFC. (Steps related to loudness variation are preceded by an asterisk [*].)

POPULATION:	Hearing impairment (children).
TECHNIQUES:	Imitation; games; modeling; cues (auditory, tactile/kinesthetic, visual); feedback (visual). (The Glossary contains definitions of the techniques.)
GOAL:	To establish vocalization skills sufficient for speech (i.e., preverbal skills).
OBJECTIVES:	1. To produce brief, loud vocalizations. 2. To produce brief, soft vocalizations. 3. To produce a whisper. 4. To produce loud, soft, or whispered vocalizations of at least 3 seconds duration. 5. To produce a series of several discrete vocalizations of varying intensities.
PROCEDURES:	*1a. The clinician plays games with client in which vocalizations of certain loudness levels permit participation. For example, the clinician and the client play "Waking Up the Teacher" or create movement in voice-activated toys.
	*b. The clinician trains the client to increase his or her loudness as the distance between the speaker and listener increases.
	*2. The clinician employs the same procedures as in Step #1 but the target is the use of a soft loudness level. Emphasis is placed on the client's ability to control others' behaviors by vocalizing.
	*3. The clinician models "forced" or "stage" whispers for clients who have sufficient residual hearing. If the client's hearing is sufficient for this task, the clinician employs tactile or visual cues (e.g., blowing out a match).
	*4. The clinician requires that each of the previously trained behaviors be sustained for at least 3 seconds. This may be accomplished by playing games, such as "Make the Teacher Walk," in which the clinician (teacher) continues to walk if the client sustains the proper loudness and duration.
	*5. The clinician and the client play additional games in which vocalizations of different loudness levels (in a single breath) represent different activities. For example, the client pretends he or she is a tiger and

PROCEDURES *(continued)*	stalks prey by whispering or attacks prey by producing loud vocalizations.
COMMENT:	Tempo (phrasing) and duration also are used indirectly in this method.

Source: The above program was derived from information provided in Ling, D. C. (1976). *Speech and the hearing-impaired child: Theory and practice* (pp. 203–206). Washington, DC: Alexander Graham Bell Association for the Deaf.

signed for children use metalinguistic tasks despite questions about the effectiveness of such techniques with children (Healey & Scott, 1991).

5. Clinicians working with **children** should consider child-oriented treatment methods that employ such age-appropriate techniques as game playing, modeling, and the pairing of motor movement with loudness levels. For treatment ideas, see the citations listed in section VI.E.

6. **Reading aloud** is a frequently used treatment technique despite the lack of evidence that loudness in reading and spontaneous speech are equivalent.

7. In this book, loudness is viewed as one of the **building blocks** for the prosodic components of tempo, intonation, stress, and rhythm. If a client has sufficient control of loudness level and variation, then loudness may be used indirectly to elicit other communicative behaviors. However, if clients experience difficulty controlling loudness and this affects the production of any of the four prosodic components, clinicians should consider treating loudness directly. Unfortunately, there currently are no criteria delineating the loudness skills speakers require for the production of acceptable prosodic components. Therefore, until research more clearly delineates the linkage between loudness and the prosodic components, clinicians must independently make decisions and verify effectiveness.

8. Few data exist verifying the **effectiveness** of loudness treatment methods. Accordingly, clinicians will want to confirm the effectiveness of treatments for their own clients and

should consider modifying undocumented programs to suit their clients' needs.

9. The **discrete organization** of this book may lead readers to assume that all treatment strategies target a single category or aspect of loudness. In fact, many approaches integrate the various categories of loudness and/or integrate loudness with the other prosodic features and the prosodic components. Refer to section VI.F for citations relating to integrative or holistic approaches for loudness.

VI. CITATIONS FOR LOUDNESS TREATMENT

A. Citations for Approaches Directly Focusing on Loudness Level

Dworkin (1991, 312, 313–314); Lodge & Yarnell (1981); Prater & Swift (1984, 112–115; 120; 160 & 189; 160, 190 & 236); Rosenbek & LaPointe (1978, pp. 300–301); Waling & Harrison (1987, p. 22); Wilson (1972, pp. 137–138).

B. Citations for Approaches Directly Focusing on Loudness Variation

Dworkin (1991, pp. 312–313, 315–316); Fairbanks (1960, pp. 141–143); Glenn, Glenn, & Forman (1989, pp. 74–80, 85–88); Moncur & Brackett (1974, pp. 77–78); Wilson (1972, pp. 175–176).

C. Citations for Approaches Indirectly Focusing on Loudness Level

Andrews (1973); Bergendal (1976); Berry & Goshorn (1983); Boone (1971, pp. 113–114, 114–115); Caligiuri & Murry (1983); Freedman & Garstecki (1973); Ham (1986, pp. 296–301, 301–305, 318–324, 324–328; 1990, pp. 296–301); Ling (1976, pp. 203–206); Minskoff (1980); Moncur & Brackett (1974, pp. 75–77, 96–98, 98, 98–99); Pindzola (1987a); Rosenbek (1978, p. 214); Sikorski (1988, pp. 2–23, 47–50, 78–81, 85–96).

D. Citations for Approaches Indirectly Focusing on Loudness Variation

Boone (1971, pp. 115–116); Glenn et al. (1989, pp. 88–90); Ling (1976, pp. 203–206, 206–211, 295–397); Simmons (1983).

E. Citations for Approaches Developed for Children

Andrews (1973); Freedman & Garstecki (1973); Ham (1990, pp. 269–301, 301–305); Ling (1976, pp. 203–206, 206–211, 295–387); Minskoff (1980); Pindzola (1987a); Waling & Harrison (1987); Wilson (1972, pp. 137–138, 175–176); Appendix B.

F. Citations for Integrative and/or Holistic Approaches

Bergendal (1976); Berry & Goshorn (1983); Caligiuri & Murry (1983); Ham (1986, pp. 318–324, 324–328); Ham (1990, pp. 301–305); Ling (1976, pp. 203–206, 206–211, 295–397); Minskoff (1980); Pindzola (1987a); Simmons (1983); Appendixes A & B.

CHAPTER

6

Treating Prosodic Features: Duration

I. NORMAL USE OF THE PROSODIC FEATURE DURATION

A. Description

Speech duration is a prosodic feature and a building block of the prosodic components of tempo, intonation, stress, and rhythm. Duration is the length of time used at the segmental, syllable, word, phrase, or sentence level.

B. Categories

The types of duration are differentiated by their function and are presented in Figure 6–1.

  1. **Inherent duration** involves length modifications that pertain to speech sounds. Some groups of speech sounds differ in their intrinsic length. Some consonants, such as fricatives or

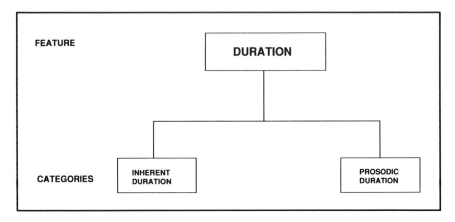

Figure 6-1. A representation of the prosodic feature duration and its categories.

nasals, may be classified as continuants and are longer in duration than obstruents, such as stop-plosives or affricates. With
respect to vowels, the so-called tense-lax distinction reflects
inherent duration. Long, sustainable vowel include /i, e, ɑ, ɔ,
u/ and diphthongs. Short vowels include /ɪ, ɛ, æ, ɒ/. Duration
of speech sounds varies relative to linguistic context. Atypical duration of speech sounds can have a detrimental impact
on overall prosody.

2. **Prosodic duration** is manifested in changes in length that are
   not related to differences among speech sounds but, nevertheless, have communicative value. Changes in prosodic duration are concerned with the production of tempo, intonation,
   stress, and rhythm. For example, prosodic duration changes
   occur for stressed words, for syllables or words at the end of
   utterances, and when speaking rate is modified.

C. Normative Information

Inherent duration and prosodic duration vary relative to a number of factors including the speech sounds produced, the syntactic
complexity, and the intentions of the speaker.

D. Communicative Roles

Inherent duration is used in the production of speech sounds; therefore, by nature, it has a communicative role. Prosodic duration
also has communicative roles.

1. It contributes to the production of the **prosodic components** of tempo, intonation, stress, and rhythm. For example, stressed words are of longer duration than unstressed words.

2. It provides **segmentation cues** to listeners. For example, the phrases below are phonemically identical but, as Borden and Harris (1984) have noted, represent two different meanings:

   - an aim
   - a name

   The /n/ in the first phrases (an aim) is slightly longer than the /n/ in the second phrase (a name). Longer duration of /n/ alerts listeners that the speech sound is ending a syllable rather than initiating one. Differences in segmentals produced in the final syllable of a phrase or sentence are another example of how duration cues contribute to segmentation.

3. We know from the work on hearing impairment using resynthesized speech that changes in aspects of duration (e.g., phoneme duration, relative duration, etc.) certainly affects **intelligibility** (Osberger & Levitt, 1979).

II. PERCEIVING THE PROSODIC FEATURE OF DURATION

The perception of variations in duration is calculated in time — the time it takes to produce the linguistic unit (e.g., word, syllable, terminal contour) in question. As with other prosodic features, there is not a one-to-one correspondence between the perception of duration and its acoustic measurement. Allen (1975) has noted, for example, that listeners are not accurate judges of duration, because they tend to underestimate long durations and overestimate short durations.

III. PRODUCING THE PROSODIC FEATURE OF DURATION

The physiological changes that occur when a speaker produces variations in duration are subject to debate in the research literature. These debates may be considered from two perspectives — "coarticulation" effects and "timing" effects. Some variations in duration arise from language specific differences, whereas others may arise at the level of motor organization of the articulators used for production. For example, when a vowel is produced in a stressed syllable position, there is greater muscle activity than for the vowel in the unstressed position. There may also be individual differences in muscle activity. For speaking rate (slow versus fast), there is conflicting evidence suggesting, on the one hand, differences in peak muscle activity and, on the other, no differences in muscle activity for the two rates. Generally, there is the notion that stressed vowels require "extra energy," but the details at the physiological level have not been worked out. The general idea suggests that this extra energy applied to the stressed vowels lasts longer and that signals to the articulators are somewhat longer. Thus, the vowel is produced farther from a neutral tract position. In an unstressed position, signals from the nervous sytem organize a vocal tract shape, and when "targets" for a subsequent phone arrive quickly, the idealized vowel target is not attained. The vowel is neutralized in comparison to its stressed pair, and the articulatory movement proceeds to the subsequent phoneme(s).

The articulatory correlates of lengthening of phonemes in the final position is a consequence of subglottal pressure changes and is discussed in Chapter 9 — Intonation.

IV. A MODEL FOR TREATING DURATION

A. A Teaching Model for Duration

The teaching model of duration is concerned with using acceptable inherent and prosodic durations when producing linguistic units (e.g., speech sounds, syllables, words, terminal contours, phrases).

B. Treatment Decisions: Duration

The accompanying Clinical Note provides guidelines for treating duration. Expanded explanations of the guidelines are provided in Chapter 2, Section III.B. In addition, the Treatment Index provides assistance in locating the purposes, focuses, objectives, hierarchies, treatment techniques, and sample programs noted in the Clinical Note and in the explanation.

CLINICAL NOTE: GUIDELINES FOR DECISION MAKING

1. **Determine the purpose** (direct, indirect) for working with duration.

2. **Identify the categories** of duration (inherent, prosodic) that will serve as the focus of therapy.
3. **Identify** specific **treatment objectives** for the targeted purpose/focus combination (PFC) (i.e., purpose from Guideline #1 and focus from Guideline #2 above).
4. **Decide how to order objectives**.
5. **Select treatment techniques** appropriate for the client and the PFCs.
6. Identify sources in which **clients with similar disorders** have similar PFCs.

V. SUMMARY OF PUBLISHED LITERATURE ON TREATING DURATION

A. Direct Purpose Treatment Strategies

1. **Approaches that focus directly on inherent duration** (i.e., direct inherent duration PFC). (**Inherent duration** = Length modifications that pertain to speech sounds.)

   a. **Population.** Direct treatment methods for effecting changes in inherent duration are designed for individuals who have hearing impairment and specific language impairment. Additionally, methods exist for normal speakers wishing to improve their overall communication skills (speech improvement) and those learning English as a second language.

   b. **Intervention**
      (1) **Content**
         (a) The **target behaviors** used to treat inherent duration consist of modifying the length of speech sounds when

         - producing strings of consonant-vowel syllables,
         - producing two word utterances,
         - reading sentences aloud, and
         - engaging in structured or spontaneous conversation.

         Table 6–1 provides an example of a typical program designed to alter inherent duration.

Table 6–1. Program for the direct inherent duration PFC

POPULATION: Specific language impairment.

TECHNIQUES: Imitation; feedback (verbal); games; cues (auditory, visual); modeling. (The Glossary contains definitions of the techniques.)

OBJECTIVES: 1. To imitate and to name spontaneously targets of increasing complexity without prolonging vowels and continuant consonants.

2. To produce connected speech in which there are no vowels or consonants with increased duration (prolongations) when describing pictures, using patterned responses, or speaking spontaneously.

PROCEDURES: 1a. The client imitates selected vowels in isolation. Example: The clinician says /o/ and the client repeats /o/ without increased duration.

b. The client imitates CV nonsense words. Example: The clinician says, "Cay," and the client repeats, "Cay," without increased duration.

c. The client spontaneously names pictured objects using CV combinations. Example: The clinician shows the client a picture of a knee and asks the prompt question, "What is this?" The client responds, "Knee," without increased duration.

d. The client imitates CVC words (real and nonsense) that contain stops in the final position. Example: The clinician says, "Say 'Top'." The client responds, "Top," without increased duration.

e. The client spontaneously names pictures of words containing CVC combinations with final stops. Example: The clinician displays a picture to the client and asks: "What is this?" The client responds, "Bag," without increased duration.

f. The client imitates real CVC words containing final fricatives, nasals, affricates, or semivowels. Example, The clinician says,

(b) A variety of **hierarchies** are used in methods that seek to improve inherent duration directly. For example, Ling's approach (1976, pp. 366–367) uses a linear hierarchy, and Hargrove, Dauer, and Montelibano (1989) (Table 6–1) use a combination hierarchy basing some of the ordering on the difficulty level of the tasks for the clients (disorder hierarchy) and basing other aspects of the ordering on the *apparent* level of difficulty (logical hierarchy).

"Say the word 'ball'." The client replies, "Ball," without increased duration.

g. The client spontaneously names the same CVC words presented in Step #1f. Example: The clinician shows the client a picture of a ball and asks the prompt question, "What is this?" The client responds "Ball," without increased duration.

h. The client spontaneously names selected disyllable words without increased duration. Example: The clinician displays a picture of a baby and asks, "What is this?" The client replies "Baby," without increased duration.

i. The client spontaneously names selected multisyllabic words without increased duration. Example: The clinician shows the client a picture of an alligator and asks, "What is this picture?" The client says, "Alligator," without increased duration.

2a. The client spontaneously describes pictured actions using at least a subject and a verb, without increased duration. Example: The clinician shows the client a picture and asks the prompt question, "What is happening in this picture?" The client answers, "A boy is kicking a ball," without increased duration.

b. The client refrains from using increased duration during structured games. Example: The clinician and the client play "Concentration" in which the client produces a single sentence about a picture without increased duration prior to completing his or her turn.

c. The client does not use increased duration during structured conversation. Structured conversation involves asking the client to describe situations or events that are removed from the "here and now."

Source: The above program was derived from information provided in Hargrove, P. M., Dauer, K. E., & Montelibano, M. (1989). Reducing vowel and final consonant prolongations in twin brothers. *Child Language Therapy and Teaching, 5,* 49–63.

(2) Table 6–2 lists treatment **techniques** used to treat inherent duration. *Imitation* and *feedback* predominate the techniques for direct inherent duration PFCs.

2. **Approaches that focus directly on prosodic duration** (i.e., direct prosodic duration PFC). (**Prosodic duration** = Changes in length that are not related to the differences among speech sounds but, nevertheless, have communicative value.) No methods for altering prosodic duration directly have been identified. Therefore, readers are referred to Appendixes A,

Table 6-2. Treatment techniques for various duration PFCs. (Definitions of all treatment techniques are provided in the glossary.)

Technique	Purpose/Focus Combinations
Amplification	indirect inherent duration
Audiotapes	indirect prosodic duration
Back-Ups	indirect inherent duration
Breathing Activities	direct inherent duration
Contrastive Sets/ Minimal Pairs	direct inherent duration, indirect inherent duration, indirect prosodic duration
Conversation	direct inherent duration
Cues	
Auditory	direct inherent duration, indirect inherent duration
Phonemic	indirect inherent duration
Rhythmic	indirect prosodic duration
Tactile/Kinesthetic	direct inherent duration, indirect inherent duration
Visual	direct inherent duration, indirect inherent duration, indirect prosodic duration
Discrimination	direct inherent duration, indirect inherent duration, indirect prosodic duration
Drill	indirect inherent duration, indirect prosodic duration
Easy Onsets	indirect inherent duration
Exaggeration	indirect inherent duration
Fading	indirect inherent duration
Feedback	
Auditory	indirect inherent duration, indirect prosodic duration
Tactile/Kinesthetic	direct inherent duration
Verbal	direct inherent duration, indirect inherent duration, indirect prosodic duration
Visual	direct inherent duration, indirect inherent duration, indirect prosodic duration
Games	direct inherent duration, indirect inherent duration

Technique	Purpose/Focus Combinations
Humming	indirect inherent duration
Imitation	direct inherent duration, indirect inherent duration, indirect prosodic duration
Labeling	indirect inherent duration
Latency	indirect inherent duration
Metalinguistics	direct inherent duration, indirect inherent duration, indirect prosodic duration
Modeling	direct inherent duration, indirect inherent duration, indirect prosodic duration
Motor Movement	indirect inherent duration, indirect prosodic duration
Narratives	indirect inherent duration, indirect prosodic duration
Negative Practice	Indirect inherent duration
Poetry Reading	indirect inherent duration, indirect prosodic duration
Query Responding	direct inherent duration, indirect inherent duration
Reading Aloud	direct inherent duration, indirect inherent duration, indirect prosodic duration
Relaxation	direct inherent duration
Review	indirect inherent duration
Rituals	indirect inherent duration
Role Playing	indirect inherent duration, indirect prosodic duration
Self-Monitoring	indirect inherent duration, indirect prosodic duration
Shadowing	indirect inherent duration
Singing/Chanting	indirect inherent duration, indirect prosodic duration
Stimulation	
Auditory	direct inherent duration, indirect inherent duration
Visual	indirect inherent duration
Unison Reading	indirect inherent duration, indirect prosodic duration
Whispering	indirect inherent duration, indirect prosodic duration

B, and E and section VI.B #2 (indirect prosodic duration PFC) for treatment ideas.

B. Indirect Treatment Strategies

1. **Approaches that focus indirectly on inherent duration** (i.e., indirect inherent duration PFC). (**Inherent duration** = Length modifications that pertain to speech sounds.)

   a. **Population.** Methods for treating inherent duration indirectly have been developed for individuals with aphasia, apraxia of speech, developmental apraxia of speech, hearing impairment, specific language impairment, stuttering, and voice disorders. Moreover, methods also are available for the improvement of the speaking skills of normal speakers (speech improvement) and for accent reduction.

   b. **Intervention**
      (1) **Content**
         (a) When inherent duration is used indirectly, the **terminal objective** of intervention has included improvement in a large number of skills:

         - articulation/phonology,
         - comprehension,
         - fluency,
         - intelligibility,
         - normalcy ratings,
         - overall communication skills,
         - overall prosody,
         - overall tempo,
         - prelinguistic vocalizations, and
         - rate.

         Table 6–3 provides an example of an approach which uses inherent duration indirectly.
         (b) **Target behaviors** of the inherent duration phases of treatment may include

         - discriminating stimuli of varying durations;
         - reading selected stimuli aloud (e.g., words, word pairs, sentences, paragraphs, poetry, etc.);

- imitating;
- hearing words and vocalizations of varying durations during play;
- producing or intoning structured sentences;
- vocalizing; and
- conversing.

(c) The most common **hierarchy** of treatment steps is the logical ordering of objectives.

(2) **Techniques** used to treat duration are presented in Table 6–2. The most commonly used techniques for indirect inherent duration involve tasks such as *imitation* and *metalinguistics*. *Modeling*, a less cognitively demanding task, also is used frequently.

2. **Approaches that focus indirectly on prosodic duration** (i.e., indirect prosodic duration PFC). (**Prosodic duration** = changes in length that are not related to the differences among speech sounds but, nevertheless, have communicative value.)

a. **Population.** Methods indirectly using prosodic duration exist for individuals with motor speech disorders and voice disorders. Methods for improving the speaking skills of normal speakers (speech improvement) and for those learning English as a second language also are available.

b. **Intervention**
   (1) **Content**
      (a) When prosodic duration is used indirectly, the **terminal objective** of intervention includes

      - improvement of overall prosody,
      - improvement of overall speaking skills,
      - improvement of tempo,
      - improvement of comprehension skills,
      - improvement of articulatory accuracy,
      - increased normalcy judgments, and/or
      - use of appropriate speaking rate.

      Table 6–4 is an example of an indirect approach using prosodic duration as its focus.

Table 6–3. Program for indirect inherent duration PFCs. (Steps related to inherent duration are preceded by an asterisk [*].)

POPULATION:	Stuttering.
TECHNIQUES:	Feedback (auditory), modeling, cues (auditory), metalinguistics, self-monitoring, easy onsets. (The Glossary contains definitions of the techniques.)
GOAL:	To increase the rate of fluency.
OBJECTIVES:	To use increased durations (prolongations) to improve speech fluency.
PROCEDURES:	1. The clinician ensures that the client has sufficient respiratory support and sufficent relaxation skills to complete this program.
	2. The clinician teaches the client to use easy onsets by stressing the release of breath and light consonant contacts.
	*3. The clinician introduces increased durations for words with initial vowels; progresses to words beginning with voiced consonants; and, finally, progresses to words beginning with voiceless consonants.
	*4. The client produces plosives with light contacts that have slightly increased durations (prolongations, stretches).
	*5. The client increases word duration using stimuli presented in the following ordering:
	• words containing all continuant, voiced sounds (e.g., "renown");
	• words containing all nonplosive sounds with some unvoiced and some voiced sounds (e.g., "sieve"); and
	• words containing both voiced and unvoiced sounds with optional plosives (e.g., "bass").

(b) When **target behaviors** are specified, they usually involve reading of selected stimuli aloud. However, many treatment methods for this PFC are vague and do not clearly describe the prosodic target behaviors.

(c) The most common **hierarchy** of treatment steps is the logical hierarchy. The method presented in Table 6–4 (Simmons, 1983), however, uses a combined logical and disorder hierarchy.

(2) **Techniques** used for treating duration are presented in Table 6–2. The most commonly used techniques for indirect prosodic duration are ***reading aloud***, ***contrastive sets***, ***unison reading***, and ***motor movements***.

*6. The client practices producing sentences using increased durations. At first, the sentences are loaded with voiced sounds. Spontaneous speech is introduced gradually.

*7. The clinician instructs the client to speak at specified rates using increased speech duration and modeling, DAF, the metronome, and so forth. This permits the client to pair increased durations with slow, moderate, and normal rates of speech.

8. Once the client achieves fluency using increased duration, the clinician models natural, normal prosody for the client.

*9. The clinician provides practice, explanations, and models to decrease the frequency and length of the increased durations. The following linguistic targets may receive attention: sentences that occur early in turns, feared words, and words following pauses.

10. The client and the clinician develop a fear hierarchy and use it in transfer activities.

11. The client becomes involved in group therapy to share problems, problem solve, and self-monitor.

12. After the termination of direct therapy, the client schedules a "booster" session in three to six months to refine skills, problem solve, and protect against relapse.

COMMENTS: Rate also is used indirectly in this program.

Source: The above program was derived from information provided in Ham, R. (1986). *Techniques of stuttering therapy* (pp. 339–344). Englewood Cliffs, NJ: Prentice-Hall.

C. Summary Points

1. Compared to other prosodic features and the prosodic components, the **number of available treatment methods for duration** is small. Some of the cited methods merely recommend changing or modeling duration and do not provide specific treatment guidelines. Considering these limitations, clinicians may direct their attention to ideas used with other aspects of prosody when seeking ideas for treating duration.

2. There is only limited **verification of effectiveness** for the treatment of duration. Researchers and clinicians need to di-

Table 6–4. Program for indirect prosodic duration PFCs. (Steps related to prosodic duration are preceded by an asterisk [*].)

POPULATION:	Dysarthria.
TECHNIQUES:	Reading aloud; feedback (auditory, verbal); metalinguistics; discrimination. (The Glossary contains definitions of the techniques.)
GOAL:	To improve overall prosody.
OBJECTIVES:	1. To vary pitch and loudness.

    2. To use appropriate stress patterns

      a. The client discriminates stressed as opposed to unstressed syllables.

      b. The client produces stress by

        • pausing before the item to be stressed,

        • lengthening the target item,

        • shortening unstressed syllables, and/or

        • decreasing the loudness of unstressed syllables.

    3. To reduce the overall length of syllables.

    4. To increase naturalness.

PROCEDURES: [**NOTE:** The client reads aloud stimuli that emphasize the behaviors targeted in the steps listed below. The overall length and complexity of the stimuli increase as the client progresses through a program encompassing syllables, words, phrases, sentences, and paragraphs. The acoustic analysis of the client's speech permits the ordering of the prosodic targets based on the *client's performance* and the identification of atypical patterns which may emerge as the result of treatment (i.e., iatrogenic problems).]

    1. The client reads stimuli aloud and attempts to increase loudness and pitch variation. The clinician evaluates the client's response and provides feedback using verbal explanations and audiotape replays.

rect their attention to providing data substantiating the value of duration treatment methods.

    3. As with other aspects of prosody, skill-oriented treatment methods predominate. The discrete organizational system employed in the Prosodic Teaching Model no doubt fosters this orientation. Clinicians interested in more **holistic or integrative methods** are referred to citations listed in section VI.D.

2a. The client discriminates stressed versus unstressed syllables using materials of increasing length and complexity. The clinician evaluates the client's response and provides feedback using verbal explanation and audiotape replays.

*b. The client reads aloud stimuli and differentiates stressed and unstressed syllables by

- pausing before the item to be stressed,

- lengthening stressed items,

- shortening unstressed items, and/or

- decreasing loudness of unstressed items.

The clinician evaluates the client's response and provides feedback using verbal explanation and audiotape replays.

*3. The client reads aloud stimuli after being instructed to reduce syllable length while maintaining stress/unstressed contrasts. The clinician can suggest that the client "under articulate" some consonants and word endings and decrease vowel length. The clinician evaluates the client's responses and provides feedback using verbal explanation and audiotape replays.

*4. The client reads aloud and attempts to

- decrease exaggerated pitch and loudness variation,

- reduce shortened words, and

- produce smooth word-to-word transitions

The clinician evaluates the client's responses and provides feedback using verbal explanation and audiotape replays.

COMMENTS: The following other aspects of prosody also are used indirectly in this approach: pitch (variation); loudness (level, variation); pause; tempo (concordance); stress; rhythm (alterations).

Source: The above program was derived from information provided in Simmons, N. N. (1983). Acoustic analysis of ataxic dysarthria: An approach to monitoring treatment. In W. R. Berry (Ed.), *Clinical dysarthria* (pp. 283–294). San Diego: College-Hill Press.

4. Most duration treatment methods are designed for adults. Citations for methods developed for **children** are listed in section VI.E.

5. Control of **duration is important to communication**. If a client has sufficient control of duration, then duration may be used for indirect purposes to elicit other communicative behaviors. However, if the client experiences difficulty in producing duration and this affects the production of any of the four prosodic components (i.e., tempo, intonation, stress, or rhythm), clinicians should consider treating duration directly prior to working on a prosodic component. Unfortunately, there are no criteria delineating minimal durational abilities necessary for the acceptable production of prosodic components. Clinicians, at this point, must determine what is appropriate for their own clients.

6. Although readers are provided with suggested treatment methods for each duration PFC, they are encouraged to develop their own methods. Table 6-2 may facilitate the development of new treatment methods by providing a listing of **commonly used treatment techniques** for the different duration PFCs. Moreover, researchers may use this table as a starting point in attempts to validate treatment effectiveness.

VI. CITATIONS FOR DURATION TREATMENT

A. Citations for Approaches Directly Focusing on Inherent Duration

Glenn, Glenn, & Forman (1989, pp. 224–230); Hargrove, Dauer, & Montelibano (1989); Ling (1976, pp. 366–367); Orion (1988, pp. 14–18); Waling & Harrison (1987, pp. 16–18, 19–21).

B. Citations for Approaches Indirectly Focusing on Inherent Duration

Fairbanks (1960, pp. 113–118); Gilbert (1984, pp. 15–16, 21–23); Glenn et al. (1989, pp. 224–230); Ham (1986, pp. 151–167, 318–324, 324–328, 339–344); Ham (1990, pp. 301–305); Helfrich-Miller (1984); Ling (1976, pp. 200–203, 203–206); Moncur & Brackett (1974, pp. 89–96); Orion (1988, pp. 14–18); Pindzola (1987a); Rosenbek, Lemme, Ahern, Harris, & Wertz (1973); Schomburg, Lippert, Johnson, Muss, & Tittnich (1989); Sparks (1981); Wilson (1972, pp. 144–146).

C. Citations for Approaches Indirectly Focusing on Prosodic Duration

Caligiuri & Murry (1983); Gilbert (1984, pp. 21–23); Glenn et al. (1989, pp. 224–230); Graham (1978); Moncur & Brackett (1974, pp.

89–96); Sikorski (1988, pp. 2–23, 47–50, 86–96); Simmons (1983); Wilson (1972, pp. 144–146); Yorkston & Beukelman (1981).

D. Citations for Integrative and/or Holistic Approaches

Caligiuri & Murry (1983); Dworkin (1991, pp. 324–326); Fairbanks (1960, pp. 146–151); Graham (1978); Ham (1986, pp. 324–328); Ham (1990, pp. 301–305); Helfrich-Miller (1984); Ling (1976, pp. 200–203, 243–244, 366–367); Moncur & Brackett (1974, pp. 89–96); Pindzola (1987a); Schomburg et al. (1989); Simmons (1983); Stern (1987, Courses #1 & #2); Yorkston & Beukelman (1981); Appendixes A & B.

E. Citations for Approaches Designed for Children

Ham (1990, pp. 301–305); Hargrove, Dauer, & Montelibano (1989); Helfrich-Miller (1984); Ling (1976, pp. 200–203, 203–206, 243–244, 366–367); Pindzola (1987a); Schomburg et al. (1989); Waling & Harrison (1987, pp. 16–18, 19–21); Wilson (1972, pp. 144–146, 178–179); Appendix B.

CHAPTER

7

Treating Prosodic Features: Pause

I. NORMAL USE OF THE PROSODIC FEATURE PAUSE

A. Description

Pause is a prosodic feature and a building block of the four prosodic components of tempo, intonation, stress, and rhythm. Pause, which involves the use of silence in speech, is physically represented as a period in time in which no acoustic signal occurs for at least 200–270 msec (Couper-Kuhlen, 1986; Gandour, Weinberg, Petty, & Dardarananda, 1986; Silliman & Leslie, 1983). Other terms used to signify pause in the speech of normal talkers include silence, hesitation, and juncture (Borden & Harris, 1984; Crystal, 1981; Deputy, Nakasone, & Tosi, 1982; Goldman-Eisler, 1964).

B. Categories

Figure 7–1 presents the two categories of pause (intraturn pause and interturn pause) which are differentiated on the traditional basis of placement in connected speech.

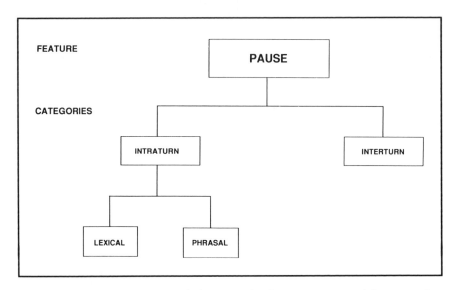

Figure 7–1. A representation of the prosodic feature pause and its categories.

1. **Intraturn pauses** are gaps in vocalization that occur within a speaker's turn. They tend to occur at the boundaries of words, phrases, or utterances (Silliman & Leslie, 1983). Some clinicians use pauses as compensatory measures to facilitate the acquisition of certain target behaviors. Pauses may provide listeners with the additional time necessary to process the degraded speech signal of some speakers with segmental and suprasegmental errors (Maassen & Povel, 1985; Osberger & Levitt, 1979). There are two variations of intraturn pauses.

   a. **Lexical intraturn pauses** occur between words or syllables. In normal, connected speech, lexical pauses usually are not perceptually salient. However, some individuals with impaired speech produce inappropriate pauses at word or syllable boundaries. These pauses may vary considerably in length from disorder to disorder.

   b. **Phrasal intraturn pauses** occur between phrases, clauses, and utterances within the same speaking turn. They may occur across natural breath groups.

2. **Interturn pauses** occur at the end of a speaker's turn when the speaker stops talking. Interturn pauses often signal the

desire to relinquish a turn or to receive a response from a listener.

C. Normative Information

Pause does not operate independently from other aspects of prosody and communication. Bolinger (1986), Clark and Clark (1977), Couper-Kuhlen (1986), and Ohde and Sharf (1992) provide examples of such interdependence.

- There tend to be more pauses in slow speech than in rapid speech.

- Distinctions such as "sin tax" and "syntax" are differentiated by phonetic, loudness, *and* pausal variations.

- Sustained exhaled air co-occurs with pauses.

- Intraturn pauses can be marked by a rising terminal contour, the use of exclamations, or various nonverbal behaviors such as tense lips, contracted eyebrows, and clicks produced on inhalation.

Variations in pauses may depend on the individual physiology of the speaker (with regard to vital capacity of breath), the type of production task (e.g., speaking versus reading), the communicative intent, and/or the stimulus length. Despite variation in pause, the following information may be helpful to clinicians attempting to determine if a client's use of pauses is within normal limits.

1. Depending on the speaking context, **normal speakers devote about 40–60% of all speaking time to pausing** (Goldman-Eisler, 1964; Johns-Lewis, 1986). It is not clear what percentage of the time is devoted to intraturn versus interturn pauses.

2. **As the complexity of linguistic units increases, the duration of the pauses increases**. Some believe this reflects the pre-planning necessary to inhale a larger quantity of air and sustain the air over phrases of varying length. Others believe it reflects the pre-planning necessary to generate complicated linguistic structures.

3. **The relationship between pauses and grammatical boundaries is context dependent**. Pause occurs at the boundaries of syntactic units (e.g., phrases or clauses) up to 100% of the time

for reading but less than 60% of the time for discussion (Goldman-Eisler, 1968; Johns-Lewis, 1986).

4. **When pauses are not at syntactic boundaries**, they often occur after the first word, usually a function word. In such cases, the rest of the phrase tends to be produced without pause (Clark & Clark, 1977).

5. Boomer (1965) reports that the **average duration of lexical intraturn pauses** (hesitations) is 750 msec, and the average duration of phrasal intraturn pauses is 1,030 msec.

D. Communicative Roles

1. Pause is used to **signal boundaries** within a speaking turn. Speakers often segment utterances or syntactic constituents in their speaking turn by pausing briefly. Such pauses assist listeners in identifying the syntactic organization of the incoming speech (Crystal, 1981; Martin, 1972). Lexical items can be differentiated through the placement of pauses. Contrast:

   • Yellowstone

   • yellow stone

   In addition, pauses can be used in more complex speech to disambiguate otherwise ambiguous utterances. In the examples below, pauses signal ellipsis.

   • she cooked and ate the stew | {The woman cooked the stew and she ate it. Elliptical: she, stew}

   • she cooked | and ate the stew | {The woman cooked an unnamed item and then she ate the stew. Elliptical = she}

2. Pauses **contribute to the production of other aspects of prosody**, especially rate. (See Chapter 8 — Tempo.)

3. Pauses can **focus information**. Couper-Kuhlen (1986) notes when speakers pause before a word, that word is perceived as more prominent or stressed.

4. Pauses can assist in **managing conversational turns**. Speakers use interturn pauses to signal that they are willing to relinquish their speaking turns (Silliman & Leslie, 1983).

5. Pauses **convey emotional information** (Crystal, 1969).

6. Pauses provide speakers time for **performance-based tasks** such as

   a. **allowing time to breathe**,

   b. **providing additional time to find a word** within a speaking turn, and

   c. **providing the opportunity to process or plan abstract linguistic information** within the speaking turn (Goldman-Eisler, 1964; Silliman & Leslie, 1983).

II. PERCEIVING THE PROSODIC FEATURE OF PAUSE

Significant issues related to the perception of pause are the length of the pause necessary to achieve perceptual saliency and the length of the pause before it facilitates (or impedes) communication.

At the segmental level, the sound of silence is a salient one. For example, the perception of stops is distinguished from other sounds by an oral occlusion heard as silence in voiceless stops /p,t,k/ or as a brief attenuation of sound in the voiced stops /b,d,g/ (along with other acoustic cues). At the prosodic level, pause (sometimes called juncture) is also cued by silence. Borden and Harris (1984, p. 194) cite the Shakespearean example from *Troilus and Cressida* in which the crowd shouts "The Troyans' trumpet!" which, if given improper juncture along with lengthening the /s/ in Troyans, would result in the crowd announcing the arrival of a prominent prostitute.

CLINICAL NOTE: The acoustic feature of pause is demonstrated to be critical in processing speech of persons with segmental and suprasegmental errors. In computer manipulation and correction of errors in hearing-impaired speakers, speech intelligibility actually decreased when pauses were significantly reduced.

III. PRODUCING THE PROSODIC FEATURE OF PAUSE

Production of this prosodic feature has not received considerable research activity. Certainly, at the segmental level, articulatory occlusion in structures such as the lips, tongue, palate, and the subsequent build up of intraoral pressure until articulatory release, must be critically timed with laryngeal abduction/adduction. At issue is what is occurring physiologically when speakers with disorders pause inappropriately. It is hypothesized that speakers may be silently blocking (e.g., stuttering); "searching" for accurate articulatory placement (e.g., as seen in neurological disorders); or breathing inappropriately (e.g., the speech of persons with hearing impairment). These notions require further investigation.

IV. A MODEL FOR TREATING PAUSE

A. A Teaching Model for Pause

The teaching model for pause is made up of the two categories (intraturn and interturn pauses) that were described in section I.B and represented in Figure 7–1.

B. Treatment Decisions: Pause

The accompanying Clinical Note presents guidelines for applying information provided in previous and subsequent sections to the treatment of pause. Explanations of the guidelines are provided in Chapter 2 (section III.A #2). Also, the Treatment Index lists the location of various purposes, focuses, hierarchies, populations, objectives, treatment techniques, and sample programs referred to in the prose.

CLINICAL NOTE: GUIDELINES FOR DECISION MAKING

1. **Determine the purpose** (direct, indirect) for working on pause.
2. **Identify pause categories** (interturn, intraturn) **that will serve as the focus of therapy**.
3. **Identify specific treatment objectives** for the targeted purpose/focus combination (PFC) (i.e., the purpose from Guideline #1 and the focus category from Guideline #2 above).
4. **Identify treatment techniques** that may be appropriate for the specific client and for the PFC.
5. **Determine the hierarcy** of treatment steps.
6. **Identify sources in which clients with similar disorders** have similar PFCs.

V. SUMMARY OF THE PUBLISHED LITERATURE ON TREATING PAUSE

A. Direct Purpose Treatment Strategies

1. **Approaches that focus directly on intraturn pauses** (i.e., direct intraturn pause PFC). (**Intraturn pauses** = Gaps in vocalization occurring within a speaker's turn.)

   a. **Population.** Methods for the direct treatment of intraturn pauses have been developed for speakers with voice disorders, for those with motor speech disorders, and for normal speakers who wish to improve their communication skills (speech improvement) or who wish to reduce foreign accent.

   b. **Intervention**
   (1) Content
       (a) The **target behaviors** for direct pause therapy involve the use of normal pause and/or abnormal pause patterns. For example, clients may be required to

   - read sentences aloud using pauses at appropriate locations,
   - disambiguate sentences by varying pause location, or
   - produce pauses before every word in word lists or in passages.

       (b) The treatment **hierarchy** usually is logical as exemplified in Table 7-1. However, this observation is based on a small number of programs and may not represent the trends in direct pause treatment literature as a whole.
   (2) The range of **techniques** for directly targeting intraturn pauses is limited due to the small number of cited methods. (See Table 7-2 for a listing of techniques used with pause PFCs.)

2. **Approaches that focus directly on interturn pauses** (i.e., direct interturn pause PFC). (**Interturn pauses** = Gaps in vo-

Table 7-1. Program for direct intraturn pause PFC

POPULATION:	Voice disorders, speech improvement.
TECHNIQUES:	Metalinguistics, reading aloud, negative practice, contrastive sets, cues (visual). (The Glossary contains definitions of the techniques.)
OBJECTIVES:	1. To use appropriate intraturn pauses. 2. To use appropriate phrasing.
PROCEDURES:	1. The clinician explains the use of pauses. 2. The client reads aloud selected passages in which the location of the pause is marked with a straight vertical line (	). Example: • Because of the snow	the high winds	and the ice	school was cancelled | 3. The client changes the pauses in the sentences from Step #2 to inappropriate locations and again reads the sentence aloud. This time, pauses are placed in inappropriate locations. 4. The client rereads aloud the sentences from Step #2 using the original pause locations. 5. The client rereads aloud the sentences from Step #2, this time using unconventional, yet meaningful, pause locations. 6. The client reads aloud sentences that progressively increase in length. The client uses only one pause for each sentence. 7. The client silently reads the sentences from Step #6 and marks two pauses in each sentence. The client then reads the sentences aloud. 8. The client marks each of the sentences from Step #6 with optimal pausing. He or she then reads the sentences aloud. 9. The client reads aloud a set of sentences that are marked to signify placement and duration of pauses. 10. The client reads aloud a paragraph containing normal punctuation. Before reading the paragraph aloud, the client marks the location of pauses in the paragraph. 11. The client reads aloud a sentence that contains no punctuation. First, the client reads the words in the paragraph in a continuous sequence. Then, he or she

marks the location of pauses and reads the paragraph aloud.

12. The client reads aloud a passage in which the location of pauses is not marked.

13. The client reads aloud sentences that are marked for length and duration of pauses.

14. Using the sentences from Step #13, the client first reads aloud all the sentences with short pauses, then with medium pauses, and finally with long pauses.

15. The clinician provides the client with sentences. The client divides each sentence into two phrases, reads each sentence aloud, and describes the meaning. The client then marks the location and duration of pauses and rereads the sentences aloud.

16. The clinician provides a paragraph with no punctuation to the client. The client marks the paragraph for pause placement and duration and reads it aloud.

17. The client reads aloud sentences containing three pauses. The second pause should be longer in duration than the first pause, and the middle phrase should be less prominent (less loudness, lower pitch, less duration) than the other two phrases. Example:

    • Rachel's car| unfortunately| has quite a bit of rust|

18. The client reorders the sentences from Step #17 so that the second phrase is at the end. Example:

    • Rachel's car| has quite a bit of rust| unfortunately|

    The client reads aloud the sentences and describes their prominent patterns.

19. The clinician provides the client with a paragraph with punctuation. The client marks pausing (placement and duration) and prominent phrases. The client then reads the paragraph aloud.

20. The clinician provides the client with a paragraph that has no punctuation. The client marks pausing (placement and duration) and prominent phrases. The client reads the paragraph aloud paying special attention to the prominent phrases.

Source: The above program was derived from information provided in Fairbanks, G. (1960). *Voice and articulation drillbook* (2nd ed., pp. 146–151). New York: Harper & Row.

Table 7–2. Treatment techniques for various pause PFCs. (Definitions of all treatment techniques are provided in the Glossary.)

Technique	Puprose/Focus Combination
Alternating Tasks	indirect intraturn
Contrastive Sets/ Minimal Pairs	direct intraturn, indirect intraturn
Conversation	direct intraturn, direct interturn, indirect intraturn
Cues	
Auditory	indirect intraturn
Tactile/Kinesthetic	indirect intraturn
Visual	direct intraturn, direct interturn, indirect intraturn
Disambiguation	direct intraturn
Discrimination	direct intraturn, indirect intraturn
Exaggeration	indirect intraturn
Fading	indirect intraturn
Feedback	
Auditory	direct interturn, indirect intraturn
Verbal	direct intraturn, indirect intraturn
Visual	direct interturn, indirect intraturn
Games	indirect intraturn
Imitation	direct intraturn, direct interturn, indirect intraturn
Metalinguistics	direct intraturn, indirect intraturn

calizing occurring at the end of a speaking turn.) No methods directly targeting improved production of interturn pauses have been identified in the literature. However, Table 7–3 provides a prototype of direct interturn pause therapy developed for a client who regularly interrupted communicative partners during conversation. Clinicians are referred to Appendixes A, B, and C for additional treatment ideas.

B. Indirect Purpose Treatment Strategies

1. **Approaches that focus indirectly on intraturn pause** (i.e., indirect intraturn pause PFC). (**Intraturn pauses** = Gaps in vocalization occurring within a single speaker's turn.)

Technique	Puprose/Focus Combination
Modeling	direct intraturn, indirect intraturn
Monologue	indirect intraturn
Motor Movement	indirect intraturn
Negative Practice	direct intraturn, indirect intraturn
Picture Description	direct interturn
Poetry Reading	indirect intraturn
Query Responding	indirect intraturn
Reading Aloud	direct intraturn, direct interturn, indirect intraturn
Rhythmic Patterning	indirect intraturn
Rhythmic Talking	indirect intraturn
Rituals	indirect intraturn
Scripts	direct intraturn
Self-Monitoring	direct intraturn, indirect intraturn
Shadowing	indirect intraturn
Singing	indirect intraturn
Stimulation *Auditory*	direct intraturn, indirect intraturn

a. **Population.** Methods that indirectly use intraturn pause to change communication skills have been developed for individuals from a variety of groups: developmental apraxia of speech, learning disability, motor speech disorders, specific language impairment, stuttering, and voice disorders. In addition, methods have been devised for normal speakers wishing to improve their overall communication skills (speech improvement) and those wishing to reduce accent.

b. **Intervention**
   (1) **Content**
       (a) **Terminal objectives** for the indirect use of intraturn pauses include

Table 7–3. Program for direct interturn pause PFC

POPULATION:	Not identified.
TECHNIQUES:	Conversation; reading aloud; visual cues; feedback (auditory, visual, verbal); picture description; self-monitoring. (The Glossary contains definitions of the techniques.)
GOAL:	1. To increase the frequency of interturn pauses during conversational speech. 2. To inhibit conversation bids in the absence of a conversational partner's pauses.
OBJECTIVES:	1. To increase the number of appropriate, visually cued pauses during a 5-minute script reading task. 2. To increase the number of appropriate pauses during a 5-minute script reading task. 3. The increase the number of appropriate pauses during a picture description task. 4. To increase the number of appropriate pauses during conversation.
PROCEDURES:	1. The clinician provides an orthographic transcription of the client's conversational speech from a previous session and instructs him or her to insert proper pause marks. One slash (l) signifies a short pause, two slashes (ll) indicate a longer pause, and three slashes (lll) signify a long pause (interturn). The client

- improved articulation,
- improved overall communication skills,
- increased fluency,
- increased intelligibility,
- improved intonation skills,
- increased lexicon,
- increased normalcy judgments,
- improved phrasing,
- improved stress,
- improved overall prosody,
- increased pitch variation,
- modified rate of speech,
- improved sound sequencing,
- improved social skills, and
- improved tempo.

(b) The **target behaviors** for intraturn pause phrases of treatment consist of

reads aloud the marked script and permits the clinician to take a turn when an interturn pause is present. The client reads his or her portion of the transcript until relinquishing the turn with an interturn pause (|||). The clinician then reads his or her portion of the transcript. The client and the clinician continue the script reading and focus on exchanging turns appropriately.

2. Same as Step #1 except the location and length of the pauses are not marked on the transcripts.

3. The clinician provides the client with a picture and asks the client questions about it. The clinician tape records the session to provide the client with feedback and to facilitate self-monitoring for interruptions (i.e., initiating a turn prior to one's conversational partner's interturn pause).

4. The clinician audiotapes the session as the client self-monitors his or her interruptions during specified tasks. Initially, the task involves a structured activity such as a board or card game. As the client progresses, the task shifts to spontaneous speech. The client tallies his or her interruptions on a counter. If he or she fails to note an interruption, the clinician signals the client to replay the tape recorder for verification.

COMMENTS: This method also uses intraturn pauses indirectly.

Source: The above program was derived from clinical information provided by Darcy Bisaillon Langstraat, Dawn Lowinske, and Susan Norsted (personal communications).

- judgments of appropriateness of pauses; or
- insertions of communicatively appropriate pauses while reading aloud or in conversation; and
- insertions of communicatively inappropriate pauses between sounds, syllables, and/or words.

The last of these pausal target behaviors is an example of teaching clients to use aberrant prosodic behavior to achieve another communication goal. An example of such a method is presented in Table 7–4.

(c) The **hierarchy** of treatment steps for indirect intraturn pause PFCs tends to be logical. However, some methods do not use a logical hierarchy. For example, Schomburg et al. (1989) and Rosenbek (1978, p. 214) use linear hierarchies.

Table 7-4. Program for indirect intraturn pause PFC. (Steps related to intraturn pause are preceded by an asterisk [*].)

POPULATION:	Dysarthria.
TECHNIQUES:	Metalinguistics, imitation, motor movement, cues (visual), feedback (auditory), pacing, reading aloud, alternating tasks, metronome, conversation, contrastive sets. (The Glossary contains definitions of the techniques.)
GOAL:	To increase speech intelligibility by reducing the rate of speech.
OBJECTIVES:	1. To use pause patterns to maximize speech intelligibility.
	2. To modify speaking rate to maximize speech intelligibility.
PROCEDURES:	1a. The clinician explains the rationale for reducing rate of speech. The clinician develops parallels between

- speaking and walking,
- articulators and weak legs, and
- unintelligibility and falling or crashing.

*b. The clinician facilitates the client's increased use of pauses by

- directing the client to produce one word (or one syllable) of a familiar phrase for each beat of a metronome;
- directing the client to read sentences using "slit cards" which overlay the sentence and expose one word at a time;
- presenting the words of a sentence on cards; and/or

(2) Although **techniques** employed when intraturn pauses are used indirectly vary markedly (Table 7-2), commonly used techniques include ***reading aloud, cues, modeling, feedback, imitation***, and ***metalinguistics***. (See Table 7-2 for a listing of the techniques used with the different pause PFCs.)

2. **Approaches that focus indirectly on interturn pause** (i.e., indirect interturn pause PFCs). (**Interturn pauses** = Gaps in vocalizing that occur at the end of a speaking turn.) Only a single program for indirect interturn pause PFC has been identified (Rosenbek & LaPointe, 1978, pp. 282–286, 300). The pausing method, however, is associated with muscle movement rather than speech. Therefore, it is not presented here. For treatment ideas, readers are referred to Appendixes A, B, and C.

- employing intersystemic reorganization. (Intersystemic reorganization pairs speaking with a rhythmic activity such as pushing a button or squeezing a ball.) The client can either produce intersystemic reorganization independently or imitate the clinician. This may result in a slowed speaking rate and equal and even stress.

2a. The client's articulation rate is increased by the use of auditory feedback with a delay (DAF) of approximately 50 msec. The length of delay should not exceed 100 msec. The type of speaking task (e.g., reading aloud, spontaneous speech, imitation) and the intensity of the delayed auditory feedback (DAF) may vary.

b. The clinician reduces the client's dependence on DAF by

- alternating production of the same task, one time using DAF and the next time not using DAF;
- comparing audiotapes of DAF and non-DAF speech; and/or
- alternating tasks such as reading and spontaneous speech while attempting to preserve reduce rate.

COMMENTS: This method also uses tempo (rate) indirectly.

Source: The above program was derived from information provided in Rosenbek, J. & LaPointe, L. (1978). The dysarthrias: Description, diagnosis, and treatment. In D. Johns (Ed.), *Clinical management of neurogenic communicative disorders* (pp. 251–310). Boston: Little, Brown.

C. Summary Points

1. By far, the most common **pause PFC** is indirect purpose with intraturn pause focus. Little information is available about the direct or indirect treatment of interturn pauses.

2. Several methods use intraturn pause as a **compensatory measure**, particularly for clients experiencing motor speech disorders such as apraxia of speech and dysarthria. In these methods, the placement of the pauses often is aberrant because clients speak one word, or even one syllable, at a time. The use of aberrant pause should be evaluated with respect to communicative cost and benefits because of its potential for negative impact on intelligibility and on judgments of normalcy (Yorkston & Beukelman, 1981).

3. Most pausal treatment methods concentrate on the acquisition of discrete behaviors. Citations for **holistic or integrative methods**, which may serve as alternatives to discrete strategies, are listed in section VI.C.

4. Many of the techniques (Table 7–2) presented in this chapter may not be appropriate for young **children**. Clinicians working with such clients may consult the citations presented in section VI.D.

5. Because of the limited **empirical support** for pause treatment methods, clinicians may develop (and ultimately validate) their own treatment methods. Information about the techniques, hierarchies, and target behaviors provided in this chapter should assist clinicians in designing treatment methods for working with pauses.

6. Clinicians who choose to treat pause should note that, at present, no data delineate **minimal pausing** skills. Accordingly, clinicians must collect their own supporting data.

VI. CITATIONS FOR PAUSE TREATMENT

A. Citations for Approaches Directly Focusing on Intraturn Pauses

Bradford (1970); Dworking (1991, p. 337); Fairbanks (1960, pp. 146–151, 167–168); Orion (1988, pp. 29–35).

B. Citations for Approaches Indirectly Focusing on Intraturn Pauses

Bellaire, Yorkston, & Beukelman (1986); Berry & Gosborn (1983); Dworkin (1991, pp. 324–326, 336–337, 338–339); Fairbanks (1960, pp. 146–151, 155–158); Glen, Glen, & Forman (1989, pp. 233–239); Ham (1986, pp. 151–167, 333–334); Macaluso-Haynes (1978); Minskoff (1980); Moncur & Brackett (1974, pp. 78–80); Orion (1988, pp. 29–35); Rosenbek (1978, p. 214); Rosenbek, Hanson, Baughman, & Lemme (1974); Rosenbek & LaPointe (1978, pp. 282–286, 300, 301–304); Rosenbek et al. (1973); Schomburg et al. (1989); Simmons (1983, pp. 144–146); Yorkston & Beukelman (1981).

C. Citations for Integrative and/or Holistic Approaches

Fairbanks (1960, pp. 146–151, 155–159, 167–168); Ham (1986, pp. 151–167); Macaluso-Haynes (1978); Moncur & Brackett (1974, pp. 78–80); Orion (1988, pp. 29–35); Rosenbek et al. (1974); Schomburg et al. (1989); Simmons (1983); Appendixes A & B.

D. Citations for Approaches Developed for Children

Macaluso-Haynes (1978); Minskoff (1980); Rosenbek et al. (1974); Schomburg et al. (1989); Weismer, Digney, Krueger, & Ricke (1990); Wilson (1972, pp. 144–146), Appendix B.

C H A P T E R

8

Treating Prosodic Components: Tempo

I. NORMAL USE OF THE PROSODIC COMPONENT TEMPO

A. Description

The term tempo represents a composite of factors that relate to the timing elements, or pace, of speech. Although tempo applies to both segmental and prosodic aspects of communication, the emphasis here is its use in prosody. Like all prosodic features and components, changes in tempo can occur at the segmental level and some of the prosodic tempo categories have their roots in segmentals.

B. Categories

The three tempo categories of speaking rate, concordance, and phrasing are described below. A visual representation of the tempo categories is presented in Figure 8-1.

128

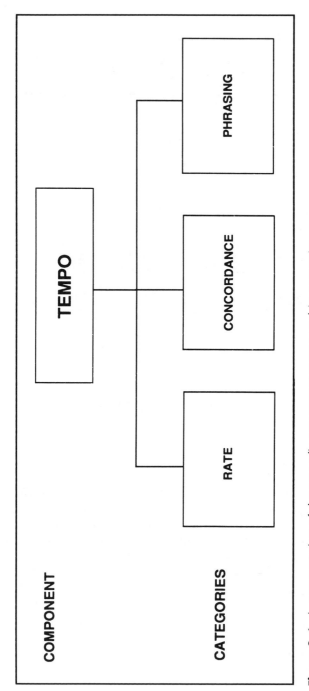

Figure 8–1. A representation of the prosodic component tempo and its categories.

1. **Speaking rate** reflects the number of syllables produced over a given amount of time. Rate varies on a continuum from fast to slow. Rate changes are accomplished by modifying the duration of segmentals (duration), inserting pauses (pause), and modifying segmentals (phonemic change).

   a. **Duration changes.** Vowels are most likely to change duration during rate modification, although durational changes also occur on consonant productions. When speaking rate is rapid, the duration of speech sounds may be shorter than when rate is slow, and there tends to be less time to achieve "target" articulatory positions. (See Chapter 6 for additional information about the prosodic feature duration.)

   b. **Pause changes.** Speakers increase speech rate by decreasing the length and number of pauses. Conversely, they decrease rate by increasing the number and length of pauses. (See Chapter 7 for additional information about the prosodic feature pause.)

   c. **Phonemic changes.** Increases in speaking rate also are accomplished by modifying speech sounds (Clark & Clark, 1977). For example:
      (1) Speakers **substitute schwas** /ə/ for unstressed vowels. Example:

         • I want to go = /aɪ want tə go/

      (2) Speakers **omit** selected consonants. Example:

         • I want to go = /aɪ wannə go/

      (3) Speakers **coalesce** speech sounds. Example:

         • Did you eat? = /dʒuit/

CLINICAL NOTE: Most speakers use a combination of duration, pause, and phonemic changes to modify rate. The modification of pauses is the most accessible skill, but it has a potentially negative impact on speech naturalness and intelligibility judgments (Maassen & Povel, 1985; Yorkston & Beukelman, 1981).

2. The use of **concordance** between the different linguistic units (e.g., syllables, words, utterances) also contributes to tempo. Concordance involves movement from one element in an utterance to the next element. An example of the use of concordance involves the differentiation of the noun phrase/word minimal pair "night rate" and "nitrate." This minimal pair has identical speech sounds, but differences in the use of concordance. "Night rate" uses an abrupt concordance, and "nitrate" has a smooth concordance (Ohde & Sharf, 1992). Two factors contribute to the quality (abruptness or smoothness) of concordances.

   a. Speakers **insert or eliminate pauses** between the linguistic units.

   b. Speakers also **phonetically blend** contiguous phonemes across elements. Phonetic blending occurs along a continuum; the two extremes of this continuum are clipped phonetic blending and drawled phonetic blending.

      (1) **Clipped phonetic blending** involves sudden movement from one speech sound to the next (Crystal, 1969). This frequently occurs with limited coarticulation and is associated with abrupt concordance.

      (2) **Prolonged phonetic blending** is a gradual, even drawled, movement from one speech sound to the next. Prolonged phonetic blending provides the opportunity for a great deal of coarticulation and is associated with smooth concordance.

3. **Phrasing** involves the speaker's marking of the beginning or the ending of phrases. Phrasing also has been called framing or enveloping and is a major factor in the division of speech into units. Phrasing involves considerable redundancy; hence, behaviors used to mark phrasing, which are listed below, need not occur concurrently for listeners to perceive a phrase.

   a. Speakers **decrease loudness** levels at the end of utterances.

   b. Speakers use a rising or a falling **terminal contour**. (See Chapter 9, Intonation, for additional information about terminal contour.)

    c. Speakers **reset pitch height** (onset) to a standard level at the beginning of each phrase. (See Chapter 9, Intonation, for additional information about onset.)

    d. Speakers **pause** at the end of utterances.

    e. Speakers **increase the duration** of vowels and continuant consonants at the end of utterances.

C. Normative Information

Tempo is not a single entity. To provide normative information about tempo, it is necessary to describe each of its categories.

    1. The **speaking rate** of normal adults varies from about 150 to 200 words per minute (wpm) or approximately three to six syllables per second (Dworkin, 1991; Ohde & Sharf, 1992). Rate is influenced by context, emotional content, cognitive complexity, the nature of the task (e.g., oral reading is generally more rapid than spontaneous speaking), and the age of the speaker (e.g., adults speak faster than the elderly and children, older children speak faster than younger children).

CLINICAL NOTE: The optimal speaking rate for persons with impaired or different communication skills may vary markedly from the above norms. Rather than targeting an idealized rate for speech, clinicians may consider identifying the rate at which speech intelligibility is optimal.

    2. The interaction of pausing and phonetic blending accounts for the variations of **concordance**. Extremely abrupt concordances are produced using pauses and clipped phonetic blending; smooth concordances are produced by minimizing pauses and using prolonged phonetic blendings. In the speech science literature, concordance has been studied in considerable detail in the form of frequency transitions. Transition times are a critical factor in the production of speech sounds (cf. Borden & Harris, 1984).

    3. Under idealized conditions, all **phrasing** behaviors coincide with phrase boundaries. That is, the syntactic units of sentences are marked by the use of the behaviors noted in section I.B #3. In spontaneous speech, the correspondence between phrasing markers and syntactic units is not perfect. Crystal

(1969), for example, determined that for speakers of Received Pronunciation (the dialect of English spoken at British public schools and major universities), phrase markers predict syntactic units less than 50% of the time. Phrasing can be influenced by the speaker's age, emotional state, or the nature of the speaking task (Shriberg, Kwiatkowski, & Rasmussen, 1990).

D. Communicative Roles

1. Tempo **contributes to the segmentation of speech** by breaking continuous speech strings into comprehensible units.

2. Tempo **facilitates intelligibility** by allowing listeners sufficient time to interpret and assimilate incoming information.

3. Tempo can be used to **express emotion**.

4. Tempo can **increase the prominence** of selected units of speech.

II. PERCEIVING THE PROSODIC COMPONENT OF TEMPO

Since the listener's overall impression of tempo is reflected by duration, concordance, and phrasing, the prosodic component of tempo is accounted for by an aggregate of cues.

III. PRODUCING THE PROSODIC COMPONENT OF TEMPO

A number of factors may be accounted for in speech production models of tempo. One coarticulatory model that considers physiological systems suggests that there is a pre-planning or "look ahead" mechanism for motor control (Borden & Harris, 1984). Speech is, therefore, not produced as "beads on a string" but, perhaps, as motor commands that are initiated over as many segments that are not in conflict. Coarticulation results from a spread of features from one phoneme to another. Recent studies concerning speech produced by young normal children who are in the process of developing speech are addressing the issue of whether the basic unit of production is at the phonetic or syllabic level. With respect to temporal ordering, since American English is a stressed-timed language, a tempo model of production might suggest that production of stressed items is planned first and given articulatory emphasis with timing, and articulatory demands of unstressed items receiving less attention. Listeners seem to "sense" the tempo of speech and use it to decode the message. Details of the production of tempo must, therefore, include segmental production, suprasegmental effects, and central processing. The ways in which these are realized productively are still being researched in speech science studies.

IV. A MODEL FOR TREATING TEMPO

A. A Teaching Model for Tempo

The model of tempo with its categories (rate, concordance, phrasing) is described in section I.B and presented in Figure 8–1.

B. Treatment Decisions: Tempo

Guidelines presented in the accompanying Clinical Note are treatment recommendations for applying information provided in previous and subsequent sections. Explanations of the guidelines are provided in Chapter 2 (section III.B) and locations of the purposes, focuses, terminal behaviors, target behaviors, hierarchies, and exemplar programs can be found in the Treatment Index.

CLINICAL NOTE: GUIDELINES FOR DECISION MAKING

1. Determine the **purpose** (direct, indirect) for working with tempo.
2. Identify the **categories of tempo** (rate, concordance, phrasing) that will serve as the focus of therapy.
3. Determine **how the client will produce** the targeted temporal category.
4. Identify **specific treatment objectives** for the targeted purpose/focus combination (PFC) (i.e., purpose from Guideline #1 and focus from Guideline #2 above).
5. Identify **treatment techniques**.
6. Determine the **rationale for the hierarchy** of steps.
7. Identify sources in which **clients with similar disorders** have similar PFCs.

V. SUMMARY OF PUBLISHED LITERATURE ON TREATING TEMPO

A. Direct Treatment Strategies

1. **Approaches that focus directly on rate** (i.e., direct rate PFC). (**Rate** = The number of syllables produced over a given amount of time.) An example of such a method is presented in Table 8–1.

   a. **Population.** Methods for the direct treatment of speaking rate have been used with people from the following groups: hearing impairment, motor speech disorders, stuttering, and voice disorders. In addition, treatment programs designed for normal speakers wishing to improve their overall speaking skills (i.e., speech improvement) are available.

   b. **Intervention**
   (1) **Content**
      (a) **Target behaviors** used when rate is the direct focus of therapy include

      • reading aloud, counting, singing, conversing, and/or imitating at specified rates.

      (b) Recommendations about how rate **changes should be produced** generally consist of manipulating duration alone or manipulating pause and direction. Because of its deleterious effect on speech judgments, pause alone is not typically used to modify rate, despite the ease with which speakers manipulate it.
      (c) The **hierarchy** of treatment steps usually is either logical or linear. The linear hierarchy occurs more frequently here than usual because of the tendency to use only a single task when directly treating rate.
   (2) **Techniques** used to treat speaking rate directly are listed in Table 8–2 which presents an overview of treatment techniques used for all tempo PFCs. There is a distinct preference for cognitively difficult tasks

Table 8-1. Program for direct rate PFC

POPULATION:	Voice disorder, speech improvement.
TECHNIQUES:	Metalinguistics; imitation; cues (visual); reading aloud; contrastive sets; modeling; discrimination; feedback (auditory, verbal). (The Glossary contains definitions of the techniques.)
OBJECTIVES:	To modify speaking rate.
PROCEDURES:	

1. The clinician explains the difference between stressed and unstressed vowels (long/short vowels).

2. The clinician describes the relative length of consonants and vowels.

3. The clinician models words of varying durations for the client to imitate. The client then

   - contrasts long and short vowels,
   - identifies the "longest" consonant, and
   - identifies the "shortest" consonant.

4. The client reads sets of disyllable and polysyllable words. The duration of the stressed syllables should be longer than the duration of the unstressed syllables.

5. The clinician explains that words of limited communicative context tend to be produced relatively quickly.

6. The client reads aloud a group of sentences that contain "filler" phrases (e.g., "by the way," "moreover," "nevertheless"). The client tries to read the "fillers" faster than the rest of the sentence.

7. The client silently reads a set of sentences and highlights the most meaningful phrases. The client then reads the sentences aloud, increasing the duration of the most meaningful phrases.

8. The clinician explains that some emotions tend to be associated with a slower rate and that other emotions are associated with faster rates. The client reads aloud a set of sentences using a rate appropriate to a designated mood.

9a. The clinician explains that although speakers generally read faster than they talk, the ideal oral reading rate is 150–180 words per minute (wpm) for maximum comprehensibility. To keep listener attention, rates

(continued)

Table 8-1 *(continued)*

PROCEDURES *(continued)*	below 150 wpm require increased stress and the careful use of pauses, and rates over 180 wpm require additional skills such as precise articulation and clear phrasing.
	b. The clinician times the client reading a nonemotional passage aloud.
	10a. The clinician informs the client that there is a relationship between meaningfulness and speaking rate.
	b. The client reads aloud two passages — one complex, one simple.
	c. The clinician times each reading from Step #10b and, then, the clinician and the client compare the two readings.
	d. If the duration of the two passages does not differ, the clinician recommends that the client use longer durations in the most meaningful portions of the complex passage.
	e. The client practices, rereads the two passages aloud, and compares the results.
	11a. The clinician informs the client that speaking rates vary considerably with the average rate ranging from 150–200 wpm.
	b. The clinician tape records a monologue by the client.
	c. The clinician tallies the number of words spoken in three one-minute segments and then averages the readings to determine wpm.
	d. The client continues to practice until the client's speaking rate is within normal limits.

Source: The above program was derived from information provided in Moncur, J. P., & Brackett, I. P. (1974). *Modifying vocal behavior* (pp. 89–96). New York: Harper & Row.

such as *metalinguistics* and *reading aloud*. This pattern persists even for approaches designed for children.

2. **Approaches that focus directly on concordance** (i.e., direct concordance PFC). (**Concordance** = The movement from one element in an utterance to the next element.) No sum-

Table 8-2. Treatment techniques for the various tempo PFCs. (Definitions of all treatment techniques are provided in the Glossary.)

Technique	Purpose/Focus Combinations
Alternating Tasks	indirect rate
Amplification	indirect rate
Breathing Activities	direct rate
Buzzing	indirect concordance
Coaching	direct rate
Contrastive Sets/Minimal Pairs	direct rate, direct phrasing, indirect rate, indirect concordance, indirect phrasing
Contrastive Stress Drill	indirect rate
Conversation	direct rate, indirect rate
Covert Rehearsal	indirect concordance
Cues	
Auditory	indirect rate
Rhythmic	indirect rate, indirect phrasing
Tactile/Kinesthetic	indirect rate
Visual	direct rate, direct phrasing, indirect rate, indirect concordance, indirect phrasing
Disambiguation	direct concordance, direct phrasing, indirect rate
Discrimination	direct rate, indirect rate, indirect concordance, indirect phrasing
Drills	direct concordance, indirect rate, indirect phrasing
Easy Onsets	indirect rate
Exaggeration	indirect rate, indirect concordance, indirect phrasing
Fading	indirect rate
Feedback	
Auditory	direct rate, indirect rate, indirect concordance, indirect phrasing
Tactile/Kinesthetic	direct rate, indirect rate
Verbal	direct rate, direct concordance, direct phrasing, indirect rate, indirect concordance, indirect phrasing
Visual	direct rate, indirect rate, indirect phrasing

(continued)

Table 8-2 (continued)

Technique	Purpose/Focus Combination
Games	indirect rate, indirect concordance
Homework	indirect concordance
Imitation	direct rate, direct concordance, indirect rate, indirect concordance, indirect phrasing
Labeling	indirect rate
Matching	indirect rate, indirect phrasing
Metalinguistics	direct rate, direct phrasing, indirect rate, indirect concordance, indirect phrasing
Modeling	direct rate, direct concordance, indirect rate, indirect concordance, indirect phrasing
Monologues	indirect rate
Motor Movement	direct rate, direct concordance, indirect rate, indirect concordance, indirect phrasing
Narratives	direct rate
Negative Practice	direct rate, direct phrasing, indirect rate, indirect phrasing
Pacing	direct rate, indirect rate
Play	indirect rate, indirect phrasing
Poetry Reading	direct rate, direct phrasing, indirect phrasing
Previews	indirect concordance
Query Led Corrections	indirect concordance
Query Responding	direct concordance, indirect rate, indirect concordance
Reading Aloud	direct rate, direct phrasing, indirect rate, indirect concordance, indirect phrasing
Reviews	indirect rate
Rhyming	indirect concordance
Role Playing	direct rate, indirect rate, indirect concordance
Routines	direct rate
Scripts	indirect phrasing
Self-Monitoring	direct rate, indirect rate, indirect concordance, indirect phrasing

Technique	Purpose/Focus Combnation
Self-Reading	indirect concordance
Sequencing Task	direct rate, indirect rate
Shadowing	indirect rate, indirect phrasing
Singing	direct rate, indirect rate, indirect phrasing
Stimulation	
Auditory	indirect rate, indirect concordance, indirect phrasing
Transcriptions	indirect phrasing
Unison Speech	indirect concordance
Whispering	indirect concordance

mary information is provided here because of the small number of pertinent methods. Table 8–3 presents a program for the direct concordance PFC. Readers also are referred to Appendixes A, B, and E for treatment ideas which may be adapted to direct concordance PFCs.

3. **Approaches that focus directly on phrasing** (i.e., direct phrasing PFCs). (**Phrasing** = The speaker's use of prosodic cues to mark the beginning or the ending of phrases.) Table 8–4 contains an example of a treatment program for treating phrasing directly.

   a. **Population.** Methods for the direct treatment of phrasing have been used with people wishing to improve their overall speaking skills (speech improvement) and for speakers with voice disorders.

   b. **Intervention**
      (1) **Content**
         (a) The **target behavior** of direct phrasing approaches usually consists of reading aloud ambiguous and/or unambiguous sentences.
         (b) Recommendations about how **phrasing should be produced** typically involve the use of pausing.

Table 8–3. Program for direct concordance PFC

POPULATION:	Phonological impairment.
TECHNIQUES:	Modeling, motor movement, imitation, drills. (The Glossary contains definitions of the techniques.)
OBJECTIVES:	1. To determine if the client is a candidate for this method.
	2. To produce consonant transitions (concordance) that link words in spontaneous, conversational speech.
PROCEDURES:	1a. The clinician presents drawings or toys to the client and produces a sentence designed to elicit a two-word target phrase containing an arresting consonant in the first word. Example:

CONTEXT	***TARGET***
Clinician displays a cookie and says: "This cookie looks really good. I am pretty hungry. What should I do?"	Eat it

b. The clinician presents at least 10 contexts.

c. The clinician scores the client's responses for the presence or absence of a smooth concordance. If the client's score is 60% or less, he or she is a candidate for therapy.

2a. The clinician develops training stimuli using the following guidelines:

• The arresting sound of the first word in the target phrase should be in the client's repertoire;

• fricatives facilitate transitions;

• clusters and morphological endings as in "walked out" or "jumped in" may be employed;

• targets should contain a variety of speech sounds; and

• content for the phrasing should refer to activities of daily living.

b. The clinician initially models two-word targets such as "may kit" for "make it" using prosodic variations in stress, loudness, duration, intonation on the second syllable. This modeling is accompanied by a picture of the second "word" in the two-word target (e.g., a kit). If necessary, the client uses a pause or prolongation between syllables until the two-word target is produced correctly. Sometimes, the transition sound is emphasized by pairing speech sound production with motor movement.

PROCEDURES *(continued)*	2c. As the client improves, the clinician fades the prolonging and pausing between the words in the two-word target and moves the consonant from the second to the first word (e.g., "make it"). Additionally, the stress pattern changes from unstressed-stressed to stressed-unstressed.
	d. The clinician models the first word of two-word targets with new second words (e.g., "make up" becomes "make it"). Although the modeling can involve drills, activities of daily living and the pairing of productions with motor activities are preferred. Example: the child says "push it" while on a swing.
	e. The criterion for correct responses becomes progressively more difficult. Thus, early in treatment the client may not be required to close the second word in the two-word phrases, but he or she will be required to do so later.
COMMENTS:	The authors claim that this program has limited effectiveness with subjects who are developmentally delayed or dysarthric. This method also indirectly uses stress, loudness, duration, and rate.

Source: The above program was derived from information provided in Johnson, H. P., & Hood, S. B. (1988). Teaching chaining to unintelligible children: How to deal with open syllables. *Language, Speech, and Hearing Services in Schools, 19,* 211–220.

(c) The **hierarchy** of treatment steps for direct phrasing approaches usually is logical.

(1) **Techniques** used to treat phrasing directly are found in Table 8–2 which presents the techniques used with all varieties of tempo PFCs.

B. Indirect Treatment Strategies

1. **Approaches that focus indirectly on rate** (i.e., indirect rate PFC). (**Rate** = The number of syllables produced over a given amount of time.)

   a. **Population.** Treatment approaches that indirectly use speaking rate have been developed for individuals from the following disorder or etiological groups: articulatory/

Table 8-4. Program for direct phrasing PFC

POPULATION:	Voice disorders, speech improvement.
TECHNIQUES:	Metalinguistic tasks, contrastive sets, reading aloud, disambiguation, feedback (verbal), cues (visual). (The Glossary contains definitions of the techniques.)
OBJECTIVES:	To employ appropriate phrasing, terminal contour, and stressing in a reading aloud task
PROCEDURES:	1a. The clinician presents the client with six sentences that have similar speech sounds but different interpretations. Example:

1a. The clinician presents the client with six sentences that have similar speech sounds but different interpretations. Example:

- The horse herd will move deer.
- The horse heard will move, dear.
  (Fairbanks, 1960, p. 167)

b. The client marks the sentences for phrasing, terminal contour, and stress.

c. The client reads the sentences aloud.

2. The client reads aloud the "Esau Wood" passage (Fairbanks, 1960, p. 167).

3a. The clinician presents the client with pairs of phrases that have similar speech sounds but different interpretations. Example:

- Flower boxes Sayle
- Flower boxes sale
  (Fairbanks, 1960, p. 168)

b. The client practices reading the phrases aloud until the different meanings are evident.

4a. The client is presented with ambiguous headlines and potential interpretations. The client reads the headlines using each of the interpretations. Example:

- NOTRE DAME BACKS GUARD PLAY

  (1) Coach defends it

  (2) They won't reveal it.
  (Fairbanks, 1960, p. 168)

Source: The above program was derived from information provided in Fairbanks, G. (1960). *Voice and articulation drillbook* (2nd ed., pp. 167-168). New York: Harper & Row.

phonological disorders, cluttering, developmental apraxia of speech, developmental delay, hearing impairment, learning disability, motor speech disorders, specific language impairment, stuttering, and voice disorders. In addition, methods have been developed for normal speakers wishing to improve their overall communication skills (speech improvement) and for those learning English as a second language.

b. **Intervention**
(1) **Content**
  (a) The **terminal objectives** used in methods that indirectly focus on speaking rate vary considerably. Some of the terminal behaviors include

  - improved intelligibility,
  - increased fluency,
  - improved articulatory/phonological skills,
  - improved loudness,
  - improved ability to sequence sounds,
  - improved social skills,
  - improved overall tempo,
  - increased lexicon, and
  - decreased use of prolongations.

  (b) The **target behaviors** for rate related steps involve a variety of behaviors such as

  - reading aloud selected passages at specified rates;
  - using a specified rate in spontaneous speech, monologues, or dialogues;
  - discriminating among speaking rates;
  - imitating various speaking rates;
  - attending to models of various speaking rates; and
  - modifying and/or maintaining speaking rate during a variety of speaking tasks (e.g., shadowing, DAF, producing commonly misarticulated words, producing words with differing rhythmic patterns, and repairing communicative breakdowns).

An example of a treatment method in which speaking rate is used indirectly is found in Table 8-5.

(c) Recommendations about the **production of rate** often are not provided in indirect rate methods. However, when recommendations are present, modification of duration is the most frequent means by which speakers change rate.

(d) When speaking rate is an intermediate step or a facilitator/constrainer, the **hierarchy** tends to be logical. Linear procedures also receive considerable use.

(2) **The wide range of techniques** used in approaches that indirectly treat speaking rate are reflected in Table 8-2, which lists techniques for each of the tempo PFCs. Frequently used techniques for indirect rate include *metalinguistics, feedback, visual cues, reading aloud,* and *motor movement.*

2. **Focusing indirectly on concordance** (i.e., indirect concordance PFC). (**Concordance** = The movement from one element in an utterance to the next element.) No summary is presented here because many of the indirect concordance methods have been presented elsewhere (e.g., Dickerson [1989] in Table 11-6; Pindzola [1987a] in Table 11-3; Simmons [1983] in Table 6-4). An additional indirect concordance method is presented in Table 8-6.

3. **Approaches that focus indirectly on phrasing** (i.e., indirect phrasing PFC). (**Phrasing** = The speaker's use of prosodic cues to mark the beginning or the end of phrases.) Table 8-7 provides an example of an approach that indirectly focuses on phrasing.

   a. **Population.** Approaches that indirectly focus on phrasing have been developed for people from the following groups: developmental delay, motor speech disorders, and stuttering. In addition, indirect phrasing has been used with normal speakers attempting to improve their overall communication skills and by speakers wishing to reduce their accents.

   b. **Intervention**

Table 8–5. Program for indirect speaking rate PFC. (Steps from the speaking rate phase of treatment are marked with an asterisk [*].)

POPULATION:	Dysarthria (ataxia).
TECHNIQUES:	Alphabet board; pacing board; cues (rhythmic, visual); reading aloud; imitation; self-monitoring; feedback (auditory, verbal, visual); monologues; modeling; metalinguistics. (The Glossary contains definitions of the techniques.)
GOAL:	To increase intelligibility by modifying speaking rate.
OBJECTIVES:	1. To speak one word at a time [Rigid Imposition of Rate].
	2. To read a passage at a speaking rate imposed by the clinician [Rhythmic Cueing].
	3. To modify pausing abnormalities [Oscilloscopic Feedback].
	4. To adopt a speaking rate at which both intelligibility and rate are maximized and to develop self-monitoring skills.
PROCEDURES:	*1. (This step is initiated soon after clients begin to emerge from comas. At that time, clients will probably experience considerable difficulty monitoring their own speech and varying degrees of confusion, distractibility, and reduced attention.) The options for speaking "one word at a time" are achieved by
	• presenting an alphabet board to the client who points to the first letter of each word as he or she reads aloud words on the board and/or
	• using a pacing board (see Helm-Estabrook, 1979). NOTE: The use of a pacing board often reduces rate by increasing pause time; this can result in decreased normalcy judgments.
	*2. (This step serves as a transition between speaking "one word at a time" and "self-monitoring.") The clinician cues the client to use a specified speaking rate by pointing to words in a passage that the client is attempting to read aloud. The clinician avoids client productions that sound as if the client is speaking "one word at a time" by

(continued)

145

Table 8-5 *(continued)*

PROCEDURES *(continued)*	• directing the client to follow slightly behind the clinician's pace and not to read ahead of the clinician.
	• instructing the client to use the same rate and rhythm as the clinician. (The clinician uses a slow speaking rate, appropriate phrasing, and appropriate pauses.)
	• cueing the client to produce stressed syllables slowly and unstressed syllables quickly.
	• gradually fading rhythmic cueing.
	*3. The clinician directs the client to increase or decrease speaking rate, as appropriate. The client attempts to produce (imitatively or spontaneously) an utterance and to "fill-up" a 5-second window on an oscilloscope while speaking. The client monitors the oscilloscope during 5 seconds of spontaneous or imitative speech.
	4. (The following can be initiated before the client completes the previous steps.)
	a. The clinician periodically instructs the client to record a passage that is unfamiliar to the clinician at a speaking rate that he or she believes will result in 95% intelligibility. The clinician transcribes the client's reading of the passage and calculates the intelligibility percentage.
	*b. The following options may be used to facilitate self-monitoring.
	• After the speaking task has been audiotaped, the client predicts the percentage of intelligible speech. This is compared to the clinician's calculation or estimation.
	• The client produces and audiotapes nonsense sentences created from a "menu" of words (e.g., adjectives, subjects, verbs, etc.) The next day, the client transcribes the audiotape and calculates his or her own intelligibility scores from the transcript.
COMMENTS:	Terms in brackets ([ ]) are the labels used by Yorkston and Beukelman (1981). The following aspects of prosody also are used indirectly in this approach: phrasing, stress (lexical), and tempo (rate).

Source: The above program was derived from information provided by Yorkston, K. M., & Beukelman, D. R. (1981). Ataxic dysarthria: Treatment sequences based on intelligibility and prosodic considerations. *Journal of Speech and Hearing Disorders, 46,* 398–404.

146

Table 8–6. Program for indirect concordance PFC. (Steps associated with concordance are preceded by an asterisk [*].)

POPULATION:	Speech improvement.
TECHNIQUES:	Metalinguistics, reading aloud, disambiguation. (The Glossary contains definitions of the techniques.)
GOAL:	To improve overall speaking skills.
OBJECTIVES:	To produce connected speech using normal overlapping speech sound productions across words.
PROCEDURES:	*1. The client reads a passage describing the need for and the characteristics of blending sounds across words (i.e., concordance) in connected speech.
	*2. The client reads aloud lists of phrases in which a speech sound in one word is "absorbed" into another [complete assimilation]. In the examples which follow, the /z/ and the /s/ take on the characteristics of the /ʃ/.
	this shore
	horse shoe
	his shirt
	(King & DiMichael, 1991, p. 343)
	*3. The client reads aloud lists containing words or two-word phrases with abutting identical stops [doubled] (e.g., get Ted, bad day, bookcase). The client attempts to produce the doubled consonants by producing only one stop but lengthens the closure time prior to the "explosion."
	*4. The client reads aloud lists containing words or two-word phrases with abutting but different stops (i.e., successive) (e.g., get down, bad coin, bookbag). The client attempts to produce the successive consonants by stopping (but not exploding) the first consonant and, then, stopping *and* exploding the second consonant.
	*5. The client reads aloud sentences containing both forms of abutted consonants. The lists provide visual cues by highlighting the abutting consonants.
	*6. The client disambiguates word or phrase sets by limiting his or her sound blending across certain syllables. Examples:
	weak aim We came
	node out no doubt
	made A May Day
	(King & DiMichael, 1991, p. 372)
COMMENTS:	This method also uses indirect pause (intraturn). Words within brackets ([ ]) are the authors' terms.

Source: The above program was derived from information provided in King, R. G., & DiMichael, E. M. (1991). *Voice and diction* (pp. 205–209, 342–344). Prospect Heights, IL: Waveland Press.

Table 8–7. Program for indirect phrasing PFC. (Steps associated with phrasing are preceded by an asterisk [*].)

POPULATION:	Speech improvement.
TECHNIQUES:	Metalinguistics, cues (visual), reading aloud, self-monitoring. (The Glossary contains definitions of the techniques.)
GOAL:	To improve overall speaking skills.
OBJECTIVES:	To read aloud sentences using appropriate phrasing.
PROCEDURES:	1. The clinician writes the word "Phrasing" on a blackboard or on a piece of paper.
	2. The clinician asks the client to share what he or she knows about phrasing.
	3. The clinician reads aloud an explanation of phrasing and instructs the client to read along silently.
	4. The client reads aloud the passage from Step #3.
	5. The clinician reads aloud sentences to the client and the client reads along silently. The clinician pauses briefly at phrases within the sentences and for a longer time at the end of sentences.
	6. The clinician rereads the sentences from Step #5 as the client marks the pauses at the phrases with one bar (l) and those at the end of a sentence with three bars (lll).
	7. The client reads aloud the sentences with the cues from Step #6. The client self-monitors his or her performance during the oral reading task.

Source: The above program was derived from information provided in English, S. L. (1988). *Say it clearly* (p. 24). New York: Collier Macmillan.

(1) **Content**

(a) The **terminal objectives** of indirect phrasing PFCs include

- increased fluency
- improved intonation
- improved intelligibility, and
- increased naturalness.

(b) The **target behaviors** for these methods consist of

- repairing communicative breakdowns using phrasing,

- reading aloud selected passages using appropriate phrasing, and
- increased naturalness.

(c) If authors provide recommendations for **production of phrasing**, they usually suggest using pause and/or duration.

(d) When the phrasing is an intermediate step or a facilitator/constrainer, the **hierarchy** tends to be linear.

(2) The **techniques** used in approaches that indirectly treat phrasing are presented in Table 8–2, which contains an overview of techniques used for each of the tempo PFCs. *Reading aloud, visual cues*, and *metalinguistics* are commonly used techniques for indirect phrasing PFCs.

C. Summary Points

1. The **number of tempo treatment methods** is decidedly in favor of indirect purposes.

2. Treatment approaches for tempo are available for individuals from **several different groups** (articulatory/phonological disorders, cluttering, developmental apraxia of speech, developmental delay, foreign accent, hearing impairment, learning disability, motor speech disorders, specific language impairment, speech improvement, and stuttering).

3. The summaries in the preceding sections indicate logical **hierarchies** are used most frequently in the ordering of treatment steps. In logical hierarchies, empirical data do not identify the most efficient method of ordering steps. Rather, developers rely on what *appears* to be an appropriate ordering. Accordingly, clinicians may consider using alternate hierarchies when planning treatment.

4. As with the other prosodic components and the prosodic features, there is a heavy emphasis on **metalinguistic tasks** such as describing or making judgments. Clinicians using metalinguistic treatment tasks should ensure such tasks are within the cognitive capacities of their clients.

5. **Clinicians working with children** should consider child-oriented treatment methods that employ age-appropriate tech-

niques. Section VI.G lists citations for tempo methods designed for children.

6. There is a strong tendency to treat tempo problems by identifying and targeting specific skills. Clinicians wishing to treat tempo using a **holistic or integrative approach** may refer to the citations in section VI.H for guidance.

7. **Reading aloud** is a frequently used treatment technique. Apparently, authors assume that reading-based skills generalize to spontaneous speech without direct training, because treatment often ends following the completion of reading objectives. Clinicians using reading-based approaches may want to monitor their clients to ensure that the skills achieved in reading generalize to spontaneous speech.

8. Little empirical data exist **verifying the effectiveness of tempo treatment methods** cited in this chapter. Accordingly, clinicians will want to confirm the effectiveness of treatments for their own clients and should not fear modifying undocumented programs to suit their own needs.

9. Clinicians are cautioned to monitor **speech "naturalness" and speech intelligibility**, because changes in tempo can result in changes in naturalness and/or intelligibility. Special attention should be directed to the effect of pauses on naturalness. Additionally, clinicians might consider monitoring, and even targeting, phonemic changes when working with rate.

10. It should be noted that for some of the cited references, the **attention to tempo is minimal**. Thus, clinicians may find only limited information pertaining to tempo in such programs.

11. Clinicians who design their own treatment methods may find Table 8-2 helpful because it provides a listing of commonly used, but usually not empirically verified, treatment **techniques**. Researchers also may find this table helpful, if they consider it a listing of techniques in need of empirical verification.

VI.   CITATIONS FOR TEMPO TREATMENT

A. Citations for Approaches Directly Focusing on Rate

Bradford (1970); Cohen (1988); Dworkin (1991, pp. 317–318, 318–320, 320–321, 321–322, 322–323, 323, 326–328, 328); Fairbanks (1960, pp. 113–118); Glenn et al. (1989, pp. 222–223); Hanson & Metter (1983); Moncur & Brackett (1974, pp. 89–96); Prater & Swift (1984, pp. 189); Riley & Riley (1985); Wilson (1972, pp. 144–146, 178–179).

B. Citations for Approaches Directly Focusing on Concordance

Johnson & Hood (1988).

C. Citations for Approaches Directly Focusing on Phrasing

Fairbanks (1960, pp. 146–151, 167–168); Glenn et al. (1989, pp. 233–239).

D. Citations for Approaches Indirectly Focusing on Rate

Berry & Goshorn (1983); Beukelman & Yorkston (1977); Dworkin (1991, pp. 323–324, 324–326); Dworkin, Abkarian, & Johns (1988); Eisenson (1972, p. 199); Fairbanks (1960, pp. 141–143); Glenn et al. (1989, pp. 222–223); Ham (1986, pp. 151–167, 308–316; 324–328, 339–344); Ham (1990, pp. 293, 301–305; 370–371); Huskins (1986, pp. 35–36); Ling (1976, pp. 243–244, 366–367); Macaluso-Haynes (1978); McDonald (1964); Minskoff (1980); Pindzola (1987a); Riley & Riley (1985); Rosenbek (1978, p. 214); Rosenbek et al. (1974); Rosenbek & LaPointe (1978, pp. 301–304); Swift & Rosin (1990); Weismer et al. (1990); Wilson (1972, pp. 137–138); Yorkston & Beukelman (1981); Yoss & Darley (1974).

E. Citations for Approaches Indirectly Focusing on Concordance

Dickerson (1989); Fairbanks (1960, pp. 141–143); Ham (1986, pp. 339–344); Orion (1988, pp. 29–35); Pindzola (1987a); Simmons (1983).

F. Citations for Approaches Indirectly Focusing on Phrasing

Bellaire et al. (1986); Brazil et al. (1980); Glenn et al. (1989, pp. 233–239); Dworkin (1991, pp. 324–326, 336–337, 338–339); Ham (1986, pp. 333–334); Orion (1988, pp. 14–18, 29–35); Swift & Rosin (1990); Yorkston & Beukelman (1981).

G. Citations for Approaches Designed for Children

Bradford (1970); Eisenson (1972); Ham (1990, pp. 293, 301–305); Ling (1976, pp. 243–244, 366–367); Macaluso-Haynes (1978); McDonald (1964); Minskoff (1980); Pindzola (1987a); Riley & Riley (1985); Rosenbek et al. (1974); Swift & Rosin (1990); Weismer et al. (1990); Wilson (1972, pp. 137–138, 144–146, 178–179); Yoss & Darley (1974); Appendix B.

H. Citations for Holistic and/or Integrative Approaches

Bellaire et al. (1986); Brazil et al. (1980); Dickerson (1989); Dworkin (1991, pp. 333–334, 338–339); Fairbanks (1960, pp. 155–159, 167–168); Glenn et al. (1989, pp. 221–239); Graham (1978); Ham (1986, pp. 151–167, 324–328); Ham (1990, pp. 301–305); McDonald (1964); Minskoff (1980); Moncur & Brackett (1974, pp. 89–96); Orion (1988, pp. 29–35); Pindzola (1987a); Riley & Riley (1985); Rosenbek et al. (1974); Schomburg et al. (1989); Simmons (1983); Swift & Rosin (1990); Appendixes A & B.

C H A P T E R

9

Treating Prosodic Components: Intonation

I. NORMAL USE OF THE PROSODIC COMPONENT INTONATION

A. Description

This chapter focuses on intonation which involves communicative changes in fundamental frequency or the linguistic use of pitch. Languages such as English, labeled intonation languages, use intonation for discourse management, the expression of attitudes, the expression of intentions, and speech registers. (Speech registers involve the use of special speech patterns in specific contexts or with specific groups of people. Child Directed Speech is one example of a register; its intonational characteristics are noted in Chapter 1.) Unlike tone languages such as Chinese, most intonation languages rarely use intonation to differentiate lexical items (Couper-Kuhlen, 1986; Cruttenden, 1986).

B. Categories

Intonation categories are divided into two major types: (1) intonation categories that have functions within utterances (internal organization) and (2) intonation categories concerned with functions across utterances (external organization). Figure 9-1 shows the categories of intonation.

1. The **internal organizational level of intonation** consists of three functional categories that must be produced in the following order: (a) onset of the fundamental frequency at the beginning of the utterance, (b) nucleus, and (c) terminal contour. All these categories must be present, although onset and terminal contour can be represented on the nucleus as in one word utterances. A fourth category is holistic and represents the entire intonational configuration of the utterance — (d) the overall contour.

    a. The **onset** of the intonation contour may be defined as the pitch height of the first full syllable in an utterance. A full syllable is a syllable that contains a full vowel. [Bolinger (1986, p. 37) considers the following to be full vowels: /i/, /ɪ/, /e/, /ɛ/, /æ/, /ʌ/, /a/, /ɔ/, /o/, /ʊ/, /u/.] Several factors impact on onset including the speaker's pitch range, the length of the utterance, the pitch height at the end of the previous utterance, and a number of pragmatic issues.

CLINICAL NOTE: Onset of the intonation contour is usually ignored by practitioners and researchers in communication disorders despite the considerable interest devoted to it by other disciplines (e.g., linguistics and teaching English as a second language).

    b. The **nucleus** is the most prominent syllable of the utterance (Crystal, 1969, 1981). Although definitions of "prominence" vary markedly, the focus in this section is the pitch direction on the syllable judged to be most prominent. The pitch direction on the nucleus may be represented by a falling (\), rising (/), falling-rising (\/), rising-falling (/\), or level (–) contour or change. These changes may result in the syllable being perceived as stressed. (Chapter 10 — Stress — contains

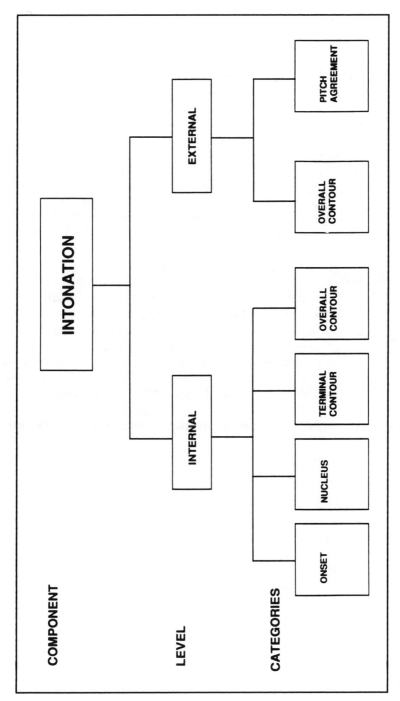

COMPONENT

LEVEL

CATEGORIES

Figure 9–1. A representation of the prosodic component intonation, its levels, and its categories.

a more thorough discussion of what makes the nucleus prominent.)

CLINICAL NOTE: Some (e.g., Crystal, 1982; Ohde & Sharf, 1992) include the height of pitch excursion in the description of the nucleus. However, due to limited research and the pitch height's considerable variability, it has only limited application at present to communication disorders.

   c. The **terminal contour** represents the completion of the pitch movement of the utterance. Cruttenden (1986) describes terminal contour as being the "last pitch direction on the last syllable" (p. 45) of the utterance. In declarative utterances, the pitch direction of the terminal contour usually falls. For many types of questions (e.g., yes/no or information verification), the pitch direction may rise.

   If the nucleus is the final syllable, the terminal contour and the nucleus are produced on the same syllable. When syllables follow the nucleus, those syllables form the terminal contour. There is a relationship between the nucleus and terminal contour even when they are separate in time, because the pitch direction of the nucleus usually continues through the terminal contour.

   Pitch direction is the primary pitch feature of the terminal contour. However, pitch slope (the amount of change in fundamental frequency over time) and pitch height also play a role.

CLINICAL NOTE: The considerable attention that terminal contour has enjoyed from speech-language pathologists is evident in the treatment section of this chapter. This attention is in stark contrast to the views of linguists such as Couper-Kuhlen (1986) who consider terminal contour to be a mere extension of the nucleus. Others suggest that the terminal contour reflects physiological events such as the decrease of subglottal air pressure.

   d. The **overall contour** of the utterance holistically represents the pitch configuration from the initiation of the utterance to its end. The overall contour includes onset, nucleus, and terminal contour and is produced using all the pitch categories: height, slope, direction and variation. While pitch at the onset or the nucleus displays considerable variation, the pitch at the endpoints varies little (Boyce & Menn, 1979). Few treatment programs exist for overall contour, despite the substantial body of literature describing the overall contour of selected groups of persons with impaired speech in terms such as "flat," "monotone," or "exaggerated intonation."

2. The **external organizational level of intonation** consists of intonation categories concerned with relations between or among different utterances. The categories are (a) cohesive devices and (b) pitch agreement.

   a. **Cohesive devices** are units of identical or related intonation patterns that extend across utterances or phrases and result in a sense of interconnectiveness among utterances. One example of a cohesive device is successive sequences which involve the repeated but selective use of a specific pitch category (e.g., lower pitch height than normal, a more gradual pitch slope than normal, or a monotone). Thus, some speakers produce specific pitch categories repeatedly during a portion of their utterance(s), but the patterns do not extend throughout all the speakers' utterances. Consolidated sequences also are cohesive devices. They leave listeners with a sense that consecutive utterances are interrelated (Couper-Kuhlen, 1986).

   b. **Pitch Agreement** reflects the degree of concordance or agreement in pitch height between the end of one utterance (termination) and the beginning of the next (relative onset level — ROL). A high termination of pitch predicts that the next utterance will be initiated with a high ROL and mid termination predicts mid ROL. Low terminations, however, do not predict ROL. Agreement (or lack of agreement) between termination and ROL impacts on the pragmatics of communication (Brazil et al., 1980).

CLINICAL NOTE: The initial pitch height of utterances is both an external and an internal organizational element because it serves dual functions. Onset (the internal element) may function as a reference point for the pitch height of the other syllables in the utterance. The relative onset level (the external element), involves the resetting of the pitch height and allows for the comparison of the pitch height of one utterance to the pitch height of the previous utterance.

C. Normative Information About Intonation

1. **Onset** (i.e., the pitch height of the first full syllable in an utterance) usually occurs in the middle of a speaker's pitch range (Couper-Kuhlen, 1986). However, onset varies considerably because of factors such as pragmatics and sentence length.

2. Crystal's (1981, p. 64) analysis of the **nucleus** (i.e., the most prominent *word* in an utterance) of British English reveals that falling pitch directions most commonly mark the nucleus (51%). The second most common pitch directed for the nucleus is the rising pitch directions (21%).

3. A falling pitch direction is the most common **terminal contour** (i.e., the final pitch direction at the end of an utterance) and is indicative of the end of phrases, sentences, or thoughts. Falling pitch direction accounts for approximately 60% of the terminal contours in English (Cruttenden, 1986; Pike, 1945).

CLINICAL NOTE: Speech-language pathologists frequently equate falling terminal contours with declarative statements. However, questions such as "Where is he going?" or "What's for dinner?" are also produced with falling terminal contours.

4. The potential number of **overall contours** (i.e., the pitch configuration from the initiation to the end of the utterance) is extensive because of the large number of variations of nuclei, onsets, and terminal contours. Some linguists (e.g., Bolinger, 1986; Pike, 1945), have reduced the configurations to a relatively small number of combinable patterns capable of representing overall pitch patterns. Bolinger, for example, describes the most frequently used overall contour as one which consists of a mid onset, a sudden jump or "step-up" in pitch on the nucleus, and a falling pitch direction with a steep slope over the remainder of the utterance.

5. At present, no normative data detail the typical use of **cohesive devices** (i.e., units of identical or related intonation patterns that extend across utterance boundaries and result in a sense of interconnectiveness among utterances).

6. As noted in the description of **pitch agreement** (i.e., the degree of concordance in pitch height between the end of an utterance and the beginning of the next), the fundamental frequency at the termination of an utterance may predict the relative onset level of pitch (ROL) of the following utterance. Thus, "normal" productions consist of meeting these expectations. Violations of these pitch expectations can convey specific messages and/or seriously impact communication. For example, if the ROL varies, the same segmental response by a child to a teacher's informational, mid termination question of "What is the site of the largest mass execution of Native Americans in American history?" may be interpreted differently. Contrast:

- (using mid ROL) Mankato| {confident}
- (using high ROL) Mankato| {requesting evaluation}
- (using low ROL) Mankato| {sullen}

D. Communicative Roles

1. Crystal (1982) suggests that intonation is used to **convey attitudes** such as warnings, boredom, surprise, and neutrality.

2. Brazil et al. (1980) claim that speakers use intonation to **signal whether information is old** (i.e., "given") or **new.** For example, some pitch directions (e.g., \ / and /) indicate that the speaker considers information as commonly known. (Some linguists label this "given" information.) Other pitch directions on the nucleus (e.g., \ or / \ ) signal that the speaker considers information new to the listener. Contrast:

- John will be *home* (\ /) in *Au*gust (\ )
- John will be *home* (\ ) in *Au*gust (\ /)

The first example indicates that the speaker thinks that the new information for the listener is the timing of John's homecoming (August). It is assumed that the listener knows where John will be (home). For the second example, the reverse is true. The speaker thinks that the new information for the listener is that John will be home and that the common knowledge is that he is doing something in August.

3. **Social status** also can be conveyed by the pitch direction of the nucleus. For example, Brazil et al. (1980) report that / and / \ pitch directions on nuclei suggest a dominant role such as a professor, physician, parent, or a police officer. The use of either of these pitch directions by persons of lower social status might be viewed as inappropriate or aggressive. These differences are particularly important in view of multicultural factors.

4. Intonation also has **grammatical functions**. Contrast the effect of different terminal contours, with the first example representing a statement and the second representing a question.

Lawrence (/)

Lawrence (\ )

5. Intonation provides information about **discourse and about speaker attitudes**. For example, high terminations of intonation can invite responses and mid terminations can close topics (Brazil et al., 1980).

II. PERCEIVING THE PROSODIC COMPONENT OF INTONATION

Although changes in fundamental frequency (F_0) are clearly the most important cue to identify differences in intonation, other acoustic cues also coincide. For example, the perception of terminal fall is cued by a decrease in F_0 that occurs at some rate over time, a decrease in amplitude, and an increase in the duration of the final syllable. The perception of a stressed or prominent syllable in the overall contour arises by an increase in F_0, an increase in loudness, and an increase in duration relative to other syllables in the overall contour. (This is the prosodic component of stress and is covered in greater detail in Chapter 10.) While numerous measures of overall contour or specific aspects of the contour have been reported in the literature, the precise mechanism that listeners use to track F_0 and perceive intonation remains elusive. Perhaps, listeners use a running average of the pitch at the zero crossings or a common denominator in a set of harmonics for a speaker (even if F_0 is absent). Classic perception studies of intonation contour have revealed that a rising intonation pattern is perceived as a question, and a falling intonation pattern as a statement for listeners of American English and Swedish even when the linguistic stimuli are ambiguous (Borden & Harris, 1984). Similar work on the perception of intonation contours produced by speakers with various disorders is limited in accounting for how F_0 alone, or in combination with other acoustic cues, may be used to convey meaningful changes in intonation.

III. PRODUCING THE PROSODIC COMPONENT OF INTONATION

Intonation can be produced on a word, phrase, or sentence in American English. The falling intonation contour occurs over what Lieberman (1967) has called the breath group, or specifically the unmarked breath group, and is characterized by a decrease in F_0 and intensity. Specifically, the decrease in subglottal air pressure results in an attenuation of the vocal fold vibration which is mirrored in the downward drift of the F_0. At issue is whether the downward drift or declination is a passive mechanism or alternatively is controlled by a decrease in cricothyroid activity. Research suggests that while cricothyroid activity may be prominent in instances of emphatic stress or segmental adjustments, it has a negligible role in accounting for the decline in intonation contours. However, when pitch rises at the end of a phrase or sentence (the marked breath group, according to Lieberman), it is characterized by an increase in cricothyroid activity. The contraction of the muscle tenses and lengthens the vocal folds so that they vibrate faster, and the perceived pitch rises. These effects are usually accompanied by an increase in subglottal pressure. Such results imply the importance of respiratory activity and breath management in the production of inappropriate intonation contours by speakers with neurological disorders or hearing impairment.

IV. A MODEL FOR TREATING INTONATION

A. A Teaching Model for Intonation

Intonation consists of a complex interaction of intonation categories (onset, nucleus, terminal contour, overall intonation contour, cohesive devices, and pitch agreement) that are described in section I.B and represented in Figure 9-1.

B. Treatment Decisions: Intonation

The guidelines in the accompanying Clinical Note are presented to assist clinicians in applying information provided in previous and subsequent sections to the task of treating intonation. Explanations of the guidelines are provided in Chapter 2 (section I.B). In addition, the Treatment Index contains a cross-reference for locating the different purposes, focuses, populations, objectives, productive characteristics, hierarchies, treatment techniques, and sample programs referred to in the accompanying Clinical Note.

CLINICAL NOTE: GUIDELINES FOR DECISION MAKING

1. Determine the **purpose** (direct, indirect) for working with intonation.
2. Identify the **categories of intonation** (nucleus, onset, terminal contour, overall contour, cohesive devices, pitch agreement) that will serve as the focus of treatment.
3. Identify how the client will **produce** the intonation category.
4. Identify specific **target behaviors** for the targeted purpose/focus combination (PFC) (i.e., the purpose from Guideline #1 and the focus from Guideline #2 above).
5. Identify **treatment techniques** that are appropriate for the client.
6. Determine the **hierarchy** of steps.
7. Identify sources in which **clients with similar disorders** have similar PFCs.

V. SUMMARY OF PUBLISHED LITERATURE ON TREATING INTONATION

A. Direct Purpose Treatment Strategies

1. **Approaches that focus directly on internal components: Onset** (i.e., direct onset PFC). (**Onset** = The pitch height of the first full syllable in an utterance.) No treatment methods have been identified that directly focus on improving onset. Readers are referred to Appendixes A, B, and E for treatment ideas.

2. **Approaches that focus directly on internal components: Nucleus** (i.e., direct nucleus PFC). (**Nucleus** = The most prominent *word* in an utterance.) No summaries are provided below because of the limited number of treatment programs relevant to this PFC. Table 9–1 provides an example of such a program.

3. **Approaches that focus directly on internal components: Terminal contour** (i.e., direct terminal contour PFC). (**Terminal contour** = The final pitch direction at the end of an utterance.) The method presented in Table 9–2 represent one approach to treating terminal contour directly. Another example, of a direct terminal contour PFC can be seen in Hargrove, Roetzel, and Hoodin (1989, Table 10–4).

   a. **Population.** Treatment approaches for terminal contour are available for individuals with developmental delay, hearing impairment, motor speech disorders, specific language impairment, and voice problems. In addition, programs have been developed for normal speakers wishing to improve their overall speaking skills (speech improvement) and for those wishing to reduce foreign accent.

   b. **Intervention**
      (1) **Content**
          (a) The **target behaviors** for terminal contour as the primary objective include

              • producing isolated multiword utterances,
              • contradicting information in questions from the clinician,
              • producing sentences relevant to the clients' activities of daily living, and
              • reading aloud sentences containing two clauses.

          (b) When suggestions for the **production** of terminal contour are provided, descriptions typically note pitch directions such as falling, rising, or level. However, Fairbanks (1960, pp. 132–134) additionally describes the pitch features of variation and slope when making production recommendations.

          (c) The **hierarchy** of steps for teaching terminal contour usually is logically ordered.

Table 9-1. Program for direct nucleus PFC

POPULATION:	Voice disorder, speech improvement.
TECHNIQUES:	Reading aloud, cues (visual), metalinguistics. (The Glossary contains definitions of the techniques.)
GOAL:	To improve production of the nucleus and the terminal contour.
OBJECTIVES:	1. To use falling pitch directions on nuclei (phrasally stressed words).
	2. To use falling pitch directions on terminal contours.
PROCEDURES:	1. The clinician explains the following about intonation to the client.
	a. There are four general pitch heights: low, middle, high, very high (rare, used only in extreme contexts).
	b. Speakers initiate contours at "pitch points" (onsets).
	c. Pauses and/or "special pitch directions" terminate contours.
	d. The "special pitch directions" are falling, rising, and level.
	e. Falling pitch direction can be used to
	• signal finality,
	• signal a positive statement,
	• demark utterance termination, and
	• demark nucleus/phrasal stress.
	2. The client reads aloud sentences that are marked with symbols depicting pitch changes for finality or a positive statement. That is, he or she uses a falling terminal contour.
	3. The client repeats Step #2, but uses only phrases (e.g., "came to a stop").
	4. The client, cued by symbols, reads aloud sentences or phrases in which the nucleus is signaled by extending the length (i.e., slope) of the falling pitch (e.g., "Positively *not*").
	5. The client reads aloud sentences in which he moves from a high general level to a lower general level within the utterance.
COMMENTS:	This approach indirectly uses pauses, pitch (slope), intonation (onset), and tempo (phrasing) and directly used intonation (terminal contour).

Source: The above program was derived from information provided in Moncur, J. P., & Brackett, I. P. (1974). *Modifying vocal behavior* (pp. 78, 80–81). New York: Harper & Row.

Table 9-2. Program for direct terminal contour PFC

POPULATION:	Hearing impairment.
TECHNIQUES:	Feedback (tactile/kinesthetic, visual); computers; discrimination; imitation; cues (auditory, tactile/kinesthetic, visual); fading. (The Glossary contains definitions of the techniques.)
OBJECTIVES:	1. To discriminate falling terminal contours on speech segments of varying complexity.
	2. To imitate falling terminal contours on speech segments of varying complexity.
	3. To produce falling terminal contours on speech segments of varying complexity.
PROCEDURES:	(For the most part, these procedures are administered hierarchically. However, at the clinician's discretion, some of the procedures may be administered concurrently.)

1. The client discriminates the presence or absence of the falling terminal contours in either the client's or the clinician's speech using stimuli that are progressively more complex (see below). For this step, clients are permitted to wear their hearing aids. The hierarchy of stimuli includes

   a. vowels in isolation,

   b. CV syllables and/or disyllable CV stimuli in which the falling terminal contour is on the first or the second syllable,

   c. three CV syllables of long-long-long duration,

   d. three CV syllables of long-short-long duration,

   e. three CV syllables of short-short-long duration,

   f. three syllable phrases (real words),

   g. two syllable phrases (real words),

   h. one syllable phrases (real words).

2. The client imitates a falling terminal contour using the hierarchy of stimuli in #1. The clinician can use (a) vibrotactile feedback and cues, (b) the Visipitch, and (c) additional sensory cues such as facial cues to guide imitation. As the client progresses, the clinician fades the cues.

3. On demand, the client produces falling terminal contours using the hierarchy of stimuli outlined in Step #1. As in Step #2, the clinician uses cues and feedback to prompt an acceptable production but fades them as soon as possible.

Source: The above program was derived from information provided in Friedman, M. (1985). Remediation of intonation contours of hearing-impaired students. *Journal of Communication Disorders, 18,* 259–272.

165

(2) The most commonly occurring **techniques** used to teach terminal contour are *metalinguistics, discrimination, cues, feedback, reading aloud,* and *imitation*. The techniques for treating terminal contour directly can be found in Table 9–3 which lists techniques for all intonation PFCs.

4. **Approaches that focus directly on internal components: Overall contour** (i.e., direct overall contour PFC). (**Overall contour** = The pitch configuration from the initiation to the end of the utterance.) Berry's (1980) and de Bot's (1983) methods are presented in Tables 9–4 and 9–5, respectively. No summaries are provided because of the relatively small number of programs that are available for this PFC. Clinicians are referred to Appendixes A, B, E and the section pertaining to indirect overall contour PFCs (section V.B #4) for additional treatment ideas.

Musically based treatment approaches may also be classified as treating overall contour directly. References for such approaches are provided in Chapter 11, sections VI.E and F.

5. **Approaches that focus directly on external components: Cohesive devices** (i.e., direct cohesive device PFC). (**Cohesive device** = Units of identical or related intonation patterns that extend across utterance boundaries and that result in a sense of interconnectiveness among utterances.) No summaries are provided because of the limited number of available methods. Table 9–6 presents one example of a direct cohesive devise PFC. In addition, readers may refer to the corresponding section for indirect treatment of cohesive devices (V.B #5) and to Appendixes A, B, and E for treatment ideas.

6. **Approaches that focus directly on external components: Pitch agreement** (i.e., direct pitch agreement PFC). (**Pitch agreement** = The degree of concordance in pitch height between the end of an utterance and the beginning of the next.) No treatment methods have been identified that directly target improved production of pitch agreement as the purpose of therapy. Clinicians may refer to the corresponding section for indirect treatment of pitch agreement (V.B #6) or to Appendixes A, B, and E for treatment ideas.

Table 9–3. Treatment techniques for the various intonation PFCs. (Definitions of all treatment techniques are provided in the Glossary.)

Techniques	Purpose/Focus Combinations
Audiotaping	indirect onset, indirect nucleus, indirect terminal contour
Backups	indirect overall contour
Breathing Activities	direct terminal contour
Coaching	indirect nucleus, indirect terminal contour, indirect overall contour
Computers	direct terminal contour
Contrastive Sets/ Minimal Pairs	direct terminal contour, indirect onset, indirect nucleus, indirect terminal contour, indirect overall contour, indirect pitch agreement
Contrastive Stress Drills	direct terminal contour, indirect terminal contour
Conversation	indirect overall contour
Cues	
Auditory	indirect terminal contour, indirect overall contour
Phonemic	indirect overall contour
Tactile/Kinesthetic	direct terminal contour, indirect onset, indirect nucleus, indirect terminal contour, indirect overall contour
Verbal	indirect onset, indirect nucleus, indirect terminal contour
Visual	direct terminal contour, indirect nucleus, indirect terminal contour, indirect overall contour, indirect cohesive devices, indirect pitch agreement
Disambiguation	direct terminal contour, indirect nucleus
Discrimination	direct terminal contour, indirect onset, indirect nucleus, indirect terminal contour, indirect overall contour, indirect pitch agreement
Dramatics	direct terminal contour, direct overall contour
Drill	indirect onset, indirect nucleus, indirect overall contour, indirect pitch agreement
Exaggeration	indirect onset, indirect nucleus, indirect terminal contour, indirect overall contour, indirect pitch agreement
Fading	direct terminal contour

(continued)

Table 9-3 *(continued)*

Techniques	Purpose/Focus Combinations
Feedback	
Auditory	direct overall contour, indirect nucleus, indirect terminal contour, indirect overall contour
Tactile/Kinesthetic	direct terminal contour
Verbal	direct terminal contour, indirect nucleus, indirect overall contour, indirect pitch agreement
Visual	direct terminal contour, direct overall contour, indirect onset, indirect nucleus, indirect terminal contour
Games	indirect overall contour
Homework	direct terminal contour
Imitation	direct terminal contour, direct overall contour, indirect onset, indirect nucleus, indirect terminal contour, indirect overall contour
Latency	indirect overall contour
Metalinguistics	direct terminal contour, direct overall contour, indirect onset, indirect nucleus, indirect terminal contour, indirect overall contour, indirect pitch agreement
Modeling	direct overall contour, indirect onset, indirect nucleus, indirect terminal contour, indirect overall contour
Monologues	indirect overall contour
Motor Movement	direct terminal contour, direct overall contour, indirect onset, indirect nucleus, indirect terminal contour, indirect overall contour
Negative Practice	indirect onset, indirect nucleus, indirect terminal contour, indirect overall contour
Oral Motor Exercise	indirect overall contour
Pantomiming	direct overall contour
Play	indirect overall contour
Poetry Reading	indirect terminal contour
Production on Demand	direct terminal contour
Pushing	direct terminal contour
Query Responding	direct terminal contour, indirect overall contour
Reading Aloud	direct terminal contour, indirect onset, indirect nucleus, indirect terminal contour, indirect cohesive devices, indirect pitch agreement

168

Techniques	Purpose/Focus Combinations
Review	indirect onset, indirect nucleus, indirect terminal contour, indirect overall contour
Rituals	indirect overall contour
Role Playing/Scripts	indirect terminal contour, indirect overall contour
Self-Monitoring	direct terminal contour, direct overall contour, indirect onset, indirect nucleus, indirect terminal contour, indirect overall contour
Shadowing	indirect overall contour
Shaping	indirect overall contour
Signing	indirect overall contour
Singing/Chanting/ Intoning	direct overall contour, indirect overall contour
Stimulation Auditory	direct terminal contour, indirect terminal contour, indirect overall contour, indirect pitch agreement
Transcription	indirect onset, indirect nucleus, indirect pitch agreement
Unison Speech/ Reading	direct overall contour, indirect terminal contour, indirect overall contour

B. Indirect Purpose Treatment Strategies

1. **Approaches that focus indirectly on internal components: Onset** (i.e., indirect onset PFC). (**Onset** = The pitch height of the first full syllable in an utterance.) Only the Brazil et al. (1980) approach has been identified as targeting improved onset as an intermediate objective of therapy or as a facilitator/constrainer. A summary of Brazil et al. may be found in Table 4–7. Clinicians may refer to Appendixes A, B, and E for additional treatment ideas.

2. **Focusing indirectly on internal components: Nucleus** (i.e., indirect nucleus PFC). (**Nucleus** = The most prominent *word* in an utterance.)

Table 9-4. Program for direct overall contour PFC — Children

POPULATION:	Specific language impairment.
TECHNIQUES:	Choral speech, metalinguistics, motor movement, modeling, pantomiming, singing, self-monitoring, dramatics. (The Glossary contains definitions of the techniques.)
OBJECTIVES:	1. To establish rhythmic motor movements.
	2. To produce rhythmic speech.
	3. To produce acceptable prosodic patterns that serve as the "envelope" into which the other aspects of language are produced and perceived.
PROCEDURES:	(This approach is recommended for use with groups of children.)

1a. The clients practice movement patterns that involve posture, motion, balance, locomotion, and action sequences (e.g., walking, jumping rope, marching, dancing to the beat of a drum, pantomiming).

b. The clients practice directional movements, for example, "turn right, turn left, now turn around." The clinician pairs clients who are weak on this task with clients who are strong.

c. The clients practice pantomime sequences depicting activities of daily living such as throwing a ball or pouring a drink. As the clients progress, the clinician increases the affective message in the sequence.

2a. The clinician teaches clients to pair motor movements with simple finger plays, chants, and verses. As the clients progress, the complexity of the motor movements increases. Verbalization during this activity should be encouraged but not required.

b. The clients pair the use of specified melodies (overall contours) and gestures while performing group recitations such as minidramas, storytelling, role playing, puppet plays, and the production of verse.

3a. The clinician presents situations which are designed to evoke overall intonation contours associated with

- emotional responses,
- directives,
- announcements of skills and achievements, and
- social exchange or routines.

b. The clinician and the clients discuss the appropriateness and inappropriateness of certain behaviors and generate suggestions for change.

Source: The above program was derived from information provided in Berry, M. F. (1980). *Teaching linguistically handicapped children* (pp. 250–255). Englewood Cliffs, NJ: Prentice-Hall.

Table 9–5. Exemplar program for direct overall contour PFC — Adult

POPULATION:	Foreign accent.
TECHNIQUES:	Feedback (auditory, visual); modeling; imitation; metalinguistics; cues (visual). (The Glossary contains definitions of the techniques.)
OBJECTIVES:	To imitate sentences using an English overall contour.
PROCEDURES:	1. The clinician explains and demonstrates the use of a pitch meter or any other instrument that provides visual feedback.
	2. The client sits in front of the pitch meter's display panel, listens to the modeled target sentence, and observes the display of its overall contour on the pitch meter.
	3. The client imitates the sentence modeled in Step #2. The pitch meter displays a visual representation of the client's overall contour below the visual representation of the modeled overall contour (from Step #2). The client has the option of hearing his or her imitation of the sentence from Step #2. The client also has the option of imitating the sentence from Step #2 and to observe its overall contour again.
	4. Steps #2 and #3 are repeated for 50 different sentences in two sessions separated by no more than 7 days.

Source: The above program was derived from information provided in de Bot, F. (1983). Visual feedback of intonation I: Effectiveness and induced practice behavior. *Language and Speech, 26,* 331–350.

a. **Population.** Nuclei serve as treatment facilitators and/or as constrainers for individuals with foreign accents, hearing impairment, motor speech disorders, and voice problems. Additionally, methods are available for normal speakers wishing to improve their overall speaking competence (speech improvement).

b. **Intervention**
   (1) **Content**
      (a) In indirect nucleus PFCs, the **terminal objectives** include

- appropriate use of pauses;
- increased normalcy judgments;

Table 9–6. Program for direct cohesive devices PFC

POPULATION:	Foreign accent.
TECHNIQUES:	Modeling, metalinguistics, imitation, reading aloud, contrastive sets, auditory stimulation, audiotapes, cues (visual). (The Glossary contains definitions of the techniques.)
OBJECTIVE:	To produce cohesive devices appropriately.
PROCEDURES:	

1. The client reads and listens to an audiotape that explains about combining phrases prosodically so that the listener realizes there are several interconnected parts. Sikorski (1988) presents the following rule: When combining phrases within a turn, each phrase has a slightly rising terminal contour except the final phrase which has a falling terminal contour. Visual cues accompany the descriptions.

2. The client listens to and, then, reads aloud lists of single syllable words (e.g., Rick, Jo, Ann, Ruth). The client attempts to use the behaviors described in Step #1.

3. The client listens to and, then, reads aloud lists of multisyllable words (e.g., Mary, Donna, Kathy, Aimee). The client attempts to use the behaviors described in Step #1.

4. The client listens to and reads aloud sentences that have lists embedded within them (e.g., Mike taught at St. Agnes, Adelphi, St. John's, and Mankato). The client attempts to use the behaviors described in Step #1.

5. The client listens to tapes and reads about the use of cohesive devices in questions. Sikorski's rule: If the speaker wishes to give options to the listener (i.e., a listing question), he or she uses rising pitch directions on each option except the last option (which has a falling terminal contour). If the speaker wishes to convey doubt or seeks listener input, he or she uses rising on *all* the options, including the final option. Visual cues accompany the descriptions.

6. The client listens to and, then reads aloud long, listing sentences. He or she attempts to use the behaviors from Step #5.

7. The client listens to and reads aloud explanations about the use of cohesive devices in complex sentences. Sikorski's rule: The falling terminal contour of the first phrase in a complex sentence does not descend as far as the falling terminal contour of the second phrase. Visual cues are provided to facilitate production of the behavior.

8. The client listens to and reads aloud sentence sets that contrast (a) simple sentences that do not use cohesive

PROCEDURES *(continued):*	devices (e.g., Alex left) and (b) complex sentences that do use cohesive devices (e.g., Alex left but she called later).
	9. The client listens to and reads aloud complex sentences that begin with connectives (e.g., when, because, since, and, after). The client attempts to apply the rule from Step #7.
COMMENT:	This method also indirectly uses intonation (terminal contour, overall contour).

Source: The above program was derived from information provided in Sikorski, L. D. (1988). *Mastering the intonation patterns of American English* (pp. 70–77). Santa Ana, CA: L. D. Sikorski & Associates.

- improved ability to express emotions, attitudes, and intentions;
- improved articulation/phonology;
- improved overall intonation or pitch; and
- improved stressing skills.

(b) The **target behaviors** of nuclear phases of treatment consist of producing a variation of the terminal behavior (such as fluent speech or accurately articulated speech) in the context of the proper production of the nucleus while

- creating sentences;
- reading aloud sentences in isolation;
- reading aloud ambiguous sentences; and
- reading aloud selected passages (sentence pairs, paragraphs, scripts, etc.).

Table 9–7 provides an example of a program using the nucleus as an intermediate objective or a facilitator/constrainer.

(c) Recommendations about the **production** of nuclei typically focus on pitch directions such as rising, falling, or "step ups" (sudden changes in pitch height).

Table 9-7. Program for indirect nucleus PFC. (Steps related to the nucleus are preceded by an asterisk [*].)

POPULATION: Foreign accent.

TECHNIQUES: Modeling, metalinguistics, cues (visual), imitation, reading aloud, self-monitoring, narratives, exaggeration, negative practice. (The Glossary contains definitions of the techniques.)

GOAL: To increase articulatory proficiency and to improve overall intonation skills.

OBJECTIVE: To increase the number of accurately articulated words in a passage.

PROCEDURES: (Stern [1987] provides an audiotape that accompanies this program.)

*1. The client listens to an audiotape that explains that prior to the nucleus, American speakers tend to increase pitch suddenly (Jump Up), and following the nucleus, they slowly reduce pitch height on each successive syllable (Step Down).

*2. The client imitates exaggerated examples of Jump Up and Step Down.

*3. The client is cautioned to

• differentiate pitch changes and loudness changes. The client should be particularly concerned with changing pitch.

• avoid pitch slides in place of Jump Ups, because pitch slides sound "foreign" to Americans.

4. The clinician explains that the final word in the phrase usually has the greatest drop in pitch height.

*5. The client reads aloud sentences from Step #2 without a model.

*6. The clinician informs the client that the nucleus can vary in different contexts.

*7. The clinician warns the client to avoid using the same pitch onset when initiating Jump Ups. In monologues, narratives, or turns of more than one utterance, such redundancy may result in sing-song speaking patterns.

*8. The client reads aloud passages in his or her current accent, translates the sentences into his or her native language, and then rereads the sentences aloud. This demonstrates to the client that he or she properly identifies the most important word in phrases or sentences (i.e., the nucleus) but may use different prosodic cues to signify the nucleus.

*9. The client repeats the sentences in Step #8 using the new (American) intonation pattern.

PROCEDURES *(continued):*	*10. The client evaluates his or her own performance in Step #9. Several questions should be answered, such as

- Were the Jump Ups noticeable?
- Did the Jump Ups involve only pitch, not loudness?
- Were the Step Downs noticeable?

*11. The client again reads aloud the sentences from Step #9.

*12. A narrative is modeled for the client using the sentences that had been taught separately in Step #9. The clinician provides the client with a script in which the nuclei are underlined.

*13. The client reads aloud the narrative from Step #12. The clinician encourages the client to experiment, exaggerate, and create plausible versions of the narrative by altering the placement of the nucleus.

14. The client reviews the entire lesson.

COMMENT:	This method also uses intonation (terminal contour) and stress (phrasal) indirectly.

Sources: The above program was derived from information provided in (1) Stern, D. A. (1987). *The sound and style of American English: A course in foreign accent reduction. Course #1.* Los Angeles: Dialect Accent Specialist and in (2) Edwards, H. T., Strattman, K. H., Cuda, R. A., & Anderson, P. J. (1990, November). *A comparison of intonation and pronunciation training in accent reduction.* Paper presented at the annual convention of the American Speech-Language-Hearing Association, Seattle, WA.

(d) When the appropriate production of the nucleus is an intermediate objective or a facilitator/constrainer, the **hierarchy** tends to be logical.

(2) The **techniques** for using the nucleus indirectly can be found in Table 9–3 which lists techniques for all intonation PFCs. Although no one technique predominates for the indirect nucleus PFCs, ***visual cues, metalinguistics,*** and ***reading aloud*** are the most frequently used techniques. In addition, the various forms of ***feedback*** appear to enjoy moderate popularity.

3. **Approaches that focus indirectly on internal components: Terminal contour** (i.e., indirect terminal contour PFC). **(Ter-**

minal contour = The final pitch direction at the end of an utterance.)

a. **Population.** Appropriate use of the terminal contour serves as an indirect objective for persons from the following groups: articulation/phonological disorders, developmental delay, dysfluency, motor speech disorders, and voice disorders. Moreover, programs have been developed for normal speakers wishing to improve their overall speaking skills (speech improvement) or to decrease their accents.

b. **Intervention**
   (1) **Content**
       (a) The **terminal objectives** for the indirect terminal contour methods include

           • improved articulatory/phonological skills,
           • decreased dysfluencies,
           • increased intelligibility,
           • improved overall intonation skills,
           • improved prosody, and
           • establishment of prelinguistic communication skills.

       (b) **Target behaviors** for the terminal contour phase of treatment include

           • reading aloud sentences, paragraphs, or passages of poetry;
           • responding to questions using a specified terminal contour;
           • imitating multiword utterances; and
           • being exposed to ritual greetings using an appropriate terminal contour.

           Table 9–8 contains an example of a typical indirect terminal contour PFC program.

       (c) Recommendations about the **production** of terminal contour focus on the use of pitch direction.
       (d) The **hierarchy** of objectives for the indirect use of terminal contours is, for the most part, logically based as exemplified in Table 9–8.

Table 9-8. Program for indirect terminal contour PFC. (Steps related to the terminal contour are preceded by an asterisk [*].)

POPULATION:	Stuttering — children.
TECHNIQUES:	Stimulation (auditory), imitation, motor movement, unison speech, fading, modeling. (The Glossary contains definitions of the techniques.)
GOAL:	To reduce the frequency of dysfluencies.
OBJECTIVE:	To produce a dysfluency-free utterance using the targeted terminal contour.

PROCEDURES:

*1a. Sentence stimuli are presented in a hierarchy progressing from single words to multiword utterances. The clinician presents all the sentence stimuli within a single session using only one terminal contour (rising, falling, or level-plus-loudness).

b. Each session is one-hour long and consists of the following:

AUDITORY STIMULATION (2 minutes), MOTOR-PLUS-INTONATION TRAINING (56 minutes), and AUDITORY STIMULATION (2 minutes).

c. The treatment format is cyclical. In cyclical treatment formats, the clinician targets several different behaviors and works on each behavior for a specified amount of time with issues such as the percentage of correct responses not influencing the switching of target behaviors. Once the client has worked on each of the targeted behaviors, the clinician again "cycles" him or her through the target behaviors, until treatment is completed (Fey, 1986). Thus, for this method, the specific motor movement and pitch direction pairs (see below) change from session to session, irrespective of the client's performance. Once all the specific motor movement and pitch direction pairs have been targeted (one cycle), the clinician starts with the beginning pair. The following constitutes one cycle:

Upper body movement plus rising terminal contour,
Upper body movement plus falling terminal contour,
Upper body movement plus level terminal contour and loudness,
Lower body movement plus rising terminal contour,
Lower body movement plus falling terminal contour, and
Lower body movement plus level terminal contour and loudness.

(continued)

TABLE 9-8 *(continued)*

PROCEDURES *(continued)*	*2. The **auditory stimulation** phase of the treatment involves the clinician's reading of sentences using the targeted terminal intonation contour. During the reading of the sentences, the client wears headphones to amplify the sentences and engages in a quiet activity.

*3. The **motor-plus-intonation training** consists of six steps.

*a. While in physical contact with the client, the clinician models an utterance using the targeted terminal intonation contour (falling, rising, or level-plus-loudness) and pairs the pitch direction with the designated motor movement. The motor movements and their associated pitch directions are

- falling pitch direction = hands down (upper body movement) or walking down steps (lower body movement);
- rising pitch direction = hands up (upper body movement) or walking up steps (lower body movement); and
- level-plus-loudness = hands crashing together as if playing cymbals (upper body movement) or staying on the same step (lower body movement).

b. While in physical contact with one another, the clinician and the client produce the targeted utterances in unison using the targeted pitch direction and the associated movement.

c. While in physical contact with the clinician, the client produces the targeted utterance using the targeted pitch direction. The clinician and the client act out the associated motor movement but the clinician does not vocalize as the client produces the target utterance using the designated pitch direction.

d. The client produces the targeted utterance, pitch direction, and motor movement. The clinician also produces the motor movement but neither touches the client nor vocalizes.

e. The client produces the targeted utterances and pitch direction with the associated motor movements. The clinician does not actively participate.

f. The client produces the targeted utterances and pitch directions without motor movements and without clinician participation. Each time the client achieves 100% accuracy on this task, the linguistic complexity of the utterance increases.

Source: The above program was derived from information provided in Grube, M. M., & Smith, D. S. (1989). Paralinguistic intonation-rhythm intervention with a developmental stutterer. *Journal of Fluency Disorders, 14,* 185–208.

(2) The **techniques** employed in approaches using terminal contour indirectly vary considerably. The most commonly used techniques are ***metalinguistics, cues, feedback, contrastive sets/minimal pairs, reading aloud,*** and ***imitation***. The techniques for using terminal contour indirectly can be found in Table 9–3 which lists techniques for all intonation PFCs.

4. **Approaches that focus indirectly on internal components: Overall contour** (i.e., indirect overall contour PFC). (**Overall contour** = The pitch configuration from the initiation to the end of the utterance.)

   a. **Population.** Overall contour has been used indirectly for persons with the following problems: aphasia, autism, developmental delay, dysfluency, hearing impairment, motor speech disorders, specific language impairment, and voice disorders. In addition, methods have been designed to improve the speaking skills of normal speakers (speech improvement) and to decrease accents.

   b. **Intervention**
      (1) **Content**
         (a) When overall contour is used indirectly, the **terminal objective** can take many forms, such as

         • improved overall communication skills,
         • increased comprehension skills,
         • improved accuracy of speech,
         • improved fluency,
         • increased intelligibility,
         • improved overall pitch or intonation skills,
         • stimulation of linguistic and prelinguistic skills,
         • modified loudness, and
         • use of pitch changes to express emotion.

         (b) **Target behaviors** for the overall contour phase of treatment vary markedly. Variations include:

         • matching of emotions or attitudes to overall contours;

- reading sentences with or without graphic cues;
- reading passages using specified overall contours;
- singing, intoning, or chanting;
- vocalizing during interactive games;
- producing speech with a restricted overall contour;
- interpreting musical symbols;
- producing memorized intonations in poems or selected passages;
- imitating intonation patterns;
- shadowing intonation;
- modifying overall contours to repair communicative breakdowns; and
- attending to speech containing exaggerated overall contours.

See Table 9–9 for an example of a program using overall contour indirectly. (Table 11–4 also presents an example of an indirect overall contour PFC method.)

   (c) When the overall contour is an intermediate objective or a facilitator/constrainer, descriptions of the **productive characteristics** often refer to intoned sentence structures, exaggerated intonations, monotones, or normal intonations. Alternately, some methods graphically describe the overall contour (e.g., Moncur & Brackett, 1974, pp. 78–80; 78, 80–81; 78, 81–82; 82–84).
   (d) The **hierarchies** of treatment procedures for indirect overall contour usually are linear or logical.
(2) The **techniques** employed when overall contour is used indirectly show considerable variety as evidenced in Table 9–3 which lists techniques for all intonation PFCs.

Approaches that use music also can be considered indirect purpose/overall contour focus. References for such approaches are provided in Chapter 11, sections VI.E and F.

Table 9–9. Program for indirect overall contour PFC. (Steps related to the overall contour are preceded by an asterisk [*].)

POPULATION: Specific language impairment — (0–2 years).

TECHNIQUES: Modeling, games, motor movements, rituals, singing. (The Glossary contains definitions of the techniques.)

GOAL: To improve overall communication skills.

OBJECTIVE: To stimulate language by engaging in interactive activities.

PROCEDURES: (Prosody is only a small part of the overall program procedures. This presentation is limited to only the prosodic features.)

*1. *Time for Talking*
During regularly scheduled interaction periods, the clinician models an overall contour that apparently matches the client's internal state.

*2. *Language Games*
The clinician plays "Peek-a-Boo" or a variation of it. During the "finding" part of the game, the clinician changes his or her intonation to reflect questions or excitement (e.g., "Where's _____?" or "I seeeeeee you. I see _____.").

*3. *Knee Bounce Game*
The clinician bounces the client on his or her lap, sings a song or tells a story or nursery rhyme, and slowly lowers the client onto his or her knees. Upon reaching a designated spot, the clinician simultaneously changes his or her overall contour. The clinician continues this until the client begins to anticipate the designated point at which the overall contour is changed.

*4. *Watch Me*
The clinician vocalizes and makes a "butterfly" by hooking together his or her thumbs. The clinician then encourages the client to track the "flight" of the "butterfly" which changes when the clinician raises his or her pitch. (The "butterfly" moves up when the pitch height increases and moves down when the pitch height decreases.)

*5. *Slide and Climb*
The clinician sings and talks while the client is on a slide. The clinician modifies his or her overall intonation contour to match the child's actions (e.g., climbing up, sliding down, catching, etc.).

(continued)

181

Table 9-9 *(continued)*

> 6. *What You Can See, I Can Tell, or Watch the Birdee*
>   When the client is attentive, the clinician carries him or her around the room and comments on objects and/or actions that appear to be of interest. The clinician pauses frequently during the vocalizations.

COMMENTS: This approach also indirectly uses pause and pitch (direction).

Source: The above program was derived from information provided in Schomburg, R., Lippert, E. L., Johnson, C., Muss, C. B., & Tittnich, E. (1989). Language activities. *Journal of Children in Contemporary Society, 21,* 67–116.

5. **Approaches that focus indirectly on external components: Cohesive devices** (i.e., indirect cohesive device PFC). (**Cohesive device** = Units of identical or related intonation patterns that extend across utterance boundaries and that result in a sense of interconnectiveness among utterances.) Only one treatment method (Table 9-10) has been identified that uses cohesive devices indirectly. Accordingly, no summaries are presented in this section.

6. **Approaches that focus indirectly on external components: Pitch agreement** (i.e., direct pitch agreement PFC). (**Pitch agreement** = The degree of concordance in pitch height between the end of an utterance and the beginning of the next.) Only two treatment approaches have been identified that have pitch agreement as an indirect objective. One of these approaches is based on the work of Brazil et al. (1980) and was presented previously in Table 4–7. The other approach is Fairbanks (1960, pp. 132–134) which is summarized in Table 9-11.

C. Summary Points

1. The **terminology** relating to intonation often is vague and confusing. On several occasions, this necessitated the placement of a single treatment method in more than one PFC because of terminological difficulties.

Table 9-10. Program for indirect cohesive devices PFC. (Steps related to cohesive devices are preceded by an asterisk [*].)

POPULATION:	Voice disorders, speech improvement.
TECHNIQUES:	Reading aloud, cues (visual). (The Glossary contains definitions of the techniques.)
GOAL:	To improve general intonation skills.
OBJECTIVE:	1. To use intonation to signify a variety of meanings.
	2. To use appropriate intonation in sequential utterances.
PROCEDURES:	1. The client reads aloud sentences to convey meaning or emotion using more than one pitch height. The pitch contour of the sentences is marked graphically.
	2. The client reads aloud sentences using a level pitch direction involving only small glides and pitch changes. The overall contour of the utterances is marked graphically.
	3. The client reads aloud sentences in which major pitch jumps mark the nucleus (phrasal stress).
	4. The client reads aloud sentences in which emotional content is signaled by manipulating pitch height.
	*5. The client reads aloud complex sentences which are interconnected by the changes in pitch height.
COMMENTS:	This approach can also be used in the indirect treatment of pitch (height), intonation (nucleus, overall contour), and stress (phrasal).

Source: The above program was derived from information provided in Moncur, J. P., & Brackett, I. P. (1974). *Modifying vocal behavior* (pp. 82-84). New York: Harper & Row.

2. The current communication disorders treatment literature primarily focuses on intonation at the **sentence level.** This is in contrast to the accent reduction language literature whose focus extends from isolated sentences to connected speech.

3. There is an uneven **distribution of treatment** methods across the different PFCs. Some combinations have no or limited treatment methods available (e.g., direct and indirect onset). Others (e.g., direct and indirect terminal contour) have an extensive number of methods available.

Table 9–11. Program for indirect pitch agreement PFC. (Steps related to the overall contour are preceded by an asterisk [*].)

POPULATION:	Speech improvement.
TECHNIQUES:	Reading aloud, metalinguistics, minimal pairs, exaggeration, cues (visual). (The Glossary contains definitions of the techniques.)
GOAL:	To improve intonation in connected speech.
OBJECTIVE:	To employ pitch agreement and a variety of terminal contours in connected speech.
PROCEDURES:	1. The client reads aloud, in an exaggerated fashion, words marked with symbols indicating falling or rising terminal contours. The words are paired with specific interpretations (e.g., "Oh" to be interpreted as "Is that so?")
	2. The client changes the interpretation of the words on the list and then rereads the list aloud with a new and appropriate terminal contour.
	3. Using a new word list, the client pairs each word with a meaning appropriate for a falling terminal contour and, then, for a rising terminal contour. The client reads aloud each set of words and exaggerates the terminal contour.
	4. The client repeats Step #3 using wide, average, and narrow pitch variations for both falling and rising terminal contours and interprets each reading.
	5. The client reads each word in Step #3 with a gradual sloping, wide falling terminal contour and then reads aloud each word with a steeply sloping, wide falling terminal contour. He or she contrasts the meanings of the different slopes.
	6. The client repeats the exercise in Step #5 using a wide rising terminal contour as the base.
	7. The client associates the words in Step #3 with the following meanings and reads the list trying to depict each of the following attitudes: uncertain, confident, impatient, bored.
	*8. Using two-word phrases (e.g., "Go home"), the client reads aloud the first word, pauses briefly, and shifts his pitch to a higher level to begin the second word. The client exaggerates the pitch shift.
	*9. The client repeats Step #8 using downward shifts.
	*10. The client reads aloud two-clause utterances with a shift (designated by a symbol) between the clauses (e.g., I couldn't do it \ even for you). The symbols alternate among upward (/), downward (\ ), and no shift (–).

| PROCEDURES (continued) | *11. The client reads aloud two-clause utterances in which the shift is not marked. He or she alternates productions among upward, downward, and no shift between clauses. |
| COMMENTS: | This also can be an indirect approach for intonation (terminal contour) and pitch (slope, variation). |

Source: The above program was derived from information provided in Fairbanks, G. (1960). Voice and articulation drillbook (2nd ed., pp. 132–134). New York: Harper & Row.

4. The larger **body of intonation literature** is designed for indirect purposes rather than for direct purposes. Despite the apparent dichotomy between direct and indirect purposes, many of the techniques that indirectly use intonation have potential for the direct treatment of intonation.

5. Indirect intonation methods sometimes are used to **stimulate** linguistic and prelinguistic communication skills. It appears that some view intonation as a way of "connecting" with preverbal children or as a prerequisite for more advanced communication skills.

6. **Music-based strategies** (e.g., singing, instrumental music, chanting, humming) enjoy widespread use in treatment. The linkage between intonation and musical melody apparently suggests that music may serve as a facilitator for intonation. Chapter 11, sections VI.E and F, provides citations for music approaches to treatment.

7. Clinicians should recall that the division of intonation into categories is an organizational tool and that speakers rarely are capable of modulating one category of intonation or even one prosodic feature or category. This suggests that **integrative or holistic approaches** for the treatment of intonation have potential. Table 9–12, Appendixes A and B, and the citations in section VI.J present sources for integrative and/or holistic approaches to intonation.

8. The majority of the intonation treatment approaches are designed for adults. Citations for approaches developed for

Table 9–12. Program for combining several aspects of intonation

POPULATION:	Motor speech disorders.
TECHNIQUES:	Reading aloud, cues (visual); negative practice; feedback (auditory, verbal); matalinguistics. (The Glossary contains definitions of the techniques.)
OBJECTIVE:	To read aloud sentences that intonationally signal requests for information.
PROCEDURES:	1. The clinician prepares index cards using the numbers one through three to signify pitch height. The sentences contain "wh" questions, a nucleus marked by increased pitch height, and a falling terminal contour. Example:

> 3   say
>
> 2 What did you
>
> 1   a moment ago?
>
> (Dworkin, 1991, p. 331)

	2. The clinician audiotapes sessions so the client can discuss his or her performance.
	3. The client reads the sentences from Step #1 aloud.
	4. The client rereads the sentences from Step #1 aloud but this time the client uses the "wrong" pitch heights to highlight the importance of intonation to interpretation.
COMMENT:	This program targets nucleus, terminal contour, and overall contour.

Source: The above program was derived from information provided in Dworkin, J. P. (1991). *Motor speech disorders: A treatment guide* (pp. 331–332). St. Louis, MO: Mosby.

children are listed in section VI.K. Many of the treatment techniques used in the child-based programs are quite abstract. Accordingly, clinicians should ensure that the tasks are appropriate for their young clients.

9. As in previous chapters, the lack of **empirical data** supporting the effectiveness of objectives, techniques, and overall treatment approaches cannot be understated.

10. With the exception of research with speakers who are dysfluent or hearing impaired, speech researchers have presented

little verification of **concomitant changes** in other aspects of communication as the result of changes in intonation. These potential relationships warrant further research.

11. Clinicians interested in developing their own intonation methods might direct particular attention to Table 9–3 which provides a listing of **treatment techniques.** By considering the listed techniques as representative of preferred practice, clinicians may gain insights about what already has been tried. Additionally, researchers may consider Table 9–3 as a listing of potential topics for investigation.

VI. CITATIONS FOR INTONATION TREATMENT

A. Citations for Approaches Directly Focusing on Nucleus

Moncur & Brackett (1974, pp. 78, 80–81).

B. Citations for Approaches Directly Focusing on Terminal Contour

Fairbanks (1960, pp. 132–134, 167–168); Friedman (1985); Hargrove, Roetzel, & Hoodin (1989); Hoodin, Conroy, & Hargrove (1988); Moncur & Brackett (1974, pp. 78, 80–81); Orion (1988, pp. 45–52); Prater & Swift (1984, p. 186); Rosenbek & LaPointe (1978, pp. 187–189, 279); Waling & Harrison (1987, pp. 23–24).

C. Citations for Approaches Directly Focusing on Overall Contour

Berry (1980, pp. 250–255); de Bot (1983); Sikorski (1988, pp. 45–46, 51–69).

D. Citations for Approaches Directly Focusing on Cohesive Devices

Sikorski (1988, pp. 70–77).

E. Citations for Approaches Indirectly Focusing on Onset

Brazil et al. (1980), Moncur & Brackett (1974, pp. 78, 80–81).

F. Citations for Approaches Indirectly Focusing on Nucleus

Brazil et al. (1980); Carlson (1989); Dworkin (1991, pp. 329–330; 331–332, 333); Edwards et al. (1990); Fairbanks (1960, pp. 167–168); Ling (1976); Moncur & Brackett (1974, pp. 78–80; 78, 81–81; 82–84; 86–89); Stern (1987, Course #1, #2).

G. Citations for Approaches Indirectly Focusing on Terminal Contour

Brown (1974); Caligiuri & Murry (1983); Dworkin (1991, pp. 329–330, 330–331, 331–332, 333); Fairbanks (1960, pp. 132–134, 155–159); Grube & Smith (1989); Grube et al. (1986); Kollman (1991); Moncur & Brackett (1974, pp. 78–80; 78, 80–81; 78, 81–82; 82–84; 86–96); Orion (1988, pp. 45–52, 53–321); Sikorski (1988, pp. 2–23, 45–69, 70–77, 86–96); Stern (1987, Course #1, #2).

H. Citations for Approaches Indirectly Focusing on Overall Contour

Brown (1974); Carlson (1989); Dworkin (1991, pp. 329–330, 330–331, 331–332, 333); Fairbanks (1960, pp. 141–143); Graham (1978); Ham (1986, pp. 308–316, 331–332, 324–328, 334–335); Ham (1990, pp. 301–305); King & DiMichael (1991); Ling (1976, pp. 196–199); Marshall & Holtzapple (1978); Miller & Toca (1979); Moncur & Brackett (1974, pp. 78–80; 78, 80–81; 82–84, 86–89); Morris (1991); Rogers & Fleming (1981); Schomburg et al. (1989); Sikorski (1988, pp. 2–23, 45–46, 51–69, 70–81, 86–96); Sparks (1981); Swift & Rosin (1990).

I. Citations for Approaches Indirectly Focusing on Cohesive Devices

Moncur & Brackett (1974, pp. 82–84).

J. Citations for Approaches Indirectly Focusing on Pitch Agreement

Brazil et al. (1980); Fairbanks (1960, pp. 132–134).

K. Citations for Integrative and/or Holistic Approaches

Brazil et al. (1980); Caligiuri & Murry (1983); Dworkin (1991, pp. 329-330, 331-332, 333, 333-334); Fairbanks (1960, pp. 155-159, 167-168); Gilbert (1984); Graham (1978); Ham (1986, pp. 324-328); Ham (1990, pp. 301-305); Marshall & Holtzapple (1978); Moncur & Brackett (1974, pp. 78-80; 78, 80-81; 81-82; 82-84; 84-86); Morris (1991); Orion (1988, pp., 45-52, 53-321); Rogers & Fleming (1981); Schomburg et al. (1989); Smith & Engel (1984); Sparks (1981); Staum (1987); Stern (1987, Course #1, #2); Swift & Rosin (1990).

L. Citations for Approaches Developed for Children

Brown (1974); Friedman (1985); Grube & Smith (1989); Grube et. al (1986); Ham (1990, pp. 301-305, 331-332); Hargrove, Roetzel, & Hoodin (1989); Kollman (1991); Ling (1976, pp. 196-199); Miller & Toca (1979); Morris (1991, pp. 251-296); Rogers & Fleming (1981); Schomburg et al. (1989); Smith & Engel (1984); Staum (1987); Swift & Rosin (1990); Thaut (1985); Waling & Harrison (1987, pp. 23-24); Appendix B.

CHAPTER

10

Treating Prosodic Components: Stress

I. NORMAL USE OF THE PROSODIC COMPONENT STRESS

A. Description

Stress, which is conveyed by varying the prosodic features of pitch, loudness, duration, and/or pause, is one of the four prosodic components of American English. In American English, normal speakers alternate stressed and unstressed syllables with stressed syllables occurring at fairly regular intervals. As a result, American English is characterized as stress-timed.

Speakers of American English use stress to change certain nouns (e.g., **ob**ject) to verbs (e.g., ob**ject**) when the stress is shifted from the first to the second syllable. In sentences, stress also can be used emphatically for contrast (e.g., "It's not **MY** problem; it's **YOUR** problem") or to change meaning (e.g., "It's not her **SIS**ter; it's her sister-in-**LAW**.")

Speakers stress by producing

- **changes in pitch direction** on the stressed syllable,
- **jumps in pitch height** prior to the stressed syllable,
- **increases in loudness** on the stressed syllable,
- **increases in the duration** of the vowel in the stressed syllable, and/or
- **pauses** before the stressed syllable.

Although several degrees of stress (e.g., primary, secondary, tertiary) have been described in the communication disorders and linguistic literature (e.g., Bronstein, 1960; Kenyon & Knott, 1953; Ohde & Sharf, 1992; Shriberg & Kent, 1982; Tiffany & Carrell, 1977), only two degrees (stressed and unstressed) are recognized here because of reliability and teachability issues (Dickerson, 1989).

A **stressed syllable** is the most prominent or noticeable syllable in a word or utterance; all other syllables are **unstressed**. There is a relationship between stressing and phonetics because only heavy syllables receive stress. (Heavy syllables are defined as containing full vowels, such as /i/, /ɪ/, /e/, or diphthongized vowels such as /aɪ/, /aʊ/, /ɔɪ/). On the other hand, unstressed syllables may be heavy or light. [Light syllables contain reduced vowels such as the schwa (/ə/), the r-colored schwa (/ɚ/), and the barred i (/ɨ/).]

B. Categories

Figure 10–1 presents the three stress categories described in this section: lexical, phrasal, and emphatic stress.

1. **Lexical stress** represents the pattern of the stressed and unstressed syllables at the word level. Lexical stress occurs in (a) multisyllabic words, (b) weak/strong forms, and (c) stress shifting.

    a. **Multisyllabic words** have only one stressed syllable and one or more unstressed syllables. In the examples below, the highlighted syllables signify lexical stress:

       - *bank*ing
       - col*lapse*

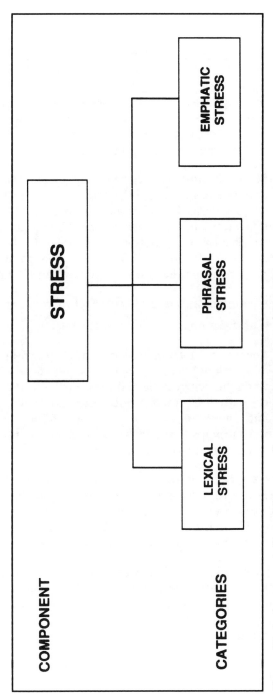

Figure 10–1. A representation of the prosodic component stress and its categories.

- em***bez***zle.

b. **Weak/strong forms** are associated with certain commonly used monosyllabic function words (e.g., "the," "a," "can," "of") that have two or more forms. The decision to use the weak or strong form depends on the linguistic or communicative context. Strong forms have full or heavy vowels, such as the /æ/ in /ænd/ for "and," whereas weak forms consist of reduced vowels or syllabic consonants, such as /ən/, /n/ for "and".

c. **Stress shifting** involves changing the placement of lexical stress in multisyllabic words because of surrounding stress patterns. Linguists such as Bolinger (1986) contend that stress shifting occurs to avoid the production of two consecutive lexically stressed syllables. In the examples of stress shift which follow, note the changes in the stress placement for the words "compact" and "antique":

- com***pact*** an***ten***na vs. ***com***pact ***mic***roscope
- an***tique*** um***bre***lla vs. ***an***tique ***tel***ephone

The first production of each of the target words (com***pact*** and an***tique***) is the normal or citation form and is used when the first syllable of the succeeding word is not lexically stressed (an***ten***na and um***bre***lla). However, if stress falls on the first syllable of the word following the target word (***mic***roscope and ***tel***ephone), the location of stress in the target word changes (***com***pact and ***an***tique).

2. **Phrasal stress.** Phrasal stress marks the most prominent syllable or word in a phrase or sentence. Several aspects of the linguistic context may influence the placement of phrasal stress. These influences form the basis for differing views about the reasons why speakers stress words in sentences.

An information-based view of phrasal stress is employed in this book. That is, speakers are viewed as using phrasal stress on words they consider relevant to listeners. The following examples illustrate the sensitivity of phrasal stress to the communicative context.

Q: Who bought the painting of the bridge?
A: My ***den***tist bought the painting of the bridge.

Q: What did your dentist buy?
A: He bought the *pain*ting.

Q: What did he do with the painting?
A: He *bought* it.

Q: Whose dentist bought the painting?
A: *Mine* did.

3. **Emphatic stress** involves a strong level of prominence and is often used to contradict the expectations of the listener. Note:

Q: Is Rachel's painting in the cabinet?
A: No, it's *ON* the cabinet.

Q: Did Lawrence take the key?
A: No, he *FOUND* it.

Couper-Kuhlen (1986) contends that emphatic stress is not separate from phrasal stress. However, in this book, emphatic stress is presented as a separate category because it has received considerable attention as a teaching technique.

C. Normative Information About Stress

1. **Lexical stress.** Because lexical stress in English seldom distinguishes between word meanings and because the placement rules are not as obvious as other languages, some suggest that English lexical stress is primarily "memorized" (Couper-Kuhlen, 1986; Edwards & Shriberg, 1983). However, lexical stress is more rule-based than is initially apparent. Cruttenden (1986), Dickerson (1989), and Ohde and Sharf (1992), among others, have developed stress placement rules that account for a large portion of the English lexicon.

2. **Phrasal Stress.** Any word in an utterance or phrase can be phrasally stressed; but certain word classes attract phrasal stress more frequently than others (Couper-Kuhlen, 1986). For example, nouns, adjectives, verbs, and adverbs are more likely to be phrasally stressed than personal pronouns and prepositions (Dickerson, 1989), and the most common placement of stress is on the last word of the sentence or phrase.

3. **Emphatic stress.** There is little information about the nature and frequency of use of emphatic stress in conversation.

D. Communicative Roles of Stress

1. To signal important or **new information**. Contrast:

   - Your **broth**er stole the money | {The speaker is indicating that he believes the listener knows the money was stolen but does not know the identity of the culprit.}

   - Your brother stole the **mon**ey | {The speaker believes the listener knows his/her brother stole something but does not know what he stole.}

2. On occasion, to **distinguish between words** or word groups. Contrast:

   - re**port** {noun} and **re**port {verb}

   - Yellow**stone** {National Park in Wyoming} and **yel**low stone {adjective-noun phrase}

   - hot **dog** {national tradition eaten at baseball games} and **hot** dog {a black Labrador Retriever during an Oklahoma summer}

3. To facilitate **imitation**. Speakers, including young children, are more likely to imitate stressed words than unstressed words (Blasdell & Jensen, 1970; Goodglass, Fodor, & Schulhoff, 1967).

CLINICAL NOTE: Clinical observation suggests that clinicians have internalized this concept. For example, which of us has not modeled utterances such as "The boy **IS** running" for a client who omits the auxiliary "be" from his or her spontaneous speech?

4. To mark **child-directed speech**. Adults reportedly use special stress patterns when speaking to children.

II. PERCEIVING THE PROSODIC COMPONENT STRESS

In normal hearers, perception of stress is primarily associated with between-word pauses, rhythmic patterns, and changes in pitch, loudness, duration, and rate of speaking (Freeman, 1982; Fry, 1955, 1958; Lehiste, 1970; Lieberman, 1967). Stress also can be conveyed by changes in the acoustic cues associated with segmentals such as aspiration of plosives or changes in the direction and extent of the formant frequency of vowels (Borden & Harris, 1984). Alternatively, the presence of a light central vowel such as the schwa (/ə/) marks an unstressed syllable (Couper-Kuhlen, 1986). Currently, the precise nature of *each* prosodic feature's contribution to the perception of stress remains the subject of considerable research.

III. PRODUCING THE PROSODIC COMPONENT STRESS

Change in fundamental frequency (F_0) is often cited as the primary means to convey stress, although normal hearing speakers use a clustering of the prosodic features (pitch, loudness, duration, and pause). F_0 usually increases for the stressed syllable as does intensity and vowel duration. This occurs because of an increase in subglottal air pressure by differentiated management of the breath stream by the larynx. F_0 also may increase because the cricothyroid muscle contracts. This muscle lengthens and tenses the vocal folds, making them thinner. Thus, the vocal folds vibrate faster and F_0, or pitch, rises. While these productive strategies occur at the laryngeal level, there are also changes in the upper articulators. Formant frequency measures, which reflect tongue position, are shown to be higher for stressed vowels than for unstressed vowels.

There may be variations in how normal speakers produce the different categories of stress (lexical, phrasal, and emphatic). For example, changes involving emphatic stress, which is frequently used as a teaching technique, may require additional physiological adjustments beyond those required to produce phrasal or lexical stress (Ohala, 1977).

> **CLINICAL NOTE:** Often the production of stress by speakers with communicative disorders (e.g., hearing impairment, neurologic impairments) resembles the production strategies employed by normal speakers for producing emphatic stress.

IV. A MODEL FOR TREATING STRESS

A. A Teaching Model for Stress

In the teaching model, stress involves perceptual prominence. Figure 7–1 and section I.B present the three stress categories (lexical, phrasal, and emphatic).

B. Treatment Decisions: Stress

The accompanying Clinical Note outlines a procedure by which clinicians can apply information provided in previous and subsequent sections to the task of treating stress. Explanation of the guidelines is provided in Chapter 2, section III.B. The location of the purposes, focuses, target behaviors, terminal behaviors, productive characteristics, hierarchies, treatment techniques, populations, and sample programs noted in the guidelines can be found in the Treatment Index.

CLINICAL NOTE: GUIDELINES FOR DECISION MAKING

1. Determine the **purpose** (direct, indirect) for working with stress.
2. Identify the **category of stress** (lexical, phrasal, emphatic) **that will serve as the focus** of therapy.
3. If using stress indirectly, identify the **terminal objectives** for treatment.
4. Identify specific **target behaviors** for the purpose/focus combination (PFC) (i.e., the purpose from Guideline #1 and the focus from Guideline #2 above).
5. Identify **treatment techniques** that are appropriate for the client.
6. If the treatment approach requires several steps to achieve the target behavior, determine the **hierarchy** of treatment steps.
7. Identify how the client will be encouraged to **produce** stress.
8. Identify treatment approaches used with **clients with similar problems**.

V. SUMMARY OF PUBLISHED LITERATURE ON TREATING STRESS

A. Direct Purpose Treatment Strategies

1. **Approaches that focus directly on lexical stress** (i.e., direct lexical stress PFC). (**Lexical stress** = The pattern of the stressed and unstressed syllables at the word level.) Table 10–1 contains a sample method for treating lexical stress directly.

   a. **Population.** Methods for improving lexical stress are available for individuals with foreign accent, hearing impairment, and voice problems. In addition, treatment

Table 10-1. Program for direct lexical stress PFC

POPULATION:	Accent reduction.
TECHNIQUES:	Reading aloud, metalinguistics, motor movements, cues (visual), imitation, discrimination, stimulation (auditory), modeling, fading. (The Glossary contains definitions of the techniques.)
OBJECTIVES:	To improve lexical stress patterns by (1) identifying the number of syllables in a word, (2) stressing the appropriate syllable in a word, and (3) producing unstressed syllables acceptably.
PROCEDURES:	1a. The clinician defines "syllable." He or she encourages the client to say a word and to tap the number of syllables in the word.
	b. While reading a word list, the client listens to audiotaped lists of words with one, two, and three or more syllables. The clinican provides a word list with highlighted vowels and syllabified words.
	c. The client imitates the clinician's production of the words in Step #1b.
	d. The client listens to the clinician read a word list and writes down the number of syllables in each word. (The clinician provides the client with the written list but no other visual cues.)
	2a. The clinician explains American stress patterns to the client and differentiates stressed from unstressed syllables. The clinician directs the client to tap out the number of syllables in selected words to identify the stressed syllables.
	b. The client listens to the clinician read words aloud. The client then produces the words and taps out the syllables and the stress patterns. (The words vary from one to six syllables.) The client is provided with a word list containing syllabifications, vowels, and stressed syllables.
	c. Replicate Step #2b, but the word list highlights only the stressed syllables and the syllabification patterns.
	d. The clinician provides the client with a word list and directs him or her to underline the stressed syllable.
	3a. The clinician explains that certain vowels (e.g., /ə/ or barred i /ɨ/ can be found in unstressed syllables.

(continued)

Table 10–1 *(continued)*

| PROCEDURES *(continued)* | b. The client listens to and imitates multisyllabic words in which /ə/ or /ɨ/ are used in the unstressed syllables (e.g., sofa, baby, brother, etc.). The clinician provides the client with a word list containing visual cues for stressed syllables and the IPA symbol for the specific unstressed vowels. |
| | c. The clinician provides the client with a word list that contains no visual cues. The client reads aloud each word and then marks the number of syllables and the stressed syllable for each word. |

Source: The above program was derived from information provided in Orion, G. F. (1988). *Pronouncing American English: Sounds, stress, and intonation* (pp. 21–28). New York: Newberry.

methods are available for normal speakers who are attempting to improve their overall speaking skills (speech improvement).

b. Intervention
 (1) Content
  (a) Target behaviors for methods that improve lexical stress include

- identifying the stressed syllable in multisyllabic words,
- producing acceptable stress in multisyllabic words, and
- producing unstressed syllables.

Although weak/strong forms and stress shift are other potential target behaviors for the direct treatment of lexical stress, no programs have been identified that treat either structure directly. Therefore, readers are referred to the following indirect methods for treatment ideas:

- for weak/strong forms (Fairbanks, 1960, pp. 141–143, 159–167; Gilbert, 1984, pp. 8–11, 16–18, 26–27; Glenn et al. 1989, pp. 230–233; Orion, 1988, pp. 36–44) and
- for stress shifting (Gilbert 1984, pp. 19–21; Sikorski, 1988, pp. 86–96).

(b) Features commonly recommended for **producing** lexical stress include

- pitch;
- loudness;
- pitch and loudness;
- phonetic cues; and
- rate, loudness, and pitch.

(c) The **hierarchy** of steps for teaching lexical stress directly usually is logically ordered. However, there is some variation regarding the nature of the initial tasks of the hierarchies. For example, Orion (1988, pp. 21–28) begins treatment at the syllable level and requires clients to tap out the number of syllables in selected words. Teaching of lexical stress to persons with impaired hearing historically involves practice at the syllabic level until automaticity in production is achieved and only then introduces linguistic variation in the treatment tasks (Ling, 1976; McGarr et al. 1992). Still other methods begin with a treatment task at the two-syllable level.

The final steps of the lexical stress hierarchies also vary. For some methods, the terminal step emphasizes multisyllabic words in isolation, but in others, the terminal step targets the production of multisyllabic words in sentence contexts.

(2) Commonly used **techniques** to teach lexical stress are *metalinguistics, visual cues,* and *reading* aloud. In addition, *motor movement* is used to facilitate syllabification and the identification of the placement of lexically stressed syllables. Treatment techniques used to treat lexical stress directly can be found in Table 10–2 which provides a listing of treatment techniques used with all stress purpose/focus combinations.

2. **Approaches that focus directly on phrasal stress** (i.e., direct phrasal stress PFC). (**Phrasal stress** = The most prominent syllable or word in a phrase or sentence.) This section is concerned with the stressing of the proper word in a sentence or

Table 10–2. Treatment techniques for the various stress PFCs. (Definitions of all treatment techniques are provided in the Glossary.)

Technique	Purpose/Focus Combination
Audiotapes	indirect lexical, indirect phrasal
Backups	indirect phrasal
Buzzing	indirect lexical, indirect phrasal
Coaching	direct phrasal, direct emphatic
Compensations	direct emphatic
Contrastive Sets/Minimal Pairs	direct lexical, direct phrasal, direct emphatic, indirect lexical, indirect phrasal, indirect emphatic
Contrastive Stress Drill	direct phrasal, direct emphatic, indirect lexical, indirect phrasal, indirect emphatic
Conversation	direct phrasal, indirect phrasal
Covert Rehearsal	indirect lexical, indirect phrasal
Cues	
Auditory	indirect lexical, indirect emphatic
Phonemic	indirect phrasal
Rhythmic	indirect lexical, indirect phrasal, indirect emphatic
Tactile/Kinesthetic	indirect lexical, indirect phrasal
Visual	direct lexical, direct phrasal, direct emphatic, indirect lexical, indirect phrasal, indirect emphatic
Disambiguation	direct phrasal
Discrimination	direct lexical, direct phrasal, direct emphatic, indirect lexical, indirect phrasal, indirect emphatic
Drill	direct phrasal, direct emphatic, indirect lexical, indirect phrasal, indirect emphatic
Exaggeration	direct phrasal, direct emphatic, indirect lexical, indirect phrasal, indirect emphatic
Fading	indirect phrasal
Feedback	
Acoustic	indirect phrasal
Auditory	direct phrasal, direct emphatic, indirect lexical, indirect phrasal

Techniques	Purpose/Focus Combination
Feedback (continued)	
Tactile/Kinesthetic	indirect lexical, indirect emphatic
Verbal	direct phrasal, direct emphatic, indirect lexical, indirect phrasal, indirect emphatic
Visual	indirect phrasal
Homework	direct emphatic, indirect lexical, indirect phrasal
Imitation	direct lexical, direct phrasal, direct emphatic, indirect lexical, indirect phrasal, indirect emphatic
Latency	indirect phrasal
Metalinguistics	direct lexical, direct phrasal, direct emphatic, indirect lexical, indirect phrasal, indirect emphatic
Modeling	direct phrasal, direct emphatic, indirect lexical, indirect phrasal, indirect emphatic
Motor Movement	direct lexical, direct emphatic, indirect lexical, indirect phrasal, indirect emphatic
Musical Instruments	indirect lexical
Narratives	direct phrasal
Negative Practice	direct phrasal, indirect lexical, indirect phrasal
Pacing	indirect lexical, indirect phrasal, indirect emphatic
Poetry Reading	direct phrasal, indirect lexical, indirect phrasal, indirect emphatic
Previews	indirect lexical, indirect phrasal
Query Led Correction	indirect lexical, indirect phrasal
Query Responses	direct phrasal, direct emphatic, indirect lexical, indirect phrasal, indirect emphatic
Reading Aloud	direct lexical, direct phrasal, direct emphatic, indirect lexical, indirect phrasal, indirect emphatic

(continued)

Table 10–2 *(continued)*

Techniques	*Purpose/Focus Combination*
Review	indirect phrasal
Rhyming	indirect phrasal
Role Playing	indirect lexical, indirect phrasal, indirect emphatic
Scripts	direct phrasal, indirect lexical, indirect phrasal
Self-Monitoring	direct lexical, direct phrasal, direct emphatic, indirect lexical, indirect phrasal, indirect emphatic
Self-Reading	indirect phrasal
Signing	indirect phrasal
Singing/Chanting	indirect lexical, indirect phrasal
Stimulation	
Auditory	direct lexical, direct phrasal, indirect lexical, indirect phrasal, indirect emphatic
Visual	indirect phrasal
Telescoping	indirect lexical, indirect phrasal, indirect emphatic
Unison Speech/Reading	direct phrasal, direct emphatic, indirect lexical, indirect phrasal, indirect emphatic
Wait Time	indirect phrasal
Whispering	indirect lexical, indirect phrasal
Writing to Dictation	indirect lexical, indirect phrasal

phrase and with how speakers make that word noticeable or prominent. Issues of the use of pitch direction on the most prominent word and the meaning of different pitch directions are discussed in Chapter 9 in the sections pertaining to the nucleus.

   a. **Population.** Phrasal stress has been a direct treatment objective for persons with the following problems: apraxia of speech, acquired dysarthria, cerebral palsy, developmental delay and voice problems. Additionally, methods have been developed for normal speakers (speech improvement) and for speakers of English as a second language who wish to improve their overall speaking skills.

b. Intervention
(1) Content

(a) Typical **target behaviors** for the direct treatment of phrasal stress involve the production of appropriate phrasal stress in

- selected sentences,
- short answers to questions that are relevant to the clients' activities of daily living,
- instructions,
- descriptions of pictures,
- answers to open-ended questions,
- scripted roles,
- spontaneous speech and/or conversation,
- paragraphs with the location of phrasal stress clearly marked, and
- ambiguous phrases such as "Adams breaks ring" and "Adam's brakes ring" (Fairbanks, 1960, p. 168).

Table 10–3 contains an example of a typical method for treating phrasal stress directly.

(b) Recommendations about how to **produce** phrasal stress vary. Although there is not sufficient research to assign primary status to any one of the prosodic features, some authors (e.g., Dworkin, 1991; Sikorski, 1988) recommend a specific prosodic feature to use when producing phrasal stress. Others recommend individualizing treatment approaches and claim that decisions about how to produce phrasal stress must be made with the skills of the individual speaker in mind. This is a particularly prominent view for those dealing with speakers who have motor speech impairments.

(c) The **hierarchical ordering** of treatment steps for phrasal stress generally is logical. Fairbanks' ordering of tasks (Table 10–3) is representative of a logical hierarchy that might be used to teach phrasal stress.

Table 10-3. Program for direct phrasal stress PFC

POPULATION:	Speech improvement.
TECHNIQUES:	Metalinguistics, reading aloud, feedback (verbal), cues (visual), self-monitoring, contrastive sets, negative practice, fading. (The Glossary contains definitions of the techniques.)
OBJECTIVE:	To read aloud selected passages using appropriate phrasal stress.
PROCEDURES:	1. The client reads an explanation of stress.

2. The client reads aloud selected sets of sentence pairs in which there are changes in the placement of the phrasally stressed word.

Example:

Mom didn't teach Cook. **Pop** taught Cook.

Pop didn't hire Cook. Pop *taught* Cook.

Pop didn't teach Smith. Pop taught **Cook**.

(Fairbanks, 1960, p. 160)

The client describes the changes in meaning associated with the changes in stress placement and notes a context appropriate to each version. For some of the sentences, the clinician describes "typical" pitch and loudness patterns used to produce phrasal stress.

3. The client reads aloud pairs of sentences stressing the highlighted words and describes changes in meaning associated with the stress changes. (Changes in intonation also are noted.) For example, "Yes, **Clair!**" and "**Yes,** Clair?"

4. The client reads aloud from a list in which compound words (e.g., "greenhouse") are contrasted with noun phrases (e.g., "green house"). The client notes the differences and produces sentences using the listed words.

5. The client reads aloud from sentence lists in which nouns, verbs, adjectives, and adverbs are highlighted and serve as phrasally stressed words and are highlighted (e.g., "The **branch** fell on the roof," "It must have been a **heavy** branch," "The roof **collapsed**," "The man fixed it **quickly**.").

6. The client reads aloud sentence lists in which auxiliary, pronouns, prepositions, conjunctions, and articles serve as phrasally stressed words and are highlighted. He or she contrasts the meanings of the

206

PROCEDURES *(continued)*	sentences from this exercise with sentences using conventional stress (as in Step #5).

7. The client reads aloud a set of sentences

   a. using conventional meanings and phrasal stress patterns (e.g., "It's **on** the dog.")

   b. stressing certain function words (e.g., "It's on the **dog**.")

8. The client reads aloud sentences with several words marked for phrasal stress. The clinician provides feedback as necessary.

9. The client replicates Step #8, but the sentences are not marked for phrasal stress.

10. The client reads aloud a passage of 100–150 words. Prior to the reading, the client marks the passage for stressing and phrasing. Then, the client reads only the underlined words and pauses at phrase marks. Next, the client reads only the words that are not underlined and produces pauses in place of the underlined words. He or she contrasts the meaning of the two readings and reads the passage aloud trying to combine all the above information.

Source: The above program was derived from information provided in Fairbanks, G. (1960). *Voice and articulation drill book* (2nd ed., pp. 159-167). New York: Harper.

(2) The **techniques** used to teach phrasal stress vary based on the abilities of the clients. For example, programs designed for cognitively normal individuals are quite complex and include ***metalinguistics, reading aloud***, and ***visual cues***. Quite appropriately, however, the program designed for a developmentally delayed client (Hoodin et al., 1988) uses less demanding tasks such as ***modeling*** and ***coaching***. Table 10-2 contains a listing of techniques used to teach phrasal stress.

3. **Approaches that reach focus directly on emphatic stress** (i.e., direct emphatic stress PFC). (**Emphatic stress** = A strong level of prominence that is often used to contradict the expectations of the listener.) Table 10-4 presents an example of a typical program designed to teach emphatic stress.

Table 10-4. Program for direct emphatic stress PFC

POPULATION:	Specific language impairment.
TECHNIQUES:	Contrastive stress drill, imitation, cues (visual), metalinguistics, feedback (verbal), self-monitoring, motor movement. (The Glossary contains definitions of the techniques.)
OBJECTIVE:	To use appropriate falling terminal contours and stress to signal contradictory information in response to questions.
PROCEDURES:	1. The clinician enacts a scene depicting a subject, verb, and object (e.g., he or she makes a boy doll, named Bill, hold a pen).
	2. The clinician asks the client a question in which one of the nouns or the verb is incorrect (e.g., "Is **Kate** holding the pencil?").
	3. The client responds to the question in Step #2 using a specified syntactic structure (e.g., SUBJECT + [IS] + VERB + ING + THE + SUBJECT], emphatic stress on the item to be contradicted, and a falling terminal intonation contour (e.g., **BILL** [is] holding the pen [\ ]).
	4. The clinician reinforces the client for correct responses. For incorrect responses, the clinician, at his or her discretion, provides a variety of cues (e.g., imitation, hand cues or gestures, explanations, self-monitoring tasks) to elicit the target response.

Source: The above program was derived from information provided in Hargrove, P. M., Roetzel, K., & Hoodin, R. B. (1989). Modifying the prosody of a language-impaired child. *Language, Speech, and Hearing Services in Schools, 20,* 245–258.

a. **Population.** The approaches that directly target emphatic stress were designed for clients with developmental delay (adult), hearing impairment, motor speech disorders, and specific language impairment.

b. **Intervention**
   (1) **Content**
      (a) Typically, the **target behaviors** for teaching emphatic stress directly involve using emphatic stress with selected sentence structures.
      (b) The descriptions of how clients should **produce** emphatic stress vary and include

- pitch,
- loudness, and
- no description.

In addition, Hoodin et al. (1988), in a post hoc analysis, determined that the client self-selected speaking rate and duration to produce emphatic stress.

(c) The **hierarchy of steps** for teaching emphatic stress often is linear. Clients attempt the treatment task with little or no gradation in the difficulty level of the task. Kollman (1991), however, recommends pretraining clients to produce the words used in the training and Hargrove, Roetzel, and Hoodin (1989) suggest preselecting lexical items in the client's productive repertoire.

(2) Table 10–2 presents the treatment techniques associated with all the stress PFCs. The most common **technique** used to teach emphatic stress directly is *contrastive sets/minimal pairs*.

B. Indirect Purpose Treatment Strategies

1. **Approaches that focus indirectly on lexical stress** (i.e., indirect lexical stress PFC). (**Lexical stress** = The pattern of the stressed and unstressed syllables at the word level.) Table 10–5 provides an example of a program that indirectly teaches lexical stress.

   a. **Population.** Lexical stress has been employed indirectly for the following problems: articulation/phonological disorders, developmental apraxia of speech, hearing impairment, motor speech disorders, stuttering, and voice disorders. Treatment programs also are available for foreign speakers and for normal speakers wishing to improve their overall speaking skills (speech improvement).

   b. **Intervention**
   (1) **Content**
      (a) For indirect lexical stress PFCs, the **terminal objective** of intervention includes

      - accurate articulation,
      - improved intelligibility,

Table 10–5. Program for indirect lexical stress PFC. (Steps related to lexical stress are preceded by an asterisk [*].)

POPULATION:	Articulation impairment — children.
TECHNIQUES:	Metalinguistics; reading aloud; imitation; contrastive stress drills; role playing; discrimination; feedback (tactile/kinesthetic, verbal); query responding. (The Glossary contains definitions of the techniques.)
OBJECTIVES:	1. To increase awareness of tactile, auditory, and proprioceptive sensations while producing target sounds in a variety of stress patterns.
	2. To increase the frequency of correct productions of target sounds by producing an acceptable version of the sound in a variety of prosodic contexts.
PROCEDURES:	*1a. The client imitates and describes articulatory patterns of spondee (equally stressed), reduplicative, CVCV syllables (e.g., **baba**) composed of sounds from his or her productive repertoire. The clinician selects one consonant and varies the vowels (e.g., **bibi, bobo**) until all CV pairs have been presented. Then, other consonants are introduced (e.g., **tata**). The client's task is to describe the movement in his oral cavity.
	*b. Using the same phonetic stimuli as in Step #1a, the client imitates, describes, and identifies the stressed syllable in iambic (unstressed, stressed) and trochaic (stressed, unstressed) productions of CVCV stimuli. Target vowels and consonants are changed as the client meets the criterion.
	*c. Using CVCV stimuli in which the consonants are identical but the vowels are different (e.g., babi), the clinician presents iambics and trochees for the client to imitate and to describe the movement in his or her oral cavity.
	*d. Step #1c is repeated; however, for this step, the vowels are stable but the consonants change (e.g., bada).
	*e. Repeating the procedures in Step #1c, the clinician presents trisyllabic stimuli for the client to imitate and describe. The placement of stress varies across syllables. At first, the speech sounds in the syllables are in the client's repertoire and involve large movement shifts. Later, the movement between syllables is reduced, and some error sounds are included in the stimuli. Speech sound production errors are not corrected at this time.

*2a. After identifying a phonetic context in which the client correctly produces the targeted speech sound, the clinician directs the client to produce the target sound in facilitating contexts using an extremely slow rate. (McDonald defines "facilitating context" as an environment in which the target phoneme is most likely to be produced correctly.) At this stage, facilitating contexts involve (i) producing two words as a noun phrase with the target speech sound at the end of the first word or the beginning of the second word and (ii) altering stress patterns.
For example:

- both syllables receive equal stress (spondee) (e.g., **bus light**)

- strong stress on the first syllable (trochee) (e.g., **bus** light)

- strong stress on the second syllable (iambic) (e.g., bus **light**)

b. The client produces the target sound in a "facilitating context" that is embedded in phrases without attending to stress or rate patterns (e.g., for /l/, the sentence might be "jump, lights are breaking"). After the client achieves criterion, he or she produces the target sound in "facilitating contexts" embedded in phrases with emphatic stress. The clinician asks questions that the client answers using a specific sentence with emphatic stress. Example:

CLINICIAN: "Did you say, **Sit**, lights are breaking?"
CLIENT: "No. I said, **JUMP**, lights are breaking."
(McDonald, 1964, p. 145)

*3a. Using new lists with the targeted speech sounds and its "facilitating contexts," the client practices the word pairs as spondees, iambics, and trochees while varying speaking rate.

*b. The client develops sentences using the lists from Step #3a. He or she produces the sentences with varying rate and phrasal stress. The clinician helps the client by asking questions, suggesting situations and attitudes that the client may want to convey, and by directing the client to modify stress. Once production of the target speech sound is stable, the client attempts to produce it without the "facilitating contexts."

(continued)

Table 10-5 *(continued)*

PROCEDURES *(continued)*	*c. The client reads the word lists and the sentences to someone other than the clinician.
	*d. The clinician directs the client to create new lists and sentences. The procedures in Step #3b are duplicated.
COMMENTS:	The following prosodic categories also are used indirectly in this method: stress (phrasal, emphatic) and tempo (rate).

Source: The above program was derived from information provided in McDonald, E. (1964). *Articulation testing and treatment: A sensory-motor approach* (pp. 138–151). Pittsburgh: Stanwix House.

- acceptable phrasal stress,
- increased normalcy judgments,
- improved overall speaking skills,
- acceptable/smooth rhythm,
- improved tempo,
- appropriate speaking rate,
- appropriate loudness,
- increased normalcy,
- improved overall prosody,
- improved comprehension, and
- improved intonation.

(b) Target behaviors may consist of production, imitation, or discrimination of

- multisyllabic words or nonsense syllables,
- frequently misstressed words,
- sets of rules which allow even nonnative speakers of English to predict the location of lexical stress in multisyllabic words,
- unstressed syllables,
- syllabification activities,
- weak/strong forms,
- stress shift contexts, and
- equal and even stress patterns.

(c) Recommendations about how to **produce** lexical stress differ greatly. The following behaviors are candidates for change:

- duration,
- pitch,
- loudness,
- pauses,
- duration and loudness,
- segmental cues,
- segmental changes and duration,
- phonetic change and pitch jumps, and
- a combination of several features (e.g., pause, duration, loudness, and segmental changes or duration, pitch, loudness and segmental changes).

In indirect treatment methods, recommendations about production of lexical stress often are tied to the terminal objective. Thus, if the terminal objective is to improve speaking rate, the recommended productive characteristics tend to be related to tempo (e.g., duration or rate), whereas, if the terminal objective is related to rhythm, the productive characteristics may involve alterations of stress sequences.

   (d) When lexical stress is used indirectly, the **hierarchy** tends to be logical.

(2) The most frequently used **techniques** for indirect lexical stress include *metalinguistics, imitation, discrimination, contrastive sets/minimal pairs, reading aloud, visual cues,* and *feedback.* Table 10–2 presents a listing of the different treatment techniques for all stress PFCs.

2. **Approaches that focus indirectly on phrasal stress** (i.e., indirect phrasal stress PFC). (**Phrasal stress** = The most prominent syllable or word in a phrase or sentence.) Table 10–6 contains an example of a program that uses phrasal stress indirectly.

   a. **Population.** Phrasal stress serves an indirect role in the treatment of persons from the following groups: accent reduction, articulation/phonological disorders, developmental apraxia of speech, developmental delay, motor speech disorders, stuttering, and voice disorders. Additionally, treatment methods have been developed for

Table 10–6. Program for indirect phrasal stress PFC. (Steps related to phrasal stress are preceded by an asterisk [*].)

POPULATION:	Foreign accent.
TECHNIQUES:	Stimulation (auditory), imitation, reading aloud, metalinguistics, cues (visual), dramatics, discrimination, poetry reading. (The Glossary contains definitions of the techniques.)
GOAL:	To increase accuracy of production of American consonants and vowels.

OBJECTIVES:

1. Using appropriate stress and intonation, the client imitates sentences loaded with targeted speech sounds.

2. Using appropriate stress and intonation, the client reads aloud sentences loaded with targeted speech sounds.

3. The client role plays using targeted speech sounds and appropriate stress and intonation.

4. The client reads aloud selected passages using targeted speech sounds, appropriate stress, and appropriate intonation.

PROCEDURE:

1. The client listens to tape recordings of sentences containing target speech sounds. He or she

   *a. listens for lexical and phrasal stress;

   *b. marks phrasal stress;

   c. listens for terminal contour;

   d. marks terminal contour; and

   *e. imitates sentences including targeted speech sounds, lexical and phrasal stress, and terminal contour.

2. The client listens to audiotapes of scripted dialogues containing targeted speech sounds. He or she

   a. listens for the target phoneme;

   *b. listens for and marks the lexical and phrasal stress;

   c. listens for and marks the terminal contour; and

   *d. listens to and imitates the entire dialogue including targeted speech sounds, lexical stress, phrasal stress, and terminal contour.

3. The client practices a dialogue with another client or the clinician.

4. The client reads aloud poetry, common phrases, or selected passages, Then he or she

PROCEDURES *(continued)*	a. checks the dictionary to determine pronunciations,
	b. underlines all words with target speech sounds,
	*c. underlines all phrasally stressed words, and
	*d. rereads the passage aloud.
	*5. The client generates sentences containing targeted speech sounds and marks them for lexical and phrasal stress. He or she again reads the sentences aloud.
COMMENTS:	Orion (1988) also employs other, nonprosodic methods to teach American consonants and vowels that are not included in this table because they are not relevant to prosody therapy. This method also uses indirectly the following aspects of prosody: intonation (terminal contour) and stress (lexical).

Source: The above program was derived from information provided in Orion, G. F. (1988). *Pronouncing American English* (pp. 53–321). New York: Newbury.

normal speakers wishing to improve their overall speaking skills (speech improvement).

b. Intervention
(1) Content
(a) The **terminal objectives** for indirect phrasal stress include improved

- articulatory accuracy or sequencing,
- comprehension,
- intonation,
- intelligibility,
- language skills,
- naturalness or normalcy,
- oral motor speech skills,
- pausing,
- overall prosody,
- phrasing,
- pitch,
- rate,
- speech fluency,

- stress, and
- vocal skills (including decreased vocal abuse).

(b) The **target behaviors** of phrasal stress aspects of treatment involve producing a version of the terminal behavior in phrasal stress contexts using

- isolated sentences;
- carrier phrases;
- extended sequences of nonsense syllables;
- spontaneous, interrelated, contiguous sentences;
- paragraphs and extended passages such as scripts, poetry, and media copy;
- the unstressed words of phrases; and
- phrases in which the words are evenly and equally stressed.

(c) Most indirect phrasal stress approaches do not provide guidelines specifying how to **produce** stress. However, when production recommendations are made, they often are tied to the terminal objective.

(d) The **hierarchy** of steps for indirect phrasal stress is, for the most part, logically based. Interestingly, in many of the methods cited in this section, lexical stress training precedes phrasal stress training. Simmons (1983) deviates from the logical hierarchy of objectives by using a disorders approach in which treatment objectives change based on the acoustic properties of the client's speech.

(2) The **techniques** used for indirect purpose and phrasal stress focus vary considerably. The most commonly used techniques are contrastive sets/minimal pairs and imitation. Table 10-2 contains a list of techniques used in all stress PFCs, including indirect phrasal stress treatment approaches.

3. Approaches that focus indirectly on emphatic stress (i.e., indirect emphatic stress PFC). (**Emphatic stress** = A strong level of prominence that is often used to contradict the expectations of the listener.) Table 10-7 provides an example of a method indirectly using emphatic stress.

Table 10-7. Program for indirect emphatic stress PFC. (Steps related to emphatic stress are preceded by an asterisk [*].)

POPULATION:	Dysarthria — acquired.
TECHNIQUES:	Minimal pairs, contrastive stress drill, imitation, metalinguistics. (The Glossary contains definitions of the techniques.)
GOAL:	To improve articulation skills.
OBJECTIVE:	To produce acceptably emphatically stressed words containing targeted speech sounds.
PROCEDURES:	*1. The clinician explains contrastive stress drills to the client.
	*2. The clinician asks a question and elicits a response from the client. The responses contain the target speech sound embedded in emphatically stressed words. For example, for the target /k/
	CLINICIAN: Do you **hate** broccoli?
	CLIENT: No. I **LIKE** it.

Source: The above program was derived from information provided in Rosenbek, J., & LaPointe, L. (1978). The dysarthrias: Description, diagnosis, and treatment. In D. Johns (Ed.), *Clinical management of neurogenic communicative disorders* (pp. 251–310). Boston: Little, Brown.

a. **Population.** Emphatic stress has been used indirectly for persons with articulation—phonological impairment, developmental apraxia of speech, dysfluencies, motor speech disorders, and specific language impairment and for normal speakers wishing to improve their overall communication skills (speech improvement).

b. **Intervention**
   (1) **Content**
      (a) In indirect emphatic stress methods, the **terminal objective** includes

   - acquisition of lexical items,
   - improved articulation/phonological skills,
   - improved comprehension,
   - increased intelligibility,
   - improved overall prosody,
   - improved phrasal stress,

- decreased dysfluencies,
- improved overall speaking skills, and
- improved tempo.

(b) For indirect emphatic stress methods, there is usually only one **target behavior** for the emphatic stress portion of the project — the use of greater than normal stress. However, the properties of the word to be emphatically stressed change relative to the terminal objective. For an articulatory terminal objective, one may load the words to be emphasized with the target phoneme; and for a terminal objective focusing on the acquisition of lexical items, clinicians may model the target lexical items using emphatic stress.

(c) The means by which emphatic stress should be **produced** often are not specified for indirect emphatic stress methods.

(d) **Hierarchies** for emphatic stress tasks tend to be logical.

(2) As shown in Table 10-2, which contains a list of techniques used in stress PFCs, clinicians employ a variety of **techniques** for indirect emphatic stress methods.

C. Summary Points

1. The balance of the treatment methods for linguistic stress is devoted to using stress indirectly. Developers of such treatment methods frequently assume that changes in stress influence other aspects of communication such as articulation, fluency, and intelligibility. Little **empirical data** are provided to support this assumed linkage.

2. With respect to treatment protocols, little attention has been directed to the use of lexical, phrasal, or emphatic stress in **conversation**. Particularly for emphatic stress, treatment usually ends at the isolated sentence level. Only methods designed for individuals with foreign accents regularly employ conversation.

3. The **hierarchy** of treatment steps for stress PFCs tends to be logical with treatment tasks beginning at apparently simple levels and becoming progressively more complex. Although treatment steps may appear to progress from easy to difficult, empirical evidence rarely supports ordering decisions.

4. The focus of therapy is on **stressed syllables**; unstressed syllables are rarely treated. Information presented in Hargrove, Roetzel, and Hoodin (1989) and in Kollman (1991) suggests that unstressed syllables may add complexity to the treatment task. Thus, for direct methods, clinicians should monitor the production of unstressed syllables and, if necessary, ensure that clients can produce unstressed syllables acceptably. For indirect methods, clinicians may consider requiring clients to produce targeted behaviors (such as fluent speech or accurate articulation) in unstressed contexts to increase task complexity. Several citations for methods that use unstressed syllables in treatment are listed in section VI.G.

5. The discrete organizational style of this book may lead one to view stress treatment strategies as isolated with singular focuses. Those wishing to attempt **integrative or holistic methods** are referred to the citations in section VI.H.

6. Although treatment methods for individuals with hearing impairment frequently use pitch, methods developed for normal hearers often ignore the issue of how to **produce** stress. Therefore, clinicians must decide if they will (a) prescribe a means by which clients will produce stress or (b) allow clients to select their own production patterns. Alternately, rather than prescribing a priori means to produce stress, clinicians may use an intriguing strategy demonstrated by Simmons (1983) in which the client's speech is periodically acoustically analyzed to assist in decision making.

7. **Speech naturalness** and ease of production must be seriously considered in treatment decisions so that clients maximize speech normalcy. Treatment for individuals with neurogenic disorders, in particular, may profit from flexibility, and clinicians would do well to consider suggesting atypical, yet achievable, patterns of prosodic features to produce stress. For example, Yorkston and Beukelman (1981) recommend that clinicians emphasize duration when working with patients with ataxic dysarthria.

8. The following **techniques** enjoy widespread usage in the teaching of stress: *metalinguistics, motor movement,* and

visual cues. Indirect methods of teaching such as ***modeling*** have only limited use which may be a function of the clinical populations for which stress treatment methods were devised. That is, most of the treatment programs cited in this chapter were developed for cognitively intact adults rather than children or developmentally delayed adults. Accordingly, the techniques listed in Table 10–2 reflect this. Clinicians are cautioned that they need to evaluate the effectiveness and/or appropriateness of each treatment technique that is used with their clients.

9. Clinicians interested in **treating children's stress** are referred to section VI.I for citations concerned with treating children. Interestingly, several of the cited approaches use ***metalinguistics*** and ***visual cues*** which are relatively cognitively complex.

10. There are only limited data supporting **program effectiveness**. Clinicians cannot assume that, because an approach has been published, it is effective. Clinicians must evaluate the progress of their clients to ensure appropriate treatment.

11. Caligiuri and Murry (1983) and Hargrove, Roetzel, and Hoodin (1989) note **deterioration** in clients' performance following the completion of certain stress objectives. Thus, clinicians may consider attending to the maintenance and stabilization of stress objectives.

12. Several methods recommend the use of **equal and even** stress as an interim step or as a compensatory strategy. (Chapter 11, section VI.I contains citations for such methods.) Clinicians who elect to employ equal and even stress need to monitor its impact on speech naturalness and on intelligibility.

VI. CITATIONS FOR STRESS TREATMENT

A. Citations for Approaches Directly Focusing on Lexical Stress

Glenn et al. (1989, pp. 28, 252–255); Kingdon (1958); McGarr et al. (1992); Moncur & Brackett (1974, pp. 96–98); Orion (1988, pp. 21–28, 29–35); Sikorski (1988, pp. 2–23, 86–96).

B. Citations for Approaches Directly Focusing on Phrasal Stress

Dworkin (1991, pp. 329–330, 330–331, 331–332, 333, 335–336, 336–337, 337, 337–338, 338–339); Fairbanks (1960, pp. 159–167, 167–168); Glenn et al. (1989, pp. 240–251); Hoodin et al. (1988); Moncur & Brackett (1974, pp. 81–82; 98–99); Orion (1988, pp. 29–35); Prater & Swift (1984, pp. 185–186); Rosenbek (1978, pp. 223–224); Rosenbek & LaPointe (1978, pp. 304–306); Sikorski (1988, pp. 47–50).

C. Citations for Approaches Directly Focusing on Emphatic Stress

Dworkin (1991, pp. 339–342); Glenn et al. (1989, pp. 233–239); Hargrove, Roetzel, & Hoodin (1989), Hoodin et al. (1988); Kollman (1991); McGarr et al. (1992); Rosenbek (1978, pp. 223–224); Rosenbek & LaPointe (1978, pp. 304–306); Sikorski (1988, 78–81, 85).

D. Citations for Approaches Indirectly Focusing on Lexical Stress

Caligiuri & Murry (1983); Dickerson (1989); Dworkin et al. (1988); Fairbanks (1960, pp. 141–143, 159–167); Gilbert (1984, pp. 8–11, 12–15, 15–16, 16–18, 19–20, 21–23); Glenn et al. (1989, pp. 230–233); Huskins (1986, pp. 36–37); Ling (1976, pp. 295–387); Macaluso-Haynes (1978); McDonald (1964); Moncur & Brackett (1974, pp. 89–96); Orion (1988, pp. 21–28, 28–35, 36–44, 45–52, 53–321); Riley & Riley (1985); Rosenbek (1978, pp. 214–215, 223–224); Rosenbek et al. (1974); Simmons (1983); Stern (1987, Course #2); Yoss & Darley (1974).

E. Citations for Approaches Indirectly Focusing on Phrasal Stress

Brazil et al. (1980); Caligiuri & Murry (1983); Carlson (1989); Dickerson (1989); Dworkin (1991, pp. 324–326); Edwards, Strattman, & Kneil (1989); Fairbanks (1960, pp. 167–168); Gilbert (1984, pp. 21–23); Ham (1986, pp. 324–328); Helfrich-Miller (1984); Huskins (1986, pp. 36–37, 83–93); Macaluso–Haynes (1978); Moncur & Brackett (1974, pp. 78–80; 78, 81–82; 82–84; 86–89; 98; 98–99); Orion (1988, pp. 29–35, 45–52, 53–321); Prater & Swift (1984, pp.

112–115); Riley & Riley (1985), Rosenbek (1978, pp. 214–215, 223–224); Rosenbek et al. (1974); Sikorski (1988, pp. 45–46, 51–69); Simmons (1983); Smith & Engel (1984); Sparks (1981); Stern (1987, Course #2); Swift & Rosin (1990); Yorkston & Beukelman, (1981); Yorkston, Beukelman, & Bell (1988, pp. 353–370); Yoss & Darley (1974).

F. Citations for Approaches Indirectly Focusing on Emphatic Stress

Carlson (1989); Dworkin et al. (1988); Glenn et al. (1989, pp. 233–239); Grube & Smith (1989); Huskins (1986, pp. 83–93); Kollman (1991); McDonald (1964); Rosenbek (1978, pp. 223–224); Rosenbek & LaPointe (1978, pp. 304–305, 305–306); Weismer et al. (1990).

G. Citations for Approaches Targeting Unstressed Syllables

Carlson (1989); Fairbanks (1960, pp. 141–143, 159–167); King & DiMichael (1991, p. 352); Gilbert (1984, pp. 16–18, 26–27); Glenn et al. (1989, pp. 230–233); Ling (1976, pp. 295–387); Moncur & Brackett (1974, pp. 89–99); Orion (1988, pp. 21–28, 36–44); Simmons (1983).

H. Citations for Integrative and/or Holistic Approaches

Brazil et al. (1980); Caligiuri & Murry (1983); Dickerson (1989); Fairbanks (1960, pp. 167–168); Glenn et al. (1989, pp. 230–233); Ham (1986, pp. 324–328); Helfrich–Miller (1984); Ling (1976, pp. 295–387); McDonald (1964); Moncur & Brackett (1974, pp. 78–80, 81–82, 82–84, 89–96); Orion (1988, pp. 21–28, 29–35, 36–44, 45–52); Prater & Swift (1984); Riley & Riley (1985); Rosenbek et al. (1974); Simmons (1983); Sparks (1981); Stern (1987); Swift & Rosin (1990); Appendixes A & B.

I. Citations for Approaches Developed for Children

Berry (1980, pp. 250–255); Grube & Smith (1989); Hargrove, Roetzel, & Hoodin (1989); Helfrich–Miller (1984); Kollman (1991);

Krauss & Galloway (1982); Ling (1976, pp. 295–387), Macaluso-Haynes (1978); McDonald (1964); Riley & Riley (1985); Smith & Engel (1984); Swift & Rosin (1990); Weismer et al. (1990); Yoss & Darley (1974); Appendix B.

CHAPTER

11

Treating Prosodic Components: Rhythm

I. NORMAL USE OF THE PROSODIC COMPONENT RHYTHM

A. Description

This chapter presents information about speech rhythm which is conveyed by prosodic features (pitch, loudness, duration, pause); prosodic components (tempo, intonation, and stress); and segmentals (speech sounds). Despite being subsumed within rhythm, the prosodic features, prosodic components, and segmentals also function independently.

The view of rhythm presented in this book focuses on stressed words and their role as the cornerstone of the rhythmic unit. The stress-based view holds that, although unequal numbers of syllables may occur between stressed syllables, the time between the stressed syllables is of approximately equal length (i.e., stress-timed).

B. Categories

With the exception of the final rhythm category (continuity), the system presented here borrows heavily from the teaching model of Dickerson (1989) in which speakers learn behaviors that result in stressed-timed speech. The categories of rhythm (stress sequence, alterations, continuity) are described below and are represented in Figure 11–1.

1. **Stress sequence.** Although stress stands on its own as a prosodic component (see Chapter 10), it also contributes to rhythm. When stress serves as a category of rhythm, the focus is on stress sequence — the occurrence of stressed syllables at regularly perceived intervals.

2. **Alterations.** Contracting and expanding the syllables and pauses between stresses also contributes to stress-timing. Speakers employ a variety of changes or alterations in tempo, intonation, and articulation when they attempt to squeeze unstressed syllables between stressed syllables or words. As the number of syllables between the stresses decreases, speakers increase the duration of the syllables and add pauses. Conversely, as the number of syllables between stresses increases, the duration of the syllables decreases and pauses are eliminated. Lieberman's (1967) classic description of durational differences and pauses between the syllables "light" and "house" in the phrases "light housekeeper" and "lighthouse keeper" illustrates the alterations.

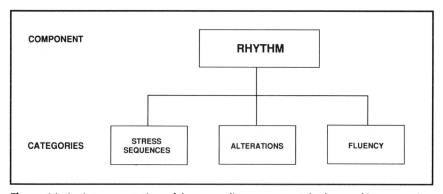

Figure 11–1. A representation of the prosodic component rhythm and its categories.

- *light house*keeper {a person who weighs 95 pounds and cleans house}

- *light*house *keep*er {the operator of a structure that provides navigational signals}

  In the first example, stress occurs on two consecutive syllables (light, house) and in the second example, stress occurs on two nonconsecutive syllables (light, keep). The pause is longer between "light" and "house" when both words are stressed (light housekeeper) than when two nonconsecutive syllables receive stress (lighthouse keeper).

3. **Continuity** represents the ability to maintain an uninterrupted flow of speech. Continuity is synonymous with fluency; however, the term fluency is avoided because of its connection with stuttering and the issue of whether fluency problems cause prosodic disruptions or if prosodic problems cause fluency disruptions (e.g., Bergmann, 1986; Borden, 1988; Ham, 1990; Harrington, 1987, 1988). Continuity is an integral part of rhythm, and disruptions in continuity influence overall rhythm. This is not to say, however, that other aspects of prosody, and even other categories of rhythm, do not impact continuity.

C. Normative Information About Rhythm

1. In English, normal rhythm is essentially stress-timed. That is, **stress sequences** are approximately equivalent despite unequal numbers of syllables in phrases. Although listeners perceive English as stress-timed, this perception is only partially supported by acoustic data.

2. In English, speakers achieve stress-timing by using **alterations** and **NOT** by making all the syllables equal lengths. As the number of unstressed syllables between stressed syllables increases, the frequency and the extent of alterations increase. Certain words are more susceptible to alterations than others. For example, auxiliaries, pronouns, and articles are more likely to be changed than are nouns and verbs.

3. Johnson, Darley, and Spriestersbach (1963) report that normal speaking adults average 0.7 to 7.0 discontinuities per 100 words across a variety of speaking tasks, thus supporting the

view that most adults have a high degree of **continuity** when speaking. Starkweather (1987) also reports relatively high degrees of continuity among children. The rate of overall discontinuities reportedly stabilizes from kindergarten through grade 12 with the average rate ranging from a high of 73 per 1000 syllables (for kindergartners) to 54 per 1000 syllables (for 12th graders). (Starkweather, however, does report that the type of discontinuity changes developmentally. Younger students are more likely to use false starts and repetitions, and older students are more likely to use parenthetical statements [e.g., "Okay," "I mean"].)

D. Communicative Roles

1. Rhythm **facilitates segmentation**. Listeners expect to hear certain rhythmic patterns. When speakers use expected rhythmic patterns and those patterns co-occur with linguistic and/or informational units, listeners do not have to monitor speech carefully to identify the units. This frees listeners for higher order tasks such as making inferences or identifying words. When speakers violate rhythmic expectations (such as using unevenly spaced stress or applying stress to every syllable), listeners find it difficult to segment the incoming speech and, therefore, devote more attention to this lower level task. This attention to segmentation slights higher level tasks and impedes communication.

2. Rhythm **facilitates intelligibility**. The occurrence of stress sequences at the expected locations/times has an impact on speech intelligibility.

3. Rhythm **facilitates certain aspect of production**. Although this view lacks empirical support, intriguing hints suggest a powerful role for rhythm. For example, Oliva and Duchan (1976) noted that a 15-year-old developmentally delayed male produced both iambic and trochaic rhythms in his spontaneous speech. They also observed that certain function words occurred less frequently when the subject used an iambic rhythm (unstressed-stressed-unstressed-stressed) than when he used a trochaic rhythm (stressed-unstressed-stressed-unstressed-stressed). The facilitating effect for rhythm can be seen in the following example in which the subject does not produce the function word "is" in the iambic context but does so in the trochaic context:

- Bill *ride* a *bike* | (iambic)
- *Bill* is *ride* a *bike* | (trochaic)
  (Oliva & Duchan, 1976, p. 125)

Additionally, Bergmann's (1986) findings demonstrate facilitating effects of a rigidly imposed stress sequence. He determined that German speakers who are moderate stutterers produce fewer dysfluencies reading a poem using iambic rhythm (i.e., a rigid, imposed stress sequence) compared to reading aloud a fable in a "natural" speaking rhythm.

II. PERCEIVING THE PROSODIC COMPONENT RHYTHM

Speech rhythm involves *acoustic events* that *regularly* occur during communication. The "acoustic events" include, but are not limited to, prosodic elements such as loudness, pause, pitch, and stress. The term "regularly" has a range of interpretations varying from "acoustic events" that occur at equal intervals to "acoustic events" that are perceived to be related because of certain patterns.

III. PRODUCING THE PROSODIC COMPONENT RHYTHM

American English is stress-timed which involves the production of stresses at regularly occurring intervals. However, the perception of regularly occurring stress is not accomplished merely by producing stresses at certain intervals. Speakers alter prosody and segmentals to achieve stress timing.

The use of alterations varies with the individual speaker and the context. The following are examples of common alterations:

- Speakers **lower pitch** on unstressed syllables.
- Speakers **increase rate** of unstressed syllables.
- Speakers use **reduced vowels** (e.g., /ə, ɚ, ɨ/) in unstressed syllables.
- Speakers insert **pauses** immediately before stressed syllables.
- Speakers **omit vowels** in unstressed syllables, as in /fæmli/for "family."

- Speakers use **coalescence** to combine two adjacent speech sounds with the resultant speech sound taking on characteristics of both original speech sounds. For example, the production of /t, d, s, z/ before /j/ may result in a new speech sound which substitutes for both the preceding consonants. Thus, "Did you read it?" might be pronounced as /dɪdʒuridit/.

- Speakers use a form of **concordance** in which speakers produce speech sounds from adjacent words as if they were part of the same word. For example, speakers may add /w/ when vowels terminate and initiate two adjacent words ("Do it" becomes /duwɪt/). In addition, if the same speech sound terminates and initiates adjacent words, the two speech sounds may be produced as one (e.g., "I've got to go" may be /aɪvgatəgo/). (Chapter 8 provides additional information about concordance.)

- Speakers employ **elision** which involves the omission of consonants or vowels in a non-phrase initial position and results in a smoother production of the word or phrase. ("We showed him around" becomes /wiʃodɪm əraund/, "he kept running" becomes /hikɛprʌnɪŋ/, or "wooden" becomes /wɒdn/.

- Speakers use **contractions** which are formalized reductions involving words such as "can't" and "don't."

- Speakers **reduce articulatory precision** on unstressed syllables.

IV. A MODEL FOR TREATING RHYTHM

A. A Teaching Model for Rhythm

The teaching model for rhythm is concerned with producing acceptable stress sequence and alterations and with using continuous speech. The model was presented in section I.B and in Figure 11–1.

B. Treatment Decision Making: Rhythm

The accompanying Clinical Note lists guidelines for a procedure that allows clinicians to apply information provided in previous and subsequent sections to treating rhythm. (The guidelines are explained in Chapter 2, section III.B.) The purposes, focuses, objectives, terminal behaviors, hierarchies, production characteristics, treatment techniques, and sample programs referenced in the guidelines are listed in the Treatment Index.

CLINICAL NOTE: GUIDELINES FOR DECISION MAKING

1. Determine the **purpose** (direct, indirect) for working with rhythm.
2. Identify the **categories of rhythm** (stress sequence, alterations, continuity) **that will serve as the focus** of treatment.
3. Identify specific **treatment objectives** for the purpose/focus combination (PFC) (i.e., the purpose from Guideline #1 and the focus from Guideline #2 above).
4. Identify **treatment techniques** that are appropriate for the client.
5. Determine the **hierarchy** of steps.
6. Identify treatment approaches used with **clients with similar etiologies** and PFCs.

V. SUMMARY OF PUBLISHED LITERATURE ON TREATING RHYTHM

A. Direct Purpose Treatment Strategies

1. **Approaches that directly focus on stress sequence** (i.e., direct stress sequence PFC). (**Stress sequence** = The occurrence of stressed syllables at regularly perceived intervals.) Table 11–1 contains an exemplar program detailing the direct treatment of stress sequence.

   a. **Population.** Methods that directly treat stress sequence are available for individuals who are hearing impaired and normal speakers who are attempting to improve their overall speaking skills (speech improvement).

   b. **Intervention**
   (1) **Content**
      (a) The **target behaviors** used in the treatment methods for direct stress sequence PFCs usually tailor therapy contexts to the skills of the client. For example, Staum (1987) alters the target behavior relative to the child's age. Thus, preschool children interpret musical notation using vowels and older children do so using phrases. On the other hand, Fairbanks (1960, pp. 118–121), who directs his methods to adults, targets the

Table 11–1. Program for direct stress sequence PFC

POPULATION:	Speech improvement.
TECHNIQUES:	Reading aloud, metalinguistics, discrimination, exaggeration, singing, poetry, writing, contrastive sets. (Definitions of techniques are provided in the Glossary.)
OBJECTIVE:	To read poetry and prose using appropriate rhythmic patterns.
PROCEDURES:	1. The client reads aloud selected poems ranked according to their rhythmic quality.
	2. The client reads aloud a passage describing rhythm variations. After the reading, the clinician and the client discuss the content of the passage.
	3. The client rereads the poems from Step #1 and the passage from Step #2 but exaggerates the rhythm. The clinician points out that in the exaggerated version, the stress patterns are sometimes "normal" or "typical" and sometimes they conflict with expectations.
	4. The client and the clinician rewrite the poems in Step #1 as prose. They preserve the lexical items but alter punctuation and capitalization. The client reads aloud the prose version with as little "poetic" rhythm as possible. The clinician points out that not all the poetic rhythm will be eliminated.
	5. The client rereads the poems from Step #1 in their original form. The stress sequence he or she employs is a compromise between the exaggerated and the prose versions.

use of appropriate rhythmic patterns while reading aloud poetry and prose.

　　(b) The **hierarchy** of steps usually is logically ordered.
　(2) No single treatment **technique** dominates direct stress sequence teaching methods. (See Table 11–2 for a listing of treatment techniques used in stress PFCs.)

　2. Approaches that directly focus on alterations (i.e., direct alteration PFC). (**Alterations** = Changes in tempo, intonation, and articulation that speakers use to produce unstressed syllables between stressed syllables or words.) No methods have been identified that directly target improved rhythmic alterations as the overall treatment objective. For treatment ideas,

6. The client categorizes selected poems as falling into one of the following groups: highly rhythmical, moderate, and temporally irregular with little overt rhythm.

7. The client sings and then reads aloud the first stanza of the song *America*. The clinician points out that it is rhythmical, rhymed, and has a definite melodic sequence.

8. Redo Step #4 with *America*.

9. The client copies the words of a popular song. He or she reads the words aloud with maximum rhythm and, then, with a normal speaking rhythm.

10. The client reads aloud a selected short passage that contains recurrent stress sequences within the passages. The client notes the contrasts in the stressed and unstressed syllables.

11. Using the paragraph from Step #2, the client identifies "Brief Rhythmic Periods" which consist of several successive reiterations of the same rhythmic pattern.

12. The client opens a book at random and identifies ten Brief Rhythmic Periods. The clinician notes that, although the phrases may be considered Brief Rhythmic Period in the citation form, such patterns may change in connected speech.

Source: The above program was derived from information provided in Fairbanks, G. (1960). *Voice and articulation drillbook* (pp. 118–121). New York: Harper.

readers are referred to section VI.B #2 which deals indirectly with alterations and to Appendixes A, B, and E.

3. **Approaches that directly focus on continuity** (i.e., direct continuity PFC). (**Continuity** = The ability to maintain an uninterrupted flow of speech.) Because of the extensive body of literature pertaining to fluency and, hence, continuity, a thorough analysis of treatment methods is beyond the scope of this book. Therefore, this section is limited to a brief survey of treatment approaches attempting to improve continuity by working on prosody.

   a. **Population.** Approaches to treating continuity problems using prosody primarily have been designed for individuals who stutter, clutter, or have motor speech problems.

Table 11-2. Treatment techniques for the various rhythm PFCs. (Definitions of all treatment techniques are provided in the Glossary.)

Technique	Purpose/Focus Combination
Audiotapes	indirect alterations
Auditory Masking	direct continuity
Backup	indirect stress sequence
Biteblocks	indirect stress sequence
Breathing Activities	indirect stress sequence
Buzzing	indirect alterations
Cloze	indirect stress sequence
Contrastive Sets/ Minimal Pairs	direct stress sequence, direct continuity, indirect stress sequence, indirect alterations
Contrastive Stress Drills	direct continuity, indirect stress sequence
Conversation	direct stress sequence, indirect stress sequence
Covert Rehearsal	indirect stress sequence, indirect alterations
Cues	
Acoustic	indirect stress sequence
Auditory	direct continuity, indirect stress sequence
Phonemic	indirect stress sequence
Rhythmic	indirect stress sequence
Tactile/Kinesthetic	direct continuity, indirect stress sequence
Visual	direct stress sequence, direct continuity, indirect stress sequence, indirect alterations
Discrimination	direct stress sequence, direct continuity, indirect stress sequence, indirect alterations
Dramatics	indirect stress sequence
Drill/Repetitions	direct continuity, indirect stress sequence, indirect alterations
Easy Onsets	direct stress sequence, direct continuity
Exaggeration	direct stress sequence, direct continuity, indirect stress sequence, indirect alterations
Fading	indirect stress sequence
Feedback	
Auditory	direct continuity, indirect stress sequence, indirect alterations

Technique	Purpose/Focus Combination
Tactile/Kinesthetic	direct continuity, indirect stress sequence
Verbal	direct continuity, indirect stress sequence, indirect alterations
Games	direct continuity, indirect stress sequence
Homework	indirect stress sequence, indirect alterations
Imitation	direct stress sequence, direct continuity, indirect stress sequence, indirect alterations
Labeling	direct continuity, indirect stress sequence
Latency	direct continuity, indirect stress sequence
Matching	indirect stress sequence
Metalinguistics	direct stress sequence, direct continuity, indirect stress sequence, indirect alterations
Modeling	direct continuity, indirect alterations
Monologues	direct continuity, indirect stress sequence
Motor Movement	direct stress sequence, direct continuity, indirect stress sequence, indirect alterations
Musical Instruments	direct stress sequence, indirect stress sequence
Music Notation	direct stress sequence
Narration	indirect stress sequence
Negative Practice	indirect stress sequence, indirect alterations
Oral Motor Exercises	indirect stress sequence
Pacing	indirect stress sequence
Pantomime	indirect stress sequence
Parallel Talk	indirect stress sequence
Play	direct continuity, indirect stress sequence
Poetry Reading	indirect stress sequence
Preview	indirect stress sequence, indirect alterations
Prompting	indirect stress sequence
Query-Led Correction	indirect stress sequence, indirect alterations
Query Responding	direct continuity, indirect stress sequence, indirect alterations

(continued)

Table 11–2 *(continued)*

Technique	*Purpose/Focus Combination*
Reading Aloud	direct stress sequence, direct continuity, indirect stress sequence, indirect alterations
Relaxation	indirect stress sequence
Review	direct continuity, indirect stress sequence
Rhyming	indirect alterations
Rituals	indirect stress sequence
Role Playing	direct continuity, indirect stress sequence, indirect alterations
Routines	indirect stress sequence
Scripts	indirect stress sequence
Self-Monitoring	direct continuity, indirect stress sequence, indirect alterations
Self-Reading	indirect stress sequence, indirect alterations
Sequencing	direct continuity, indirect stress sequence
Shadowing	direct continuity, indirect stress sequence
Shaping	direct continuity, indirect stress sequence
Signing	indirect stress sequence
Singing	direct stress sequence, direct continuity, indirect stress sequence
Stimulation	
Auditory	direct continuity, indirect stress sequence, indirect alterations
Generalized	indirect stress sequence
Visual	indirect stress sequence
Telescoping	indirect alterations
Unison/Choral Speech or Reading	direct continuity, indirect stress sequence, indirect alterations
Whispering	indirect stress sequence, indirect alterations
Writing	indirect alterations

b. Intervention
(1) Content
    (a) Prosodically based **target behaviors** for achieving continuity employ a range of features (pitch, loudness, duration, pause) and components (tempo, stress, intonation). The underlying assumption of these approaches is that modification in prosody can induce continuity. Clients may be exposed to any of the following:

- stylized forms of stress sequence such as speaking to the beat of a metronome or other timing device;
 using a smooth, even stress during treatment tasks; or
 using a bounce technique in which the client repeats a target syllable (usually the first stressed syllable) using a slow, slightly exaggerated rhythm.
- modifications of terminal contours.
- using several aspects of prosody concurrently.

    Table 11-3 presents a procedure for direct purpose and continuity focus.
    (b) For the most part, the **hierarchy** for the achievement of continuity using prosody is logically ordered.
(2) A wide variety of treatment **techniques** are used to induce continuity. (See Table 11-2 which lists treatment techniques used for rhythm PFCs.)

B. Indirect Purpose Treatment Strategies

1. Approaches that indirectly focus on stress sequence (i.e., indirect stress sequence PFC). (**Stress sequence** = The occurrence of stressed syllables at regularly perceived intervals.)

    a. Population. Programs that indirectly use stress sequence have been developed for the following: aphasia, autism, developmental apraxia of speech, developmental delay, foreign accent, hearing impairment, motor speech disorders, specific language impairment, stuttering, and voice disorders.

Table 11-3. Program for direct continuity PFC

POPULATION:	Stuttering—children.
TECHNIQUES:	Metalinguistics, query responding, reviews, cues (visual), motor movement, imitation, games, feedback (verbal), modeling, labeling, contrastive sets, reading aloud, exaggeration. (The Glossary contains definitions of the techniques.)
GOAL:	To produce fluent speech.

OBJECTIVES:

1. To use a slow speaking rate[1] when producing combined monosyllabic words.
2. To reduce loudness[2] when producing combined monosyllabic words.
3. To use a slow speaking rate and reduced loudness when producing combined monosyllabic words.
4. To use a slow speaking rate and reduced loudness in polysyllabic words.
5. To use smooth concordance[3] when producing polysyllabic words.
6. To use a slow speaking rate, reduced loudness, and smooth concordance in phrases and short sentences.
7. To use a slow speaking rate, reduced loudness, and smooth concordance in sentences that require two breaths.
8. To use a slow speaking rate, reduced loudness, and smooth concordance in multiple utterances.
9. To use a slow speaking rate, reduced loudness, and a smooth concordance in spontaneous speech.

PROCEDURES:

1a. The clinician explains that the purpose of therapy is to learn a new way of speaking and to recognize that learning requires practice.

 b. The clinician models and labels a slow rate of speech. The clinician prolongs a monosyllabic word or the first syllable of a multisyllabic word.

 c. The clinician provides the following visual cues for reduced rate
   - a rubber band,
   - a balloon, or
   - a picture of one of the above.

 d. Using a reduced speaking rate, the client imitates the clinician's labeling of picture cards or reading of single words. If necessary, the clinician provides the visual cues from Step #1c.

 e. The client spontaneously names picture cards or reads aloud words using reduced speaking rate. The clinician may initially present some cards or pictures containing visual cues and some cards or pictures without visual cues.

    f. Using reduced speaking rate, the client imitates the clinician's productions of combined monosyllabic words (e.g., tree-house, ice-toy).

    g. The client and clinician review progress to date.

    h. Repeat Step #1f.

    i. In the context of games, the client practices spontaneously producing or reading monosyllabic words using a reduced speaking rate.

2a. The clinician and the client review the previous work.

    b. The clinician models a loud versus a reduced loudness level while speaking.

    c. The client imitates the clinician's productions of combined monosyllable words using a reduced loudness level.

    d. The client spontaneously reads aloud or labels combined monosyllable words using a reduced loudness level.

3a. The client imitates the clinician's reduced rate and volume during production of combined monosyllabic words.

    b. The clinician reviews the descriptions of reduced rate and reduced loudness. He or she quizzes the client about the terms.

    c. The client spontaneously reads aloud or labels combined monosyllable words using reduced rate and loudness levels.

    d. The client's caregiver models and scores the client's imitation of combined monosyllabic words using reduced rate and loudness.

    e. The clinician models polysyllabic words for the client to imitate using reduced rate and loudness.

    f. The client spontaneously reads aloud or labels polysyllabic words using reduced rate and loudness.

    g. The clinician and the client review progress to date.

    h. The client's caregiver models and scores the client's imitation of polysyllabic words using reduced rate and loudness.

4a. The clinician introduces the concept of smooth concordance:

- by describing,
- by drawing representations of waves as visual prompts with each wave representing a syllable, and
- by modeling.

(continued)

Table 11–3 *(continued)*

b. The client imitates the clinician's production of polysyllabic words using smooth concordance.

c. The client spontaneously reads aloud or labels polysyllabic words using a smooth concordance.

d. The clinician reviews the definitions of reduced rate and loudness and of smooth concordance. He or she ascertains the client's level of understanding through questioning.

e. Repeat Step #4c.

5a. The client imitates the clinician's models of polysyllabic words using a smooth concordance and reduced loudness and rate. Visual cues can be used as needed.

b. Without a model, the client reads aloud or labels polysyllabic words using smooth concordance, reduced loudness, and reduced rate. Visual cues can be used as needed.

c. The client's caregiver directs the session and replicates Step #5b.

d. The client imitates the clinician's production of phrases and short sentences with no audible pauses (i.e., in one breath) using smooth concordance, reduced loudness, and reduced rate. Visual cues can be used as needed.

e. In the context of a game, the client spontaneously produces phrases and short sentences with no audible pauses using smooth concordance, reduced loudness, and reduced rate. Visual cues can be used as needed.

f. The clinician reviews the definitions of smooth concordance, reduced loudness, and reduced rate and quizzes the client to determine his or her level of understanding. Visual cues can be used as needed.

g. Repeat Step #5e. The visual cue of the wave should be altered to associate one word or one bisyllable with each wave.

h. The caregiver directs and replicates Step #5g.

6a. The client imitates the clinician, producing longer sentences that contain one pause while using smooth concordance, reduced loudness, and reduced rate.

b. The clinician reviews the definitions of smooth concordance, reduced loudness, and rate.

c. Repeat Step #6a

d. The client spontaneously produces longer sentences (i.e., those requiring a pause) using smooth concordance, reduced loudness, reduced rate. This step should be practiced repeatedly with a variety of targets.

e. The clinician reviews the definitions of smooth concordance and reduced loudness and rate.

f. Repeat Step #6d using more naturalistic tasks such as role playing. Visual cues should be faded.

g. The client's caregiver directs the task using the procedures in Step #6f.

h. The clinician reviews the definitions of smooth concordance, reduced loudness, and reduced rate.

i. Repeat Step #6f with new activities.

7a. The client imitates the clinician's productions of multiple utterances spoken with appropriate pauses and breaths using smooth concordance, reduced loudness, and reduced rate.

b. The client spontaneously produces multiple utterances spoken with appropriate pauses and breaths using smooth concordance, reduced loudness, and rate. The clinician should increase the naturalness of the sentences and the context.

c. Repeat Step #7b with a variety of sentences and activities. The clinician fades the exaggeration of the cues.

d. The clinician reviews the definitions of smooth concordance, reduced loudness, and rate. She quizzes the client to ascertain his or her level of comprehension.

e. Repeat Step #7c

f. The client's caregiver directs the session using Step #7c procedures.

8a. The client uses smooth concordance, reduced loudness, and rate when producing spontaneous speech in a variety of naturalistic contexts. The clinician varies activities considerably.

b. The client's caregiver directs the session using Step #8a procedures.

COMMENTS: This is an example of integrating several aspects of prosody to achieve a goal. In addition to treating continuity directly using prosody, this method indirectly treats loudness (level), duration, tempo (rate, concordance), and pause (intraturn). Moreover, this method has been used for people with phrasing, stress (phrasal), and rhythmic (stress sequences) problems.

---

[1] Pindzola labels this "slow stretched speech."

[2] Pindzola labels this "soft speech."

[3] Pindzola labels this "smooth talking."

Source: The above program was derived from information provided in Pindzola, R. (1987a). *Stuttering intervention program: Age 3 to grade 3.* Tulsa, OK: Modern Education Co.

b. Intervention
(1) Content
(a) For indirect stress sequence PFCs, the **terminal objective** of intervention can include

- decreased production of hard glottal attacks,
- decreased use of palilalia,
- improved articulation,
- improved comprehension skills,
- improved fluency,
- improved gross motor skills,
- improved intelligibility,
- improved memorization,
- improved naturalness,
- improved overall language,
- improved overall speech skills,
- improved pitch and/or intonation,
- improved pragmatics,
- improved prelinguistic skills,
- improved overall rhythm,
- improved semantics,
- improved stress,
- improved tempo,
- improved voice quality, and
- modifications of speaking rate.

Table 11-4 provides an example of an approach that indirectly uses stress sequence.

(b) The **target behaviors** of the stress sequencing phase of treatment involve producing, imitating, or discriminating a variation of the desired terminal objective in one of the following contexts:

- stylized stress sequences. These are employed in a number of ways and in a number of treatment approaches. The assumption is that speakers find it easier to speak using a preset, predetermined pattern of stress sequences rather than using a normal speaking prosody. Examples:

  equal and even stress
  forms of intoning

singing
sprechgesang
speaking to the beat of a metronome

Not only are stylized stress sequences used to facilitate the production of targeted behaviors, but they also are used during "warm-up" sessions prior to traditional therapy sessions.

- **motoric stress sequences.** These capitalize on the link between motor and speech rhythm by requiring the client to speak while motorically marking specified beats (i.e., stress sequence). Examples:

Clients perform activities such as finger tapping or head nodding to a metronome's beat.

Clients sing songs while tapping out the beat (stress sequence) with their hands.

Clients rhythmically produce certain physical activities while vocalizing vowels, consonants, words, or phrases.

- **normal stress sequences.** Although these are used to achieve nonrhythmic terminal objectives, for the most part, the focus on normal stress sequences comes only after having met criterion for stylized or motoric sequences.

(c) The most common **hierarchy** for the indirect treatment of stress sequences is logical ordering. Notable exceptions to the logical hierarchy are Rosenbek (1978, pp. 221–223) (who uses a linear hierarchy) and Cartwright and Huckaby (1972), Hoskins (1988), and Walker (1972) (who employ horizontal orderings of objectives in which several major objectives are concurrently taught).

(2) The **techniques** used to teach stress sequence indirectly vary as noted in Table 11–2 which presents the techniques used in all rhythm PFCs. The most commonly used techniques include *motor movement, music, imitation, cues, feedback, metalinguistics*, and *reading*. Although the technique *singing* is not unique to this section, all approaches that use sing-

Table 11–4. Program for indirect stress sequence PFC. (Steps related to stress sequences are preceded by an asterisk [*].)

POPULATION:	Accent reduction.
TECHNIQUES:	Modeling; choral reading; role-playing; cues (rhythmic, visual); metalinguistics; feedback (verbal); imitation; motor movement; drill. (The Glossary contains definitions of the techniques.)
GOAL:	To improve American English speaking and comprehension skills.
OBJECTIVES:	To express feelings or emotions by manipulating stress, intonation and rhythm.
PROCEDURES:	(NOTE: This procedure is designed for use with a group. Graham [1978] provides a book of readings and audiotaped presentations of the passages. Each passage focuses on specific skills or concepts.)

    1. The clinician explains the context and purpose of the targeted passage. He or she provides definitions of vocabulary in the passage and describes contexts in which the terms might be used.

    *2a. The clinician models a line from the passage using normal rate, intonation, and stress sequences and then directs the clients to read the line in unison.

    *b. The clinician models each line several times, the clients imitate the clinician's model, and the clinician corrects their intonation and/or articulation.

    *3. The clinician repeats Step #2 but highlights the stress.

---

ing, chanting, or intoning are included within this section because of the special interrelation between singing and rhythm. Table 11–5 describes the use and function of singing-based treatment programs.

2. **Approaches that indirectly focus on alterations** (i.e., direct alteration PFC). (**Alterations** = Changes in tempo, intonation, and articulation that speakers use to produce unstressed syllables between stressed syllables or words.)

    a. **Population.** By far, the most frequent population for which rhythmic alterations are indirectly used is individuals with foreign accents. However, alterations also are the focus of treatment for dysarthria, stuttering, voice disorders, and speech improvement.

sequence (beat) of the passage by clapping, using rhythm sticks, or using hand cues to mark each stress.

*4. The clinician divides the clients into two groups and presents the first line of the passage using normal rate and intonation while highlighting the stress sequences with hand cues. The first group imitates the first line of the passage, and then the second group imitates the second line. This pattern continues throughout the entire passage.

*5. The clinician produces the first line of the chant, highlighting the stress sequences with hand cues. As a single group, the clients read aloud the second line of the passage. As clients become increasingly familiar with the passage, they reduce their use of the written materials and rely more on memory. This pattern continues throughout the passage.

*6. The clinician divides clients into two groups. The clinician highlights the stress sequences using hand cues prior to and during the groups' production of the passage. (The clinician does not talk during this phase.) The first group produces the first line, and the second group produces the second line. The pattern continues until the end of the passage.

COMMENTS: This method may also be used indirectly with tempo (rate), intonation (overall contour), and stress (phrasal).

Source: The above program was derived from information provided in Graham, C. (1978). *Jazz chants: Rhythms of American English for students of English as a second language.* New York: Oxford University Press.

b. Intervention
(1) Content
(a) The **terminal objective** for indirect alterations PFCs may involve the improvement of a variety of communicative behaviors including

- articulation,
- comprehension,
- duration,
- fluency,
- intelligibility,
- normalcy judgments,
- overall prosodic skills,
- rate,
- tempo, and
- voice quality.

Table 11-5. Using music to improve communication skills

RATIONALE:	1. Music and prosody have common features (e.g., rhythm, intonation, tempo).
	2. In treatment contexts, music and its various forms (e.g., humming, intoning singing, chanting, instrument playing) differ from spontaneous speaking in that music has a more limited range of pitches, is slower, is more "lyrical," has a more predictable rhythm, and has more predictable stress sequences. Thus, the use of music during treatment may simplify the task of speaking. It is important to note, however, that this is only one view of why music may facilitate learning. Schuster and Mouzon (1982), for example, suggest that music's positive influence may be due to its ability to induce relaxation.
	3. The overlapping features may facilitate the learning of both music and prosody.
	4. Particularly for children, music can be a non-threatening, playful means of interacting and learning.
	5. Zoller (1991) cites studies that support the effectiveness of music in improving communication skills.
BACKGROUND:	1. Music has been used for the following communication-related purposes:
	• to promote relaxation,
	• to increase the use of imagery, and
	• to improve language skills.
	2. Music can be used in treatment with only homemade instruments, the clinician's voice, or taped and recorded music. Formal training is not a prerequisite for success.
	3. Zoller provides guidelines to help clinicians achieve appropriate matches between clients' abilities (e.g., cognitive level, physical/motor skills, attention level, emotional functioning, musical talent) and music activities.
	4. Space limitation can influence the choice of music activities.
GENERAL GUIDELINES:	1. Music frequently is employed following the establishment stage of treatment when the client produces the target behavior on demand but evidences limited generalization and maintenance.
	2. Repetition is paramount.

3. The client should be able to mark his or her own beat before imitating the beat of another or the beat of an instrument.

4. The following hierarchy of treatment steps is suggested.

   a. The client claps his or her hands, stomps his or her feet, or pats his or her thighs using a beat that is comfortable and natural. First, the beat is internal; then it can be external (from a source other than oneself).

   b. The client wiggles his or her hands or fists, claps hands in front or in back of himself or herself, or twists his or her upper body to a comfortable and natural beat.

   c. The client uses "locomotion movements" to an external beat. Locomotion movements include behaviors such as rolling, walking, running, and hopping (Zoller, 1991). If appropriate, the clinician labels the client's actions.

   d. The client moves to an external beat using nonlocomotion movements such as stooping, bending, rocking, pulling, and shaking (Zoller, 1991). If appropriate, the clinician labels the client's actions.

5. The clinician exposes the client to a range of tempos, loudnesses, and rhythms.

INDIRECT USE OF SONGS:

1. Singing is a developmental skill that reportedly begins during infancy and is not completely mastered until the middle grades.

2. Potential target behaviors include

   • improved eye contact by having the clinician sing clients' names using a "calling melody,"

   • improved articulation and sequencing of speech sounds by singing words with the target sounds or sequences in songs,

   • improved word order,

   • improved auditory perception by using "call-and-response" singing (Zoller, 1991, p. 274),

   • improved imitation,

   • improved vocabulary using "fill-in-singing" (Zoller, 1991, p. 274)

(continued)

Table 11-5 *(continued)*

- improved auditory memory by repetitively using the same linguistic units in refrains,
- improved word retrieval, and
- improved socialization using group singing.

3. Singing guidelines

   a. For younger or severely impaired clients, initiate treatment using only two or three notes with simple rhythm and limited vocal range.

   b. As the client progresses, increase the vocal range to five and then to six or eight notes.

   c. Initiate treatment at a relatively low pitch height (C–A). Gradually increase the pitch height.

   d. Particularly with young children or severely impaired clients, use songs that

      - encourage movement,
      - repeat melody,
      - repeat words,
      - contain the clients' names,
      - involve activities of daily living, or
      - contain common lexical items and syntactic forms.

   e. Ensure that the client comprehends the lexical items (vocabulary) and the syntactic forms used in the songs. If necessary, define and explain the meaning of the songs.

   f. When introducing a song, use the following hierarchy:

      - The clinician initially presents the melody only by encouraging the client to mark the beat (stress sequence) using hand clapping, knee patting, thigh slapping, etc.
      - The clinician directs the client to sing the song using a neutral syllable ("lah").
      - The clinician sings the song phrase by phrase. The client must correctly imitate the target phrase before moving to the next phrase.
      - The client and the clinician sing the entire song in unison.

   g. The clinician writes the words of the songs for the client or draws pictures for the nonreading client. As the client sings, the clinician points to the words or the pictures.

h. If necessary, the clinician may simplify the vocabulary or syntactic structure of songs.

i. If a client is reluctant to participate, the clinician may request that he or she plays an instrument or acts out the lyrics of the song.

j. The clinician may provide visual cues. Examples:

- Hand height may represent pitch height.
- Arcs drawn in the air or on a board may represent duration.
- The size of words or pictures may represent loudness.
- Underlining may represent stress.

k. Use of instruments should involve simple activities. For example, the clinician may use a single finger to play instruments.

l. Clients should know songs thoroughly before adding the use of musical instruments.

EXEMPLARS OF MUSIC ACTIVITIES:

To identify body parts. The clinician introduces songs (e.g., "Looby Loo" and "Hokey Pokey") that repetitively involve and label body parts.

To increase the frequency and complexity of vocalization. The clinician involves the client in a variety of activities. Examples:

- The clinician models proper breathing and highlights the outward motion of the ribs and abdomen and the lack of shoulder movement by placing her hand at the bottom of the rib cage.
- The clinician models the production of a single syllable word using one stable pitch height.
- The client attempts to imitate the clinician's model.
- As the client's skills increase, the complexity of the words that the clinician models increases.
- The clinician monitors the client to ensure he or she is using the optimum pitch height.
- The clinician models a sustained vowel that is from the middle of the client's pitch range.
- The client imitates the clinician.
- The clinician models consecutive vowels while using the pitch height identified above.
- The client imitates the clinician.

(continued)

Table 11-5 *(continued)*

- The clinician models different CV syllables maintaining the same consonant but changing the vowel.

To improve articulation. The clinician establishes the correct production of the target sound(s) using traditional speech therapy techniques.

- The clinician selects songs that contain the target sound.

- The clinician sings songs and intentionally misarticulates some words containing the target sound.

- The client sings the song. At first, the client may only sing the words that contain the target sound.

- Some clients experience difficulty producing multisyllabic words. Such clients might attempt to sing each syllable of multisyllabic words at different pitch heights.

- The clinician encourages the client to read aloud poetry and to accompany the reading with motor movements such as clapping, stomping, or walking.

- The clinician writes out words containing the target sounds in songs and in poetry.

To increase vocabulary.

- The clinician sings but omits the target vocabulary item.

- To teach opposites and prepositions, the clinician presents specific songs:

  - up/down: "The Eensy Weensy Spider Went up the Water Spout"

  - left/right: The clinician cuts out representations of left and right feet and places them on the floor. The client then reads aloud or recites a poem highlighting direction.

  - verbs and sequences: The clinician and the client sing a song and act out the motor movements in the song.

  - auxiliary verbs: The clinician modifies songs to stress targeted auxiliary verbs emphatically.

Source: The information in this table is derived from Zoller, M. B. (1991). Use of music activities in speech-language therapy. *Language, Speech, and Hearing Services in Schools, 22,* 272–276.

(b) The **target behaviors** of the rhythmic alteration phases of indirect treatment approaches include producing or reading aloud passages containing

- contractions,
- elisions,

- concordance,
- coalescence,
- reduced loudness for unstressed syllables,
- increased rate for unstressed syllables, and
- vowel reductions on unstressed syllables.

Dickerson's (1989) approach for indirect rhythmic alteration is particularly well developed. He considers alterations an integral part of the rhythmic model and targets alterations in words and phrases as a means to improving the intelligibility. A brief summary of Dickerson's impressive array of objectives and activities to improve alterations is presented in Table 11–6.

(c) The most common **hierarchy** used for indirect rhythmic alterations is the linear hierarchy. The methods designed for speakers with foreign accents present several exceptions to this trend. Dickerson (Table 11–6), for example, requires his students to progress through a series of objectives to achieve appropriate rhythmic skills and he targets several goals simultaneously. Thus, Dickerson's method qualifies as a combined approach using both logical and horizontal hierarchies.

(2) The **techniques** used to teach rhythmic alterations indirectly vary considerably. A relatively large number of techniques are appropriate for groups, perhaps due to the preponderance of approaches designed for foreign speakers. (Table 11–2 presents treatment techniques for all rhythm PFCs.)

3. **Indirectly focusing on continuity.** No methods have been identified that use continuity to improve other aspects of communication. Clinicians apparently perceive the task of achieving continuity to be as or more difficult than achieving other communication objectives. This makes the use of continuity as a facilitator marginal.

C. Summary Points

1. To date, rhythm methods for speakers with **foreign accents** are more linguistically sophisticated than those developed for individuals with communication disorders. This may be related to the complexity of the treatment task, the difficul-

Table 11-6. Program for indirect alteration PFC. (Steps related to rhythmic alteration are preceded by an asterisk [*].)

POPULATION:	Foreign accent — high intermediate to advanced levels.
TECHNIQUES:	Covert rehearsal, metalinguistics, homework, self-reading, cues (visual), previews, reading aloud, self-monitoring, query responding, imitation, motor movement, unison speech, whispering, query-led corrections, buzzing, reviewing. (The Glossary contains definitions of the techniques.)
GOAL:	To improve speaking intelligibility[1] and comprehension.[2]
OBJECTIVES:	1. At the phrase level, to predict, perceive, and produce
	*• the contrast between function and content words;
	*• vowel reductions, vowel omissions,[3] contractions, concordance, coalescence,[4] and elisions;[3] and
	• location of phrasal stress.
	2. At the word level, to predict, perceive, and produce
	• location of lexical stress,
	• the stressed vowel,
	*• the vowels to the right of the stressed vowel, and
	*• the vowels to the left of the stressed vowel.
PROCEDURES:	NOTE: This method is designed for use with a group of clients. A typical fifty minute session consists of the following:
	• *Twenty minutes of vowel/consonant articulation or phrase level work.* (Topics presented during phrase level work are summarized in the Objectives #1.)
	a. The clinician presents information.
	b. The clinician presents examples.
	c. The client practices oral exercises that usually take the form of dialogues.

ty of achieving stress-timing consciously, or the lack of rhythmic problems among communicatively impaired individuals. This is an area that can profit from additional research.

2. The use of ***singing*** (including chanting, humming, intoning, etc.) has been classified as a rhythmic technique. The rationale for using singing as a treatment method appears to be pred-

- *Twenty minutes of word level work.* (Topics presented during word level work are presented in the Objectives #2.)
  a. Oral work
     (1) Content:
         - reading of phrases/sentences loaded with the target structure
         - exercises including reading passages, dialogues, matching, competitions, etc.
     (2) Teacher strategies:
         - reiteration of significant information
         - rhyme activities to emphasize target structures. During rhyming activities the clinician may employ **motor movements, reading aloud, buzzing, unison reading, metalinguistics**.
         - **query-led corrections** to promote **self-monitoring**
         - **visual cues**
  b. Review
- *Five minutes of **previewing** the content of the oral work for the next session.
- *Five minutes of miscellaneous activities* such as assigning, explaining, and returning homework (which is regularly assigned).

COMMENTS: This method may also be indirectly used for stress (lexical, phrasal) and tempo (concordance).

1 Dickerson's term is production.
2 Dickerson's term is perception.
3 Dickerson's term is trimmings.
4 Dickerson's term is linkings.
Source: The above program was derived from information provided in Dickerson. W. B. (1989). *Stress in the speech stream: The rhythm of spoken English. Teacher's manual.* Urbana, IL: University of Illinois Press.

icated on the belief that singing provides speakers with predictable, stylized rhythmic patterns (stress sequences) which frees them to attain other communicative goals. That is, clients who are singing do not have to contend with determining their own rhythmic pattern and can devote more attention to controlling other behaviors. Citations for publications describing the use of singing as a treatment technique are provided in the section VI.F.

3. Although the logical **hierarchy** remains the most popular format for ordering objectives, alternative orderings for rhythm therapies include the linear and horizontal hierarchies. Several authors (e.g., Cartwright & Huckaby, 1972; Dickerson, 1989; Hoskins, 1988; Walker, 1972) have employed the horizontal hierarchy which clinicians may consider as an alternative to the logical hierarchy. Additionally, clinicians also may create their own empirically ordered hierarchies basing the ordering of objectives on levels of difficulty that have been validated for the individual client.

4. There is little documentation of the **effectiveness** of objectives, hierarchies, and techniques for treating rhythm. Accordingly, clinicians will need to expend considerable energy critically evaluating the impact of treatment approaches on their clients. This area also warrants additional research.

5. Treatment approaches that have been designed for **children** are cited in section VI.G.

6. The organization of this book, may lead readers to view rhythm therapy as primarily skill based and/or as an entity that profits from the treatment of discrete units. In fact, several methods, which are cited in section VI.H, approach rhythm treatment in an **integrative or a holistic** manner.

7. Clinicians planning to develop their own rhythm methods may consider the **treatment techniques** in Table 11-2 as a listing of preferred practices for each of the rhythmic PFCs. Likewise, researchers may consider the lists of techniques in Table 11-2 to be potential research ideas.

8. Some clinicians employ **equal and even stress** which may be viewed as a form of stylized stress sequencing. Clinicians using equal and even stress should take care to attend to naturalness and intelligibility issues. (Section VI.I contains citations for methods using equal and even stress.)

VI. CITATIONS FOR RHYTHM TREATMENT

A. Citations for Approaches Directly Focusing on Stress Sequences

Fairbanks (1960, pp. 118-121); Staum (1987); Wilson (1972, pp. 178-179).

B. Citations for Approaches Directly Focusing on Continuity

Grube & Smith (1989); Ham (1986, pp. 151–167, 308–316, 318–324, 324–328, 331–332, 333–334, 334–335, 339–344; Ham (1990, pp. 293, 293–294, 296–301, 301–305, 321–322, 331, 370–371); Pindzola (1987a); Riley & Riley (1985).

C. Citations for Approaches Indirectly Focusing on Stress Sequences

Bergendal (1976); Berry (1980); Brown (1974); Cartwright & Huckaby (1972); Cohen (1988); Dickerson (1989); Dworkin (1991, pp. 318–320, 320–321, 321–322, 323–324, 324); Dworkin et al. (1988); Dworkin et al. (1990); Gilbert (1984, pp. 16–18); Graham (1978); Ham (1986, pp. 308–316, 318–324); Ham (1990, pp. 293, 293–294); Harding & Ballard (1982); Helfrich-Miller (1984); Helm (1979); Hoskins (1988); Ingham & Sato (1990); Keith & Aronson (1975); Krauss & Galloway (1982); Kruse (1990); Macaluso-Haynes (1978); Marshall & Holtzapple (1978); Miller & Toca (1979); Morris (1991); Orion (1988, pp. 29–35); Pindzola (1987a); Prater & Swift (1984, pp. 118–119); Riley & Riley (1985); Rogers & Fleming (1981); Rosenbek (1978, pp. 221–223); Rosenbek et al. (1973); Sparks (1981); Spencer (1988, #1, #2); Swift & Rosin (1990); Tavze (1990); Thaut (1985); Walker (1972); Wilson (1972, pp. 172–175, 178–179); Witt & Steele (1984); Yorkston & Beukelman (1981).

D. Citations for Approaches Indirectly Focusing on Alterations

Dickerson (1989); Gilbert (1984, pp. 16–18, 21–23, 24–26, 26–27); Glenn et al. (1989, pp. 230–233); Graham (1978); Moncur & Brackett (1974, pp. 86–96, 98); Orion (1988, pp. 14–18, 21–28, 29–35, 36–44); Pindzola (1987a); Simmons (1983); Stern (1987, Course #2); Yorkston & Beukelman (1981).

E. Citations for Approaches Using Music

Brown (1974); Harding & Ballard (1982); Morris (1991); Saperston (1973); Spencer (1988); Staum (1987); Thaut (1985); Waling & Harrison (1987, p. 22); Wilson (1972, pp. 172–175, 175–176, 178–179); Witt & Steele (1984).

F. Citations for Approaches Using Singing

Cartwright & Huckaby, 1972); Cohen (1988); Dworkin (1991, pp. 306–308, 308–309, 310, 312–313); Dworkin et al. (1988); Fairbanks (1960, pp. 118–121); Gilbert (1984, pp. 21–23); Glenn et al. (1989, 80–84); Graham (1978); Ham (1986, pp. 333–334); Hanson & Metter (1983); Harding & Ballard (1982); Helfrich-Miller (1984); Hoskins (1988); Keith & Aronson (1975); Krauss & Galloway (1982); Kruse (1990); Macaluso-Haynes (1978); Marshall & Holtzapple (1978); Miller & Toca (1979); Moncur & Brackett (1974, pp. 77–78); Prater & Swift (1984, pp. 118–119); Rogers & Fleming (1981); Schomburg et al. (1989); Sparks (1981); Spencer, 1988); Swift & Rosin (1990); Walker (1972); Wilson (1972, pp. 172–175, 175–176, 178–179).

G. Citations for Approaches Designed for Children

Berry (1980, pp. 250–255); Brown (1974); Cartwright & Huckaby (1972); Cohen (1988); Ham (1986, pp. 308–316, 333–334); Ham (1990, pp. 293, 293–294, 296–301, 301–305, 321–322, 331); Harding & Ballard (1982); Helfrich-Miller (1984); Hoskins (1988); Krauss & Galloway (1982); Macaluso-Haynes (1978); Morris (1991); Pindzola (1987a); Riley & Riley (1985); Rogers & Fleming (1981); Spencer (1988); Staum (1987); Swift & Rosin (1990); Tavze (1990); Thaut (1985); Wilson (1972, pp. 172–175, 178–179); Witt & Steele (1984); Appendix B.

H. Citations for Integrative and/or Holistic Approaches

Berry (1980, pp. 250–255); Brown (1974); Cartwright & Huckaby (1972); Gilbert (1984); Graham (1978); Ham (1986, pp. 318–324, 324–328, 334–335, 339–344); Ham (1990, pp. 301–305, 308–316, 321–322); Harding & Ballard (1982); Helfrich-Miller (1984); Marshall & Holtzapple (1978); Orion (1988, pp. 14–18, 21–28, 29–35, 36–44, 53–321); Pindzola (1987a); Riley & Riley (1985); Rogers & Fleming (1981); Simmons (1983); Smith & Engel (1984); Sparks (1981); Spencer (1988); Staum (1987); Stern (1987, Course #1 and #2); Swift & Rosin (1990); Walker (1972); Appendixes A & B.

I. Citations for Approaches Using Equal and Even Stress

Dworkin (1991, pp. 318–320, 320–321; 321–322, 323–324); Dworkin et al. (1988); Dworkin et al. (1990); Ham (1986, pp. 308–316); Ham

(1990, pp. 293–294); Macaluso-Haynes (1978); McDonald (1964); Riley & Riley (1985); Rosenbek (1978, pp. 214–215, 223–224); Rosenbek et al. (1973); Rosenbek et al. (1974); Rosenbek & LaPointe (1978, pp. 301–304, 304–306).

APPENDIX

A

Sample Integrative/Holistic Program for Older Children and Adults

COMMENT:	The focus of this approach may be adapted to any prosodic feature or prosodic component.
POPULATION:	Older children or adults who use too much stress, too much pausing, and/or inappropriate phrasing. (Such speech has been labeled "choppy," "staccato," "equal and even stress," and "one-word or syllable structured." This may be present in speech of individuals with communication impairments or in those who are learning English as a second language).
OBJECTIVES:	1. To provide auditory stimulation using targets before attempting or being expected to produce them.
	2. To produce the targeted behaviors during role playing.
	3. To clarify and correct the production of prosody based on the clinician's requests for clarification during spontaneous conversation.
TECHNIQUES:	Stimulation (auditory), scripts, modeling, reading aloud, cues (visual), clarification requests, conversation, motor movement.
PROCEDURES:	1. *AUDITORY BOMBARDMENT.* Prerecorded audio- or videotaped lists of words and phrases spoken with correct stress, phrasing, and pausing are provided to the client who listens to them several times a day. Such auditory stimulation continues for several weeks before productive treatment begins and can continue throughout production treatment.
	2. *DAILY LIVING ROLE PLAYING.* Scripted dialogue modeling normal prosody during activities of daily living (e.g., ordering food at a restaurant, asking for assistance in a store, introducing people) is videotaped. Following the viewing of the videotapes, individuals or groups of people are assigned the task of reading the dialogue from a script. The "play" proceeds with the "actors" reading the script along with the audiotaped model. The clients may use motor movements to simulate the prosodic components being targeted (e.g., a rising pitch direction is paired with raising of a hand).
	3. *CLARIFICATION REQUESTS (INREAL, 1988).* Once the client is able to produce correct pausing, phrasing, terminal contour, and/or stress in activities similar to those described in Step #2, the clinician uses requests for clarification during conversation to elicit the target behavior. The clinician's use of the

PROCEDURES	request for clarification (repeating exactly what was
(continued)	said by the client, including the incorrect prosody)
	provides a direct model of what was said. It is hoped
	that the client will hear the difference between the
	production and the "ideal" and repeat the original
	production using an acceptable prosodic pattern.
	Example:

Client:	I⎸ like cookies (/)⎸
	[said in a context suggesting the client was making a statement.]
Clinician:	I⎸ like cookies (/)⎸
Client:	No (\)⎸ I like cookies (\)⎸

Source: Lund, B. (1992, personal communication)

Note: Legend for symbols is provided in the Glossary under the entry "Symbols."

APPENDIX

B

Sample Integrative/Holistic Program for Preverbal Children

COMMENT:	The focus of this approach may be adapted to any prosodic feature or prosodic component.
POPULATION:	Preverbal (and low verbal) children
TECHNIQUES:	Imitation, modeling, expansion, wait time
OBJECTIVES:	1. To match the prosodic output of the preverbal child.
	2. To model the pairing of words and prosodic patterns in response to the infant's preverbal requests.
	3. To employ "Wait Time."
PROCEDURES:	1. For the preverbal and low verbal child, the caregiver's effective use of the prosodic features and components of language is essential. These may be the first aspects of language that represent meaning to the infant. Caregivers exhibiting a wide variety of prosodic features meaningfully vary their pitch, loudness, duration, pauses, tempo, intonation, stress, and rhythm. Thus, when the infant coos, the caregiver not only matches the segmental attributes (speech sounds) of the cooing but also the prosodic aspects of it. The caregiver "enters the infant's world" and establishes a communicative bond. Such communicative acts are the foundation and the beginning of meaningful interchanges of language. The infant's attentiveness, facial expressions, and continued turn-taking will signify that this is a desired activity. Example:

Infant: ah (/ \:) {Prolonged production of "ah" using a rising and then falling pitch direction.}

Caregiver: ah (/ \:) {Prolonged production of "ah" using a rising and then falling pitch direction.}

2. Once the infant regularly engages in prosodic interchanges, the caregiver models words paired with the prosodic, preverbal acts of the infant, as in the following dialogue:

Infant: emits a cry signifying hunger (hunger cry)

Caregiver: imitates the hunger cry with special attention to the prosodic pattern and says, "Baby hungry?"

Without the caregiver's imitation of the infant's prosody, the infant might not have a reason to tune into the caregiver's message.

| **PROCEDURES** *(continued)* | 3. An essential, often overlooked, aspect of the caregiver's prosody is the consistent use of effective pauses, sometimes referred to as "wait time" or "latency." The caregiver's use of pauses allows the infant to process the incoming information and communicate to his or her maximum ability. Not only is it important for the caregiver to pause after vocalizing or verbalizing, it is also important for the caregiver to pause after the infant vocalizes/verbalizes. This final pause stimulates the infant to expand his or her vocalization or verbalization. The following exchanges exemplify this phenomenon: |

EXAMPLE 1

Infant:	ba, ba, ba, o (\:) {Prolonged production of "o" using a falling pitch direction}
Caregiver:	ba, ba, ba, o (\:) {Prolonged production of "o" using a falling pitch direction}
Infant:	ba, ba, ba, o (\:) {Prolonged production of "o" using a falling pitch direction}
Caregiver:	pauses
Infant:	ba, ba, ba, o (\:), ah (\:)

EXAMPLE 2

Infant:	(Produces "happy" coos)
Caregiver:	pauses (Waits for the infant to elaborate or continue the coo.)
Infant:	(Produces "happy" coos)
Caregiver:	Imitates the infant's happy coos and says, "Happy Baby." (The caregiver then pauses to permit the infant to process and respond before repeating the vocalization.)

Source: Lund, B. (1992, personal communication).

265

APPENDIX

C

Measures for the Assessment of Prosody

I. SCREENERS/EVALUATIONS

A. *Prosody-Voice Screening Profile (PVSP)*
(Shriberg et al., 1990)

    1. Methods. The PVSP screens selected aspects of prosody and voice. Clinicians analyze spontaneous speech samples and follow explicit directions for segmentation, inclusion, exclusion, and coding of utterances. Training tapes and exercises ensure acceptable intra- and interjudge reliability. The PVSP is appropriate for speakers from a variety of disorder, etiological, and age groups.

    2. Content. The PVSP assesses the following aspects of prosody: rhythm (continuity); rate; duration; stress (lexical, phrasal); loudness; and pitch. Aspects of prosody that extend beyond the sentence level are not within the scope of the PVSP.

3. **Supporting data.** Validity and reliability data are reported (Shriberg, Kwiatkowski, & Rasmussen, 1989a, 1989b, 1990; Shriberg, Kwiatkowski, Rasmussen, Lof, & Miller, 1992).

4. **Questions answered**

   a. **Problem/no problem.** The PVSP is designed to screen prosody and voice. However, the range of measures, the thoroughness of the training tapes, and the lack of another major evaluative measure will probably result in the PVSP being used to determine problem/no problem.

   b. **Nature.** Although the purpose of the PVSP is to screen prosody, strengths and weaknesses can be identified in aspects of prosody that are rated by the instrument.

   c. **Causes.** The PVSP does not examine causes of prosodic problems.

   d. **Facilitating/constraining effects.** The PVSP identifies neither facilitating nor constraining effects.

   e. **Therapy effectiveness.** Although the PVSP is not designed to assess treatment effectiveness, the information obtained has potential for describing communicative changes resulting from treatment.

B. *Profile of Prosody* (PROP)
(Crystal, 1982)

1. **Methods.** The PROP is used to analyze spontaneous language samples. The procedures are described clearly and a tape is available to illustrate various components of the PROP. The tape, however, is not appropriate for training listeners to judge prosodic errors reliably.

2. **Content.** The primary focus of the PROP is intonation (direction of pitch on the nucleus), tempo (phrasing), stress (phrasal), and strategies for producing stress. Parts of the PROP permit considering prosody beyond the sentence level.

3. **Supporting data.** Normative, reliability, and validity data are not provided for the PROP. However, age ranges, guidelines, and examples of impaired prosody are presented.

4. Questions answered

a. **Problem/no problem.** Clinicians can be guided in making problem/no problem decisions based on the information provided by the PROP and the text that accompanies it. Because of limited empirical information, clinicians are cautioned against sole use of the PROP to make judgments about the presence or absence of a problem.

b. **Nature.** Information about some aspects of the nature of prosodic problems, such as intonation and phrasal stress, are illuminated by the PROP. Other aspects of prosodic problems, such as rhythmic or rate problems, are not highlighted.

c. **Causes.** The PROP does not examine causes of prosodic problems.

d. **Facilitating/constraining effects.** The PROP identifies neither facilitating nor constraining effects.

e. **Therapy effectiveness.** Although the PROP is not designed to assess treatment effectiveness, the information obtained has potential for describing communicative changes resulting from treatment.

C. *Tennessee Test of Rhythm and Intonational Patterns (T-TRIP)* (Koike & Asp, 1981; Shadden, Asp, Tonkovich, & Mason, 1980)

1. **Methods.** The T-TRIP requires clients to imitate 25 prerecorded presentations produced with selected prosodic variations.

2. **Content.** The following prosody categories are used in the TRIP: tempo (rate, pause); pitch (direction, slope); and rhythm (stress sequence).

3. **Supporting data.** Koike and Asp (1981) and Shadden et al. (1980) report that interobserver reliability for the T-TRIP is over 90%. The clinical utility of this information is questionable because interobserver reliability was achieved using the criterion of two of three judges rating a response as correct.

Koike and Asp provide evidence that the T-TRIP is sensitive to developmental differences.

4. Questions answered

  a. **Problem/no problem.** Because the T-TRIP provides no normative data, its usefulness in making problem/no problem decisions is limited.

  b. **Nature.** The T-TRIP can be used to determine relative strengths and weaknesses in the aspects of prosody that are the focus of the test. Because the TRIP is an imitative test, if prosody functions in a manner similar to segmental phonology, it may provide a measure of stimulability.

  c. **Causes.** The T-TRIP does not examine causes of prosodic problems.

  d. **Facilitating/constraining effects.** The T-TRIP identifies neither facilitating nor constraining effects.

  e. **Therapy effectiveness.** No claims are made about the T-TRIP's ability to assess treatment effectiveness. As an imitative task, it has only limited benefit in describing communicative effectiveness.

D. *Voice Assessment Protocol (VAP)*
(Pindzola, 1987b)

  1. **Methods.** The VAP assesses selected aspects of prosody by rating five parameters analyzing spontaneous speech, performance on selected tasks, and case history information. The VAP provides tape recorded samples to assist clinicians in making the pitch discriminations necessary for voice evaluations.

  2. **Content.** The VAP analyzes the following aspects of prosody: pitch (height, variability); loudness (level, variability); duration (inherent); and tempo (rate).

  3. **Supporting data.** Normative, reliability, and validity data are not provided.

4. Questions answered

  a. Problem/no problem. Clinicians are provided with guidelines to make decisions about the presence or absence of prosodic problems.

  b. Nature. The VAP identifies strengths and weaknesses for the categories included in the profile.

  c. Causes. For the most part, this system does not examine causes of prosodic problems. However, important etiological information may be acquired as part of the interview, the case history questionnaire, the Breath Features parameter of the instrument, and a suggested medical/laryngeal examination.

  d. Facilitating/constraining effects. This system identifies neither facilitating nor constraining effects.

  e. Therapy effectiveness. Although not designed to assess treatment effectiveness, the information obtained from the VAP has potential for describing communicative changes resulting from treatment.

E. *The TAKI Task*
(Allen, 1983)

  1. Methods. The TAKI Task, which was developed for experimental purposes, uses nonsense objects and words to assess the client's production and perception of lexical stress. The examiner labels two different objects with nonsense names that differ only in the location of stress (e.g., ta*ki* versus *ta*ki) and involves the client in tasks to assess his or her ability to comprehend and produce the differing stress placements.

  2. Content. The TAKI Task assesses lexical stress.

  3. Supporting data. Normative, reliability, and validity data are not provided.

  4. Questions answered

  a. Problem/no problem. Although the TAKI was developed as an experimental task, it has potential for clinical use. Clinicians who develop local norms may use the TAKI to make decisions about the presence or the absence of a problem.

b. **Nature.** The TAKI does not explore the relative strengths and weaknesses of the client's lexical stress system.

c. **Causes.** The TAKI does not attempt to identify the causes of problems in lexical stress.

d. **Facilitating/constraining effects.** The TAKI identifies neither facilitating nor constraining effects.

e. **Therapy effectiveness.** Although not designed to assess treatment effectiveness, the TAKI has potential for describing communicative changes resulting from treatment.

II. INFORMAL GUIDELINES

A. *Decision-Making Guidelines for Adults*
(Yorkston, 1988)

1. **Methods.** The procedure involves moving through a decision-making tree to determine if an adult client's speech passes or fails the aspect of prosody examined. Clinicians identify specific prosodic problems and then determine their underlying cause(s).

2. **Content.** The following aspects of prosody are analyzed: intonation (overall contour); tempo (rate, phrasing); stress (phrasal); duration; pausing; loudness; and pitch. Yorkston recommends evaluating prosody within and across sentences.

3. **Supporting data.** No normative, reliability, and validity data are provided.

4. **Questions answered**

a. **Problem/no problem.** The rater relies on clinical judgment and experience as a speaker/listener to make judgments about the presence or absence of a problem.

b. **Nature.** Prosodic strengths and weaknesses can be identified using this tool.

c. **Causes.** Causality is explored by determining if the client has sufficient cognitive ability and respiratory support to sustain prosody and by identifying compensatory strategies used to produce various aspects of prosody.

d. **Facilitating/constraining effects.** Yorkston deals with this issue by identifying the prosodic behaviors that can be used to develop compensatory strategies.

e. **Therapy effectiveness.** Although Yorkston's approach is not designed to assess treatment effectiveness, information derived from it has potential for describing communicative changes resulting from treatment.

B. *Decision-Making Guidelines for Children*
(Kent, 1988).

1. **Methods.** This procedure was developed for use with young children who are capable of producing multisyllable speech. It involves the use of a decision-making tree to explore the client's ability on tasks of varying complexity. Kent (1988) recommends instrumental analysis as a supplement to perceptual appraisal.

2. **Content.** This procedure explores loudness (level, variation); duration; pitch (height, variation); stress (phrasal); and rate at the syllable, word, and sentence level. Additionally, it assesses structure and function to determine if the client has sufficient respiratory and laryngeal control to sustain speech and prosody.

3. **Supporting data.** Normative, reliability, and validity data are not provided.

4. **Questions answered**

a. **Problem/no problem.** By relying on clinical judgment, experience as a speaker/listener, and instrumentation, clinicians can make judgments of problem/no problem.

b. **Nature.** The procedure allows for judgments of prosodic strengths and weakness in the aspects of prosody that are measured.

c. **Causes.** The issue of causality is addressed in two ways. First, the procedure identifies the competency of the physiological mechanisms that are needed to produce prosodic components. Second, the clinician determines if the prosodic features that serve as the building blocks for the prosodic components are intact.

d. **Facilitating/constraining effects.** The constraining or facilitating effects of prosody on other aspects of communication are not explored. However, Kent recommends exploring the effects of articulatory impairment on the speaker's prosody.

e. **Therapy effectiveness.** Although Kent's approach is not designed to assess treatment effectiveness, information derived from it is potentially useful in describing communicative changes resulting from treatment.

C. *Prosodic Teaching Model Checklist*

The purpose of the Prosodic Teaching Model Checklist (Appendix D) is to provide guidance to clinicians using this book by identifying the aspect(s) of prosody that may be in need of intervention.

1. **Methods.** When using this checklist, clinicians observe clients speaking spontaneously in natural contexts. They, then, determine if each prosodic category is produced acceptably by classifying performance in the different categories as appropriate, inappropriate, or not judged. Normative information is not provided.

2. **Content.** All the categories of the prosodic features and components in this book are analyzed by the Prosodic Teaching Model Checklist.

3. **Supporting data.** Normative, reliability, and validity data are not provided.

4. Questions answered

    a. **Problem/no problem.** Because no normative data are provided, the judgment of problem/no problem is based on the individual clinician's knowledge of normal speaking patterns.

    b. **Nature.** This procedure permits determining the strengths and weaknesses of the speaker's prosodic system.

    c. **Causes.** No attempt is made to assess the underlying physiological causes of prosody problems.

    d. **Facilitating/constraining effects.** The constraining and/or facilitating effects of prosody on other aspects of communication are not explored.

    e. **Therapy effectiveness.** The checklist is not designed to assess treatment effectiveness. Information derived from it has potential for describing communicative changes resulting from treatment.

APPENDIX

D

Prosodic Teaching Model Checklist

NAME: _____ SEX: _____ AGE: _____

DATE: _____ EVALUATOR: _____

Feature/Component	Appropriate	Inappropriate	Not Judged
PITCH			
Height			
Slope/Declination			
Direction			
Variation			
LOUDNESS			
Level			
Variation			
DURATION			
Inherent			
Prosodic			
PAUSE			
Intraturn			
Interturn			
TEMPO			
Rate			

Feature/Component	Appropriate	Inappropriate	Not Judged
TEMPO *(continued)*			
Concordance			
Phrasing			
INTONATION			
Internal			
Onset			
Nucleus			
Terminal Contour			
Overall Contour			
External			
Cohesive Devices			
Pitch Agreement			
STRESS			
Lexical			
Phrasal			
Emphatic			
RHYTHM			
Stress Sequences			
Alterations			
Continuity			

APPENDIX

E

Sample Generic Approaches for Treating Prosody

NOTE:	The treatment methods listed below represent examples of generic approaches designed to be adapted to a variety of prosodic features and prosodic categories.
METHOD #1:	FEEDBACK (adapted from Boone, 1971, pp. 132–134).
TECHNIQUES:	Metalinguistics; feedback (auditory, tactile/kinesthetic, verbal); self-monitoring; amplification. (Definitions of techniques are presented in the Glossary.)
OBJECTIVE:	To use feedback to facilitate production of target behaviors.
PROCEDURES:	1. The clinician describes and demonstrates tactile (e.g., runs fingertips over prongs of a fork), kinesthetic (e.g., closes eyes, lifts and extends arm), and auditory feedback.
	2. The clinician demonstrates a device that permits the immediate replaying of what the client says (e.g., a Language Master or the replay button of a tape recorder).
	3. The clinician directs the client to produce the target behavior, records the vocalization, and replays the tape for the client. The clinician evaluates the vocalization and encourages the client to do so.
	4. The clinician amplifies the client's production of targeted behaviors. After listening to several amplified productions, the client describes them.
METHOD #2:	EXPLANATIONS (adapted from Boone, 1971, pp. 130–132).
TECHNIQUES:	Metalinguistics, modeling.
OBJECTIVE:	The client understands what he or she is doing incorrectly and the rationale for change.
PROCEDURES:	1. The clinician describes the behaviors that are "in error," the general direction of therapy, goals of therapy, and the prognosis.
	2. If the problem is not organic, the clinician demonstrates the target behavior.
	3. If the problem is organic, the clinician describes the pathology, its origin, and its outcome, if possible.
	4. This treatment can be administered concurrently with or prior to other treatments.
COMMENT:	Boone warns clinicians to avoid blame statements such as "Wrong." Rather, clinicians should describe the inappropriate behavior (e.g., "The terminal contour is falling.")

282

METHOD #3:	NEGATIVE PRACTICE (adapted from Boone, 1971, pp. 137–138).
TECHNIQUES:	Discrimination; metalinguistics; negative practice; feedback (auditory, tactile/kinesthetic, verbal); self-monitoring.
OBJECTIVE:	To facilitate the production of the target behavior.
PROCEDURES:	1. After the client is capable of producing a new behavior on command, the clinician directs the client to use his old, incorrect prosodic pattern.
	2. The clinician audiotapes 20 second segments of both the old and new behaviors. The client analyzes the two recordings and describes the "sound" and "feel" of the behaviors.
	3. The client identifies contexts in which the new pattern is relatively easy to produce and agrees to produce the old pattern in these contexts. The client then contrasts and evaluates the new and old patterns.
METHOD #4:	LISTENING TRAINING (adapted from Wilson, 1972, pp. 103–105).
TECHNIQUES:	Metalinguistics, discrimination, cues (visual), modeling.
OBJECTIVES:	1. To identify incorrect productions of the target behavior in others.
	2. To label samples of speech as having correct or incorrect productions of the target behavior. If the production is incorrect, the error type is described.
	3. To make fine discriminations of the target behavior.
PROCEDURES:	1a. The clinician describes and models unacceptable examples of the target behavior.
	b. The clinician produces correct and incorrect examples of the target behavior. The client identifies the productions as correct or incorrect.
	2a. The clinician describes the basic features of acceptable and unacceptable productions of the target behavior.
	b. The clinician presents a pair of speech samples (live, on tape, or on the Language Master), and the client judges the pair as same or different.

(continued)

c. The client labels the type of error noted in Step #2b.

3a. The clinician models and describes error types of the target behavior.

b. The client discriminates among three representations of the target behavior (one correct, two errors). As the client progresses, the magnitude of the differences among the representations decreases.

G L O S S A R Y

Activities of Daily Living: A treatment technique involving organized replications of tasks typically used in the course of a day.

Alterations: Changes in tempo, intonation, and articulation that speakers use when they produce unstressed syllables between stressed syllables or words.

Alternating Tasks: A treatment technique that involves changes in the treatment activity (e.g., switching from speaking to reading and back to speaking in a DAF task).

Amplification: A treatment technique involving increasing the loudness of the acoustic signal.

Audiotapes: A treatment technique that involves the audiotaping of parts or all of the session.

Auditory Cues: See Cues–Auditory.

Auditory Feedback: See Feedback–Auditory.

Auditory Masking: A treatment technique that consists of the client receiving sufficient auditory stimulation through earphones to prevent attention to environmental noises.

Auditory Stimulation: See Stimulation–Auditory.

Backup: A treatment technique involving repetitions of previous steps.

Biteblocks: A treatment technique that involves inserting a solid object into the client's mouth and requesting the client to grip the item with his or her teeth.

Bouncing: A treatment technique that consists of the client repeatedly producing a target syllable using a slow, slightly exaggerated rhythm.

Breath Chewing: A treatment technique involving the production of exaggerated chewing motions while vocalizing.

Breathing Exercises: A treatment technique that focuses on achieving adequate respiratory support for speech.

Buzzing: A treatment technique involving the simultaneous reading aloud of rhyming sentences by a group.

Chanting: A treatment technique involving vocalizations of repetitive tones.

Choral/Unison Reading: A treatment technique involving two (unison) or more (choral) speakers simultaneously reading selected passages aloud.

Choral/Unison Speech: A treatment technique that consists of the client speaking simultaneously with one (unison) or more (choral) speakers.

Clarification Requests: One communicative partner signals to the other that there has been a communicative breakdown.

Cloze: A treatment technique that consists of "filling in the blanks" in sentences or phrases presented by the clinician.

Coaching: A treatment technique that involves reminding the client about performing previously practiced behaviors.

Cohesive Device: Units of identical or related intonation patterns that extend across utterance boundaries and that result in a sense of interconnectiveness among utterances.

Combination Hierarchy: This involves the use of two or more of the different hierarchy types to order treatment steps.

Compensatory Strategies: A treatment technique involving the use of atypical patterns to achieve the target behavior.

Computers: Any treatment technique that uses a computer.

Concordance: The movement from one element in an utterance to the next element.

Constrainer: The prosodic context that makes a task more difficult or more complex.

Continuity: The ability to maintain an uninterrupted flow of speech.

Contrastive Sets/Minimal Pairs: A treatment technique that involves the client being exposed to two (minimal pairs) or more (contrastive sets)

sets of stimuli that differ in only one dimension. Usually, the client is expected to discriminate between the sets of stimuli.

Contrastive Stress Drills: A treatment technique involving one speaker contradicting his or her partner using emphatic stress.

Conversation: A treatment technique that involves spontaneous verbal interactions among two or more participants.

Covert Rehearsal: A treatment technique that consists of practicing targeted behaviors when alone.

Cues-Auditory: A treatment technique in which the clinician provides sounds or vocalizations (but not verbalizations) as prompts or hints.

Cues-Rhythmic: A treatment technique that involves the providing of prompts or hints to the client by exaggerating or highlighting the beat.

Cues-Tactile/Kinesthetic: A treatment technique involving the use of prompts or hints that rely on the sense of touch or the sense of bodily movement and position.

Cues-Verbal: A treatment technique in which the clinician uses spoken words to provide hints or prompts to the client.

Cues-Visual: A treatment technique involving the use of prompts or hints that rely on the sense of seeing.

Direct Purpose: Treatment attempts to change a prosodic behavior.

Disambiguation: A treatment technique involving the use of prosody to differentiate ambiguous utterances.

Discrimination: A treatment technique that consists of directing the client to judge if two or more stimuli are the same or different.

Disorder Hierarchy: The ordering of treatment steps is based on monitoring the individual client's progress throughout the treatment process, evaluating changes that occur (presumably as the result of treatment), and altering treatment procedures and objectives in response to the changes in the client's speech.

Disyllable: Two syllables.

Dramatics: A treatment technique that involves one or many forms of theatrical arts such as acting, poetic interpretation, pantomiming, or story telling.

Drill/Repetitions: A treatment technique involving repetitive presentations of the training task.

Easy Onsets: A treatment technique that involves producing speech by (1) directing breath through relaxed vocal folds; (2) initiating vocalization and; then, (3) initiating articulatory movements.

Ellipsis: Omitting redundant parts of utterances.

Emphatic Stress: A strong level of prominence that is often used to contradict the expectations of the listener.

Empirical Hierarchy: The ordering of treatment steps has been verified as progressing from easy to difficult, or the program instructs clinicians to determine which tasks are relatively easy and/or difficult for the *specific client.*

Exaggeration: A treatment technique involving the overemphasis of a selected prosodic behavior.

Facilitator: The prosodic context that makes a task easier or simpler.

Fading: A treatment technique involving the gradual decreasing of the cues or prompts to the client.

Feedback–Auditory: A treatment technique in which the clinician provides nonverbal acoustic information to the client regarding the acceptability of his or her attempts or replays of the client's own productions using audiotapes.

Feedback–Tactile/Kinesthetic: A treatment technique that involves relying on the sense of touch or the sense of bodily movement to provide information about the acceptability of the client's attempts.

Feedback–Verbal: A treatment technique involving the clinician using words (speech or graphemes) to provide information to the client about the acceptability of his or her attempts.

Feedback–Visual: A treatment technique involving the use of visible information such as gestures, instrumental printouts, or lights to provide information to the client about the acceptability of his or her attempts.

F_0: See fundamental frequency.

Fundamental Frequency: The lowest frequency component of a complex tone (Borden & Harris, 1984, p. 282).

Games: A treatment technique involving engagement in playful activities that have rules and a certain degree of structure.

Glide: Pitch height changes within syllables.

Habitual Pitch: The average pitch most frequently used by a speaker.

Heavy Syllables: Syllables that contain full vowels, such as /ʊ/, /ɪ/, /e/, or diphthongized vowels such as /aɪ/, /au/, /ɔɪ/).

Holistic Approaches: Treatment approaches that focus on an array of functionally related behaviors.

Homework: A treatment technique that consists of the clinician assigning work for the client to complete outside the treatment context.

Horizontal Hierarchy: These consist of the simultaneous treatment of two or more objectives.

Humming: A treatment technique involving the production of a single continuing speech sound such as /m/ or /n/.

Imagery: A treatment technique involving the use of visualization to facilitate the production of the target behavior.

Imitation: A treatment technique that involves reiterations of modeled or previously produced behaviors.

Indirect Purpose: Treatment manipulates a prosodic behavior which, in turn, causes other dimensions of communication to improve. The prosodic behavior is a secondary goal or even a procedure used to achieve the primary goal.

Indirect Speech Acts: The intention of the speaker is not directly interpretable from the surface structure.

Inherent Duration: Length modifications that pertain to speech sounds.

Integrated Approaches: Treatment approaches that target more than one PFC.

Intersystemic Reorganization: A treatment strategy that pairs speaking with a rhythmic activity such as pushing a button or squeezing a ball.

Interturn Pauses: Gaps in vocalizing that occur at the end of a speaking turn when the speaker stops talking.

Intonation Questions: Questions that are signaled by changes in intonation rather than by changes in syntax.

Intoning: A treatment technique that consists of vocalizing or verbalizing while maintaining a simple intonation contour.

Intraturn Pauses: Gaps in vocalization that occur within a single speaking turn.

Jump Ups: Sudden increase in pitch height.

Kinesthetic Cues: See Cues–Tactile/Kinesthetic.

Kinesthetic Feedback: See Feedback–Tactile/Kinesthetic.

Labeling: A treatment technique that consists of the client producing the name of the item on demand.

Latency: A treatment technique consisting of deliberately requiring the speaker to wait a specified period of time before responding.

Lexical Stress: The pattern of the stressed and unstressed syllables at the word level.

Light Syllables: Syllables that contain reduced vowels such as the schwa (/ə/), the r-colored schwa (/ɚ/), and the barred i (/ɨ/).

Linear Hierarchy: The treatment consists of only a single step or objective without increases or decreases in task complexity.

Logical Hierarchy: The ordering of treatment steps is arranged in an assumed order of difficulty. This is the most commonly used ordering of treatment steps.

Long Vowels: /i/, /e/, /a/, /ɔ/, /u/.

Loudness Level: Magnitude of the excursion from an arbitrary reference point.

Loudness Variation: Change in loudness from greatest (loudest) to least (softest) level for any linguistic unit.

Metalinguistics: A set of treatment techniques involving the thinking and talking about language (e.g., explanations, discrimination, self-monitoring).

Metronome: See Cues–Rhythmic.

Minimal Pairs: See Contrastive Sets/Minimal Pairs.

Modeling: A treatment technique involving the clinician presenting ideal examples of the target behavior.

Monologues: A treatment technique that consists of one person speaking or reading aloud about a selected topic.

Motor Movement: A treatment technique involving the pairing of physical movements with the production of a specific prosodic behavior (e.g., the speaker moves his or her hand up and down to signify changes in pitch height or timing gestures representing the production of stressed syllables).

Multisyllable: Words containing three or more syllables.

Musical Instruments: A treatment technique that involves the playing of devices that produce music.

Music Notation: A treatment technique that involves teaching clients to read musical symbols.

Naming: See Labeling.

Narration: A treatment technique involving the production of monologues along a story line.

Negative Practice: A treatment technique involving the purposeful production of errors.

Nonrestrictive Clauses: The information in the clause merely elaborates on the topic.

Nucleus: The most prominent *word* in an utterance.

Onset: The pitch height of the first full syllable in an utterance.

Optimum Pitch: The client's most efficient average pitch height.

Overall Intonation Contour: This represents the pitch configuration from the initiation to the end of the utterance.

Pacing: A treatment technique that consists of using an external source to cue the rate of speaking.

Palilalia: Speech in which words and phrases are repeated using increasingly rapid rates and decreasingly accurate articulation.

Pantomiming: A treatment technique involving the use of facial and bodily gestures to express meaning.

PFC: See purpose/focus combination.

Phrasal Stress: This represents the most prominent syllable or word in a phrase or sentence.

Phrasing: The use of prosodic cues to mark the beginning or the ending of phrases.

Physical Manipulation: A treatment technique that consists of the clinician touching and moving the client's body parts.

Pitch Agreement: The degree of concordance in pitch height between the end of an utterance and the beginning of the next.

Pitch Declination: Change in fundamental frequency over time.

Pitch Direction: Perceived pitch change.

Pitch Height: Average pitch level.

Pitch Range: See pitch variation.

Pitch Slides: A smooth movement from one pitch height to another.

Pitch Slope: Change in fundamental frequency over time.

Pitch Variation: The range of pitch heights from lowest to highest.

Play: A treatment technique involving enjoyable and spontaneous activities.

Poetry Reading: A treatment technique that consists of the reading aloud of verse.

Polysyllable: Three or more syllables.

Production on Demand: See Labeling.

Prompting: A treatment technique in which the client provides hints or cues.

Prosodic Component(s): Tempo, intonation, stress, and/or rhythm.

Prosodic Duration: Changes in length that are not related to the differences among speech sounds but, nevertheless, have communicative value.

Prosodic Feature(s): Pitch, loudness, duration, and/or pause.

Purpose: Reason for working with prosody. There are two distinct purposes: direct and indirect.

Pushing: A treatment technique that involves the speaker pressing against an immovable object while vocalizing.

Query Led Corrections: A treatment technique that consists of the clinician asking a series of questions to facilitate the client's correction of his or her own errors.

Query Responding: A treatment technique that involves answering questions.

Rate: The number of syllables produced over a given amount of time.

Reading Aloud: A treatment technique involving interpreting orally written materials by the client or by the clinician.

Received Pronunciation: The dialect of British English spoken by those attending public schools (the equivalent of private schools in the United States) and universities such as Oxford and Cambridge.

Relaxation: A treatment technique involving the reduction of tension.

Repetitions: See Drill/Repetitions.

Restrictive Clauses: The information in the clause qualifies the meaning of the topic.

Review: A treatment technique involving the studying of treatment information two, three, or more times.

Rhythmic Cues: See Cues–Rhythmic.

Rituals: A treatment technique involving prosodic behaviors in the context of well-rehearsed and frequently repeated acts.

Role Playing: A treatment technique involving a form of dramatics in which the client adopts the character of a real or imagined person.

Segmentals: Speech sounds.

Self-Monitoring: A treatment technique involving the client's evaluation of his or her own performance.

Scripts: See Role Playing.

Shadowing: A treatment technique that consists of a speaker repeating the verbalizations of a model one or two syllables behind the model.

Shaping: A treatment technique involving the clinician reinforcing behaviors that are progressively closer to the target behavior.

Short Vowels: /ɪ/, /ɛ/, /æ/, /ɒ/.

Signing: A treatment technique that uses sign language.

Singing: A treatment technique involving the vocal production of musical sounds.

Speech Improvement: Treatment programs for normal speakers wishing to improve their overall speaking skills.

Sprechgesang: A treatment technique involving verbalizing using an exaggerated rhythm and stress but a normal intonation. This is often a component of Melodic Intonation Therapy.

Speech Register: The use of special speech patterns in specific contexts or with special groups of people.

Step: Each syllable has a different pitch height.

Step Down: Small, graded reductions in pitch height on successive syllables.

Step Up: Sudden changes in pitch height.

Stimulation Activities: Follow-up tasks requiring the use of materials such as glue, tape, crayons, glitter, and scissors that emphasize the session's target concept or structures.

Stimulation–Auditory: A treatment technique that involves repeated exposures to auditory models of a target behavior. There is no expectation that the client will produce the target behavior.

Stimulation–Rhythmic: A treatment technique involving repeated exposures to patterned beats or stresses. There is no expectation that the client will produce the rhythm.

Stressed Syllable: The most prominent or noticeable syllable in a word or utterance.

Stress Sequence: The occurrence of stressed syllables at regularly perceived intervals.

Story (Re)telling: A treatment technique involving narrating an original or repeated version of an event.

Symbols:

\	falling pitch direction
/	rising pitch direction
/ \	rising-falling pitch direction
\ /	falling-rising pitch direction
/+\	rise-plus-fall pitch direction
\+/	fall-plus-rise pitch direction
—	level pitch direction
{ }	information within the braces is an interpretation of the previous phrase.
/ /	phonemic transcription
[ ]	phonetic transcription
( )	symbol within the parentheses pertains to the preceding word or phrase.
|	utterance boundary
:	prolongation
word	{Word; in bold italics; upper and lower cases, as appropriate} Lexical stress is used.
WORD	{Word, in bold italics, all upper case} Emphatic stress is used.

Tactile Cues: See Cues–Tactile/Kinesthetic.

Tactile Feedback: See Feedback–Tactile/Kinesthetic.

Tag Questions: A question added to the end of a statement.

Telescoping: A group treatment technique that consists of speakers taking turns reading aloud a series of sentences.

Terminal Countour: The final pitch direction at the end of an utterance.

Unison Reading: See Choral/Unison Reading.

Unison Speech: See Choral/Unison Speech.

Unstressed Syllable: Any syllable in a word or utterance that is not the most prominent syllable.

Verbal Cues: See Cue–Verbal.

Verbal Feedback: See Feedback–Verbal.

Visual Cues: See Cues–Visual.

Visual Feedback: See Feedback–Visual.

Vocative: A word representing the individual to which a message is addressed (e.g., the name "Godiva" in "Godiva, don't eat the chocolates.")

Wait Time: See Latency.

Whispering: A treatment technique that involves the use of articulated speech produced using a breathstream without vocalization (i.e., the vocal folds do not approximate).

Writing to Dictation: A treatment technique that involves graphically encoding messages produced by another.

REFERENCES

Abe, I. (1980). How vocal pitch works. In L. R. Waugh & C. H. van Schooneveld (Eds.), *The melody of language: Intonation and prosody* (pp. 1–24). Baltimore: University Park Press.

Allen, G. D. (1975). Speech rhythm: Its relation to performance universals and articulatory timing. *Journal of Phonetics, 3,* 75–86.

Allen, G. D. (1983). Linguistic experience modifies lexical stress perception. *Journal of Child Language, 10,* 535–549.

Allen, G. D., & Hawkins, S. (1978). The development of phonological rhythm. In A. Bell & J. B. Hooper (Eds.), *Syllables and segments* (pp. 173–185). Amsterdam: North-Holland.

Allen, G. D., & Hawkins, S. (1979). Trochaic rhythm in children's speech. In H. Hollien & P. Hollien (Eds.), *Amsterdam studies in the theory and history of linguistic science VI: Current issues in the phonetic sciences* (Vol. 9, pp. 927–933). Amsterdam: John Benjamins.

Allen, G. D., & Hawkins, S. (1980). Phonological rhythm: Definition and development. In G. H. Yeni-Komshian, J. F. Kavanagh, & C. A. Ferguson (Eds.), *Child phonology. Volume I: Production* (pp. 227–255). New York: Academic Press.

Andrews, M. L. (1973). Voice therapy with a group of language-delayed children. *Journal of Speech and Hearing Disorders, 38,* 510–513.

Baken, R. (1987). *Clinical measurements in speech and voice.* San Diego: College-Hill Press.

Baltaxe, C. A. M. (1981). Acoustic characteristics of prosody in autism. In P. Mittler (Ed.), *Frontiers of knowledge in mental retardation. Vol. 1 Social, educational, and behavioral aspects* (pp. 223–233). Baltimore: University Park Press.

Bellaire, K., Yorkston, K., M., & Beukelman, D. R. (1986). Modifications of breath patterning to increase naturalness of a mildly dysarthric speaker. *Journal of Communication Disorders, 19,* 271–280.

Bergendal, B.-I. (1976). Musical talent used as a prognostic instrument in voice treatment. *Folia Phoniatrica, 28,* 8–16.

Bergmann, G. (1986). Studies in stuttering as a prosodic disturbance. *Journal of Speech and Hearing Research, 28,* 290–300.

Bernstein Ratner, N. (1985, November). *Cues which mark boundaries in mother-child speech.* Paper presented at the annual convention of the American Speech-Language-Hearing Association, Washington, DC.

Berry, M. F. (1980). *Teaching linguistically handicapped children.* Englewood Cliffs, NJ: Prentice Hall.

Berry, M. D., & Erickson, R. L. (1973). Speaking rate: Effect on children's comprehension of normal speech. *Journal of Speech and Hearing Research, 16,* 367–374.

Berry, W. R., & Goshorn, E. L. (1983). Immediate visual feedback in the treatment of ataxic dysarthria: A case study. In W. R. Berry (Ed.), *Clinical dysarthria* (pp. 253–265). San Diego: College-Hill Press.

Beukelman, D. R., & Yorkston, K. (1977). A communication system for the severely dysarthric speaker with an intact language system. *Journal of Speech and Hearing Disorders, 17,* 265–270.

Blasdell, R., & Jensen, P. (1970). Stress and word position as determinants of imitation in first-language learners. *Journal of Speech and Hearing Research, 13,* 193–202.

Blount, B. G., & Padgug, E. J. (1977). Prosodic, paralinguistic, and interactional features in parent child speech: English and Spanish. *Journal of Child Language, 4,* 67–86.

Bolinger, D. (1986). *Intonation and its parts: Melody in spoken English.* Stanford: Stanford University Press.

Bonvillian, J. D., Raeburn, V. P., & Horan, E. A. (1979). Talking to children: The effects of rate, intonation, and length on children's sentence imitation. *Journal of Child Language, 6,* 459–467.

Boomer, D. S. (1965). Hesitation and grammatical encoding. *Language and Speech, 8,* 148–158.

Boone, D. R. (1971). *The voice and voice therapy.* Englewood Cliffs, NJ: Prentice-Hall.

Boone, D. R. (1980). Voice disorders. In T. J. Hixon, L. D. Shriberg, & J. H. Saxman (Eds.), *Introduction to communication disorders* (pp. 311–351). Englewood Cliffs, NJ: Prentice-Hall.

Borden, G. J. (1988). Commentary on J. Harrington's paper "Stuttering, delayed auditory feedback, and linguistic rhythm." *Journal of Speech and Hearing Research, 31,* 136–137.

Borden, G. J., & Harris, K. S. (1984). *Speech science primer: Physiology, acoustics, and perception of speech* (2nd ed.). Baltimore: Williams & Wilkins.

Boyce, S., & Menn, L (1979). *Peaks vary, endpoints don't: Implications for linguistic theory.* Paper presented at the 5th annual meeting of the Berkeley Linguistics Society.

Bradford, L. J. (1970). The use of operant procedures to reduce rates of reading and speaking. In F. L. Girardeau & J. E. Spradlin (Eds.), *A functional analysis approach to speech and language* (pp. 19–23). (ASHA Monograph, No. 14). Washington, DC: American Speech and Hearing Association.

Brazil, D., Coulthard, M., & Johns, C. (1980). *Discourse intonation and language teaching.* Essex, England: Longman.

Broen, P. (1972). *The verbal environment of the language learning child.* (ASHA Monographs, 17). Washington, DC: American Speech and Hearing Association.

Bronstein, A. J. (1960). *The pronunciation of American English.* New York: Appleton-Century-Crofts.

Brown, J. (1974). The psychophysical responses to music therapy of some very young retarded children. *British Journal of Music Therapy, 3,* 57–64.

Brown, R. (1973). *A first language: The early stages.* Cambridge, MA: Harvard University Press.

Caligiuri, M. P., & Murry, T. (1983). The use of visual feedback to enhance prosodic control in dysarthria. In W. R. Berry (Ed.), *Clinical dysarthria* (pp. 267–282). San Diego: College-Hill Press.

Carlson, L. R. (1989, April). *Contrastive stress drills: Treatment and generalization effects in a mildly apraxic speaker.* Paper presented at the Spring Convention of the Minnesota Speech-Language-Hearing Association, Minneapolis.

Cartwright, J., & Huckaby, G. (1972). Intensive preschool language program. *Journal of Music Therapy, 9,* 137–146.

Chiat, S. (1989). The relation between prosodic structure, syllabification and segmental realization: Evidence from a child with fricative stopping. *Clinical Linguistics and Phonetics, 3,* 223–242.

Clark, H. H., & Clark, E. V. (1977). *Psychology and language: An introduction to psycholinguistics.* New York: Harcourt Brace Jovanovich.

Cohen, N. S. (1988). The use of superimposed rhythm to decrease the rate of speech in a brain-damaged adolescent. *Journal of Music Therapy, 25,* 85–93.

Colmar, S., & Wheldall, K. (1985). Behavioral language teaching: Using the natural language environment. *Child Language Teaching and Therapy, 1,* 199–216.

Colton, R., & Casper, J. (1990). *Understanding voice problems.* Baltimore, MD: Williams & Wilkins.

Cooper, M. (1973). *Modern techniques of vocal rehabilitation.* Springfield, IL: Charles C. Thomas.

Couper-Kuhlen, E. (1986). *An introduction to English prosody.* Baltimore: Edward Arnold.

Cruttenden, A. (1986). *Intonation.* Cambridge: Cambridge University Press.

Crystal, D. (1969). *Prosodic systems and intonation in English.* Cambridge: Cambridge University Press.

Crystal, D. (1975). *The English tone of voice: Essays in intonation, prosody and paralanguage.* London: Edward Arnold.

Crystal, D. (1978). The analysis of intonation in young children. In F. D. Minifie & L. L. Lloyd (Eds.), *Communicative and cognitive abilities — Early behavioral assessment* (pp. 257–271). Baltimore: University Park Press.

Crystal, D. (1980). The analysis of nuclear tones. In L. R. Waugh & C. H. van Schooneveld (Eds.), *The melody of language: Intonation and prosody* (pp. 55–70). Baltimore: University Park Press.

Crystal, D. (1981). *Clinical linguistics.* New York: Springer-Verlag/Wien.

Crystal, D. (1982). *Profiling linguistic disability.* London: Edward Arnold.

Darley, F. L., Aronson, A. E., & Brown, J. R. (1975). *Motor speech disorders.* Philadelphia: W. B. Saunders.

de Bot, F. (1983). Visual feedback of intonation I: Effectiveness and induced practice behavior. *Language and Speech, 26,* 331–350.

Deputy, P. N., Nakasone, H., & Tosi, O. (1982). Analysis of pauses occurring in the speech of children with consistent misarticulations. *Journal of Communication Disorders, 15,* 43–54.

Dickerson. W. B. (1989). *Stress in the speech stream: The rhythm of spoken English. Teacher's manual.* Urbana, IL: University of Illinois Press.

du Preez. P. (1974). Units of intonation in the acquisition of language. *Language and Speech, 17,* 369–376.

Dworkin, J. P. (1991). *Motor speech disorders: A treatment guide.* St. Louis, MO: Mosby.

Dworkin, J. P., Abkarian, G. G., & Johns, D. F. (1988). Apraxia of speech: The effectiveness of a treatment regimen. *Journal of Speech and Hearing Disorders, 53,* 280–294.

Dworkin, J. P., Petrucci–Coley, T., Abkarian, G. G., & Culatta, R. A. (1990, November). *Use of rhythmic stimulation in the treatment of apraxia.* Paper presented at the annual convention of the American Speech-Language-Hearing Association, Seattle, WA.

Edwards, H. T., Strattman, K. H., Cuda, R. A., & Anderson, P. J. (1990, November). *A comparison of intonation and pronunciation training in accent reduction.* Paper presented at the annual convention of the American Speech-Language-Hearing Association, Seattle, WA.

Edwards, H. T., Strattman, K. H., & Kneil, T. R. (1989, November). *Prosodic training effects on non-native speakers of English.* Paper presented at the annual convention of the American Speech-Language-Hearing Association, St. Louis, MO.

Edwards, M. L., & Shriberg, L. D. (1983). *Phonology: Applications in communicative disorders.* San Diego: College-Hill Press.

Eisenson, J. (1972). *Aphasia in children.* New York: Harper & Row.

English, S. L. (1988). *Say it clearly.* New York: Collier Macmillan.

Fairbanks, G. (1960). *Voice and articulation drillbook* (2nd ed.). New York: Harper & Row.

Fernald, A., Taeschner, T., Dunn, J., Papousek, M., de Boysson–Bardies, B., & Fukui, I. (1989). A cross-language study of prosodic modifications in mothers' and fathers' speech to preverbal infants. *Journal of Child Language, 16,* 477–501.

Fey, M. E. (1986). *Language intervention with young children.* Boston: Little, Brown.

Freedman, S. R., & Garstecki, D. C. (1973). Child-directed therapy for a nonorganic voice disorder: A case study. *Language, Speech, and Hearing Services in Schools, 4,* 8–12.

Freeman, F. J. (1982). Prosody in perception, production, and pathologies. In N. J. Lass, L. V. McReynolds, J. L. Northern, & D. E. Yoder (Eds.), *Speech, language and hearing. Vol. III. Pathologies of speech and language* (pp. 652–672). Philadelphia: W. B. Saunders.

Friedman, M. (1985). Remediation of intonation contours of hearing-impaired students. *Journal of Communication Disorders, 18,* 259–272.

Fry, D. B. (1955). Duration and intensity as physical correlates of linguistic stress. *Journal of the Acoustical Society of America, 27,* 765–768.

Fry, D. B. (1958). Experiments in the perception of stress. *Language and Speech, 1,* 126–152.

Furrow, D. (1984). Young children's use of prosody. *Journal of Child Language, 11,* 203–213.

Gandour, J., Weinberg, B., Petty, S. H., & Dardarananda, R. (1986). Rhythm in Thai esophageal speech. *Journal of Speech and Hearing Research, 29,* 563–568.

Garnica, O. K. (1977). Some prosodic and paralinguistic features of speech to young children. In C. E. Snow & C. A. Ferguson (Eds.), *Talking to children: Language input and acquisition* (pp. 63–88). Cambridge: Cambridge University Press.

Gilbert, J. B. (1984). Clear speech: Pronunciation and listening comprehension in American English — Teacher's manual and answer key. Cambridge: Cambridge University Press.

Glenn, E. C., Glenn, P. J., & Forman, S. H. (1989). *Your voice and articulation* (2nd ed.). Englewood Cliffs, NJ: Prentice-Hall.

Goldman–Eisler, F. (1964). Hesitation, information, and levels of speech production. In A. V. S. de Reuck & M. O'Connor (Eds.), *Disorders of language* (pp. 96–111). Boston: Little, Brown.

Goldman–Eisler, F. (1968). *Psycholinguistic experiments in spontaneous speech.* New York: Academic Press.

Goodglass, H., Fodor, I. G., & Schulhoff, C. (1967). Prosodic factors in grammar — Evidence from aphasia. *Journal of Speech and Hearing Research, 19,* 5–20.

Graham, C. (1978). *Jazz chants: Rhythms of American English for students of English as a second language.* New York: Oxford University Press.

Grube, M. M., & Smith, D. S. (1989). Paralinguistic intonation-rhythm intervention with a developmental stutterer. *Journal of Fluency Disorders, 14,* 185–208.

Grube, M. M., Spiegel, B. B., Buchhop, N. A., & Lloyd, K. L. (1986). Intonation training as a facilitator of intelligibility. *Human Communication Canada, 10*(5), 17–24.

Hadding–Koch, K., & Studdert–Kennedy, M. (1964). An experimental study of some intonation contours. *Phonetica, 11,* 175–185.

Ham, R. (1986). *Techniques of stuttering therapy.* Englewood Cliffs, NJ: Prentice-Hall.

Ham, R. E. (1990). *Therapy of stuttering: Preschool through adolescence.* Englewood Cliffs, NJ: Prentice-Hall.

Hanson, W. R., & Metter, E. J. (1983). DAF speech rate modification in Parkinson's disease: A report of two cases. In W. R. Berry (Ed.), *Clinical dysarthria* (pp. 231–251). San Diego: College-Hill Press.

Harding, C., & Ballard, K. D. (1982). The effectiveness of music as a stimulus and as a contingent reward in promoting the spontaneous speech of three physically handicapped preschoolers. *Journal of Music Therapy, 19,* 86–101.

Hargrove, P. M., Dauer, K. E., & Montelibano, M. (1989). Reducing vowel and final consonant prolongations in twin brothers. *Child Language Teaching and Therapy, 5,* 49–63.

Hargrove, P. M., Roetzel, K. A., & Hoodin, R. B. (1989). Modifying the prosody of a language-impaired child. *Language, Speech, and Hearing Services in Schools, 20,* 245–258.

Harrington, J. (1987). Stuttering, delayed auditory feedback, and linguistic rhythm. *Journal of Speech and Hearing Research, 30,* 36–47.

Harrington, J. (1988). Reply to G. Borden's comments. *Journal of Speech and Hearing Research, 31,* 138–140.

Healey, E. C., & Scott, L. A. (1991, November). *Young stutterers' and nonstutterers' understanding of rate reduction strategies.* Paper presented at the annual convention of the American Speech-Language-Hearing Association, Atlanta, GA.

Helfrich–Miller, K. R. (1984). Melodic intonation therapy with developmentally apraxic children. *Seminars in Speech and Language, 5,* 199–226.

Helm, N. A. (1979). Management of palilalia with a pacing board. *Journal of Speech and Hearing Disorders, 44,* 350–353.

Hoodin, R. B., Conroy, L., & Hargrove, P. M., (1988, November). *Prosodic modulation and generalization in a cerebral palsied adult.* Paper presented at the annual convention of the American Speech-Language-Hearing Association, Boston, MA.

Hoskins, C. (1988). Use of music to increase verbal response and improve expressive language abilities of preschool language delayed children. *Journal of Music Therapy, 25,* 75–84.

Huskins, S. (1986). *Working with apraxic clients: A practical guide to therapy for apraxia.* Tucson: Communication Skill Builders.

Ingham, R. J., & Sato, W. (1990, November). *The modification of stutterers' speech naturalness during rhythmic stimulation conditions.* Paper presented at the annual convention of the American Speech-Language-Hearing Association, Seattle, WA.

INREAL. (1988). *INREAL training evaluation model.* Boulder, CO: Author.

Jacobson, J. L., Boersma, D. C. Fields, R. B., & Olson, K. L. (1983). Paralinguistic features of adult speech to infants and small children. *Child Development, 54,* 436–442.

Johns–Lewis, C. (1986). Prosodic differentiation of discourse modes. In C. Johns–Lewis (Ed.), *Intonation in discourse* (pp. 199–219). San Diego: College-Hill Press.

Johnson, H. P., & Hood, S. B. (1988). Teaching chaining to unintelligible children: How to deal with open syllables. *Language, Speech, and Hearing Services in Schools, 19,* 211–220.

Johnson, W., Darley, F. L., & Spriestersbach, D. C. (1963). *Diagnostic methods in speech pathology.* New York: Harper & Row.

Keith, R. L., & Aronson, A. E. (1975). Singing as therapy for apraxia of speech and aphasia: Report of a case. *Brain and Language, 2,* 483–488.

Kent, R. D. (1988). Prosody in the young child. In D. E. Yoder & R. D. Kent (Eds.), *Decision making in speech-language pathology* (pp. 144–145). Toronto: Decker.

Kenyon, J. S., & Knott, T. A. (1953). *A pronouncing dictionary of American English.* Springfield, MA: Merriam.

King, R. G., & DiMichael, E. M. (1991). *Voice and diction.* Prospect Heights, IL: Waveland.

Kingdon, R. (1958). *The groundwork of English stress.* London: Longmans, Green and Co.

Klein, H. B (1981). Early perceptual strategies for the replication of consonants from polysyllabic lexical models. *Journal of Speech and Hearing Research, 24,* 535–551.

Klein, H. B., & Spector, C. C. (1985). Effect of syllable stress and serial position on error variability in polysyllabic productions of speech-delayed children. *Journal of Speech and Hearing Disorders, 50,* 391–402.

Koike, K. J. M., & Asp, C. W. (1981). Tennessee Test of Rhythm and Intonation Patterns. *Journal of Speech and Hearing Disorders, 46,* 81–87.

Kollman, P. A. (1991). *Modifying the prosody of a child with impaired phonology.* Unpublished Master's Thesis, Kansas State University, Manhattan, KS.

Krauss, T., & Galloway, H. (1982). Melodic Intonation Therapy with language delayed apraxic children. *Journal of Music Therapy, 19,* 102–113.

Kruse, K. (1990). *Musical melodies versus rote memorization: A comparison study of strategies for teaching word definitions.* Unpublished Alternate Plan Paper, Mankato State University, Mankato, MN.

Lehiste, I. (1970). *Suprasegmentals.* Cambridge, MA: MIT Press

Lieberman, P. (1967). *Intonation, perception and language.* Cambridge, MA: MIT Press.

Lieberman, P. (1980). The innate, central aspect of intonation. In L. R. Waugh & C. H. van Schooneveld (Eds.), *The melody of language: Intonation and prosody* (pp. 187–199). Baltimore: University Park Press.

Ling, D. C. (1976). *Speech and the hearing-impaired child: Theory and practice.* Washington, DC: Alexander Graham Bell Association for the Deaf.

Lodge, J. M., & Yarnell, G. D. (1981). A case study of vocal volume reduction. *Journal of Speech and Hearing Disorders, 46,* 317–320.

Maassen, B., & Povel, D. J. (1985). The effects of segmental and suprasegmental corrections on the intelligibility of deaf speech. *Journal of the Acoustical Society of America, 78,* 877–886.

Macaluso–Haynes, S. (1978). Developmental apraxia of speech: Symptoms and treatment. In D. F. Johns (Ed.), *Clinical management of neurogenic communicative disorders* (pp. 243–250). Boston, MA: Little, Brown.

Marshall, N., & Holtzapple, P. (1978). Melodic intonation therapy: Variations on a theme. In R. Brookshire (Ed.). *Clinical aphasiology: Collected proceedings 1972–1976* (pp. 285–308). Minneapolis: BRK Publications.

Martin, J. G. (1972). Rhythmic (hierarchical) versus serial structure in speech and other behavior. *Psychological Review, 79,* 487–509.

McDonald, E. T. (1964). *Articulation testing and treatment: A sensory-motor approach.* Pittsburgh: Stanwix House.

McGarr, N. S. (1989). Speech training and sensory aids. *Volta Review, 91,* 197–207.

McGarr, N. S., Youdelman, K., & Head, J. (1992). *A guidebook for remediation of voice pitch problems in hearing impaired persons.* Englewood, CO: Resource Point.

McReynolds, L. V., & Kearns, K. P. (1983). *Single subject experimental designs in communication disorders.* Baltimore: University Park Press.

Miller, S. B & Toca, J. M. (1979). Adapted melodic intonation therapy: A case study of an experimental language program for an autistic child. *Journal of Clinical Psychiatry, 40,* 201–203.

Minskoff, E. H. (1980). Teaching approach for developing nonverbal communication skills in students with social perception deficits. Part II. Proxemic, vocalic, and artifactual cues. *Journal of Learning Disabilities, 13,* 203–208.

Moncur, J. P., & Brackett, I. P. (1974). *Modifying vocal behavior.* New York: Harper & Row.

Morris, S. E. (1991). Facilitation of learning. In M. B. Langley & L. J. Lombardino (Eds.), *Neurodevelopmental strategies for managing communication disorders in children with severe motor dysfunction* (pp. 251–296). Austin, TX: Pro-Ed.

Moskowitz, A. I. (1973). The two-year-old stage in the acquisition of English phonology. In C. A. Ferguson & D. I. Slobin (Eds.), *Studies of child language development* (pp. 52–69). New York: Holt, Rinehart, and Winston.

Nicolosi, L., Harryman, E., & Kresheck, J. (1989). *Terminology of communication disorders: Speech-language-hearing* (3rd ed.). Baltimore: Williams & Wilkins.

Ohala, J. (1977). The physiology of stress. *Southern California Occasional Papers in Linguistics, 4,* 145–168.

Ohde, R.N., & Sharf, D. J. (1992). *Phonetic analysis of normal and abnormal speech.* New York: Merrill.

Oliva, J., & Duchan, J. (1976). Structural regularities in the intonation of an abnormal speaker: Psycholinguistic implications. In P. A. Reich (Ed.), *The second Lacus Forum 1975* (pp. 120–128). Columbia, SC: Hornbeam Press.

Orion, G. F. (1988). *Pronouncing American English.* New York: Newbury

Osberger, M. J., & Levitt, H. (1979). The effect of time errors on the intelligibility of deaf children's speech. *Journal of the Acoustical Society of America, 66,* 1316–1324.

Peters, A. M. (1983). *The units of language acquisition.* Cambridge: Cambridge University Press.

Pike, K. L. (1945). *The intonation of American English.* Ann Arbor, MI: University of Michigan Press.

Pindzola, R. (1987a). *Stuttering intervention program: Age 3 to grade 3.* Tulsa, OK: Modern Education.

Pindzola, R. H. *(1987b). VAP: A voice assessment protocol for children and adults.* Tulsa, OK: Modern Education

Prater, R. J., & Swift, R. W. (1984). *Manual of voice therapy.* Boston: Little, Brown.

Remick, H. (1976). Maternal speech to children during language acquisition. In W. von Raffler-Engel & Y. Lebrun (Eds.), *Baby talk and infant speech* (pp. 223–233). Amsterdam: Swets & Zeitlinger.

Riley, G. D., & Riley, J. (1985). *Oral motor assessment and treatment: Improving syllable production.* Austin: Pro-Ed.

Ringler, N. (1978). A longitudinal study of mothers' language. In N. Waterson & C. Snow (Eds.), *The development of communication* (pp. 151–158). New York: John Wiley.

Rogers, A., & Fleming, P. L. (1981). Rhythm and melody in speech therapy for the neurologically impaired. *Music Therapy: The Journal of the American Association for Music Therapy, 1,* 33–38.

Rosenbek, J. (1978). Treating apraxia of speech. In D. F. Johns (Ed.), *Clinical management of neurogenic communication disorders* (pp. 191–241). Boston: Little, Brown.

Rosenbek, J., Hansen, R., Baughman, C. H., & Lemme, M. (1974). Treatment of developmental apraxia of speech: A case study. *Language, Speech, and Hearing Services in Schools, 5,* 13–22.

Rosenbek, J. C., & LaPointe, L. L. (1978). The dysarthrias: Description, diagnosis, and treatment. In D. F. Johns (Ed.), *Clinical management of neurogenic communication disorders* (pp. 251–310). Boston: Little, Brown.

Rosenbek, J. C., Lemme, M. L., Ahern, M. B., Harris, E. H., & Wertz, R. T. (1973). A treatment for apraxia of speech in adults. *Journal of Speech and Hearing Disorders, 38,* 462–472.

Rubin-Spitz, J., & McGarr, N. S. (1990). Perception of terminal fall contours in speech produced by deaf persons. *Journal of Speech and Hearing Research, 33,* 174–180.

Saperston, B. (1973). The use of music in establishing communication with an autistic mentally retarded child. *Journal of Music Therapy, 10,* 184–188.

Sachs, J., Brown, R., & Salerno, R. (1976). Adult speech to children. In W. von Raffler-Engel & Y. Lebrun (Eds.), *Baby talk and infant speech* (pp. 240–245). Amsterdam: Swets & Zeitlinger.

Schomburg, R., Lippert, E. L., Johnson, C., Muss, C. B., & Tittnich, E. (1989). Language activities. *Journal of Children in Contemporary Society, 21,* 67–116.

Schuster, D. H., & Mouzon, D. (1982). Music and vocabulary learning. *Journal of the Society for Accelerative Learning and Teaching, 7,* 82–108.

Shadden, B. B., Asp, C. W., Tonkovich, J. D., & Mason, D. (1980). Imitation of suprasegmental patterns by five-year-old children with adequate and inadequate articulation. *Journal of Speech and Hearing Disorders, 45,* 390–400.

Shriberg, L. D., & Kent, R. D. (1982). *Clinical phonetics.* New York: John Wiley.

Shriberg, L., Kwiatkowski, J., & Rasmussen, C. (1989a, November). *The Prosody-Voice Screening Profile (PVSP): I. Description and psychometric studies.* Paper presented at the annual convention of the American Speech-Language-Hearing Association, St. Louis, MO.

Shriberg, L., Kwiatkowski, J., & Rasmussen, C. (1989b, November). *The Prosody-Voice Screening Profile (PVSP): II. Reference data and construct validity.* Paper presented at the annual convention of the American Speech-Language-Hearing Association, St. Louis, MO.

Shriberg, L., Kwiatkowski, J., & Rasmussen, C. (1990). *Prosody-Voice Screening Profile.* Tucson: Communication Skill Builders.

Shriberg, L. D., Kwiatkowski, J., Rasmussen, C., Lof, G. L., & Miller, J. F. (1992). *The Prosody-Voice Screening Profile (PVSP): Psychometric data and reference information for children* (Tech. Rep. No. 1). Tucson, AZ: Communication Skill Builders.

Shute, B., & Wheldall, K. (1989). Pitch alterations in British motherese: Some preliminary acoustic data. *Journal of Child Language, 16,* 503–512.

Sikorski, L. D. (1988). *Mastering the intonation patterns of American English.* Santa Ana, CA: Lorna D. Sikorski and Associates.

Silliman, E. R., & Leslie, S. P. (1983). Social and cognitive aspects of fluency in the instructional setting. *Topics in Language Disorders, 4*(1), 61–74.

Simmons, N. N. (1983). Acoustic analysis of ataxic dysarthria: An approach to monitoring treatment. In W. R. Berry (Ed.), *Clinical dysarthria* (pp. 283–294). San Diego: College-Hill Press.

Smith, P. D., & Engel, B. J. (1984). *Melodic apraxia training: Stop consonants.* Tucson, AZ: Communication Skill Builders.

Sparks, R. W. (1981). Melodic intonation therapy. In R. Chapey (Ed.), *Language intervention strategies in adult aphasia* (pp. 265–283). Baltimore: Williams & Wilkins.

Spencer, S. L. (1988). The efficiency of instrumental and movement activities in developing mentally retarded adolescents' ability to follow directions. *Journal of Music Therapy, 25,* 44–50.

Stark, J., Poppen, R., & May, M. Z. (1967). Effects of alterations of prosodic features on the sequencing performance of aphasic children. *Journal of Speech and Hearing Research, 10,* 849–855.

Starkweather, C. W. (1987). *Fluency and stuttering.* Englewood Cliffs, NJ: Prentice-Hall.

Staum, M. J. (1987). Music notation to improve the speech prosody of hearing impaired children. *Journal of Music Therapy, 24,* 146–159.

Stern, D. A. (1987). *The sound and style of American English: A course in foreign accent reduction. Course #1.* Los Angeles: Dialect Accent Specialists.

Stern, D. N., Spieker, S., Barnett, R. K., & MacKain, K. (1983). The prosody of maternal speech: Infant age and context related changes. *Journal of Child Language, 10,* 1–15.

Subtelny, J., Orlando, N., & Whitehead, R. L. (1981). *Speech and voice characteristics of the hearing impaired.* Washington, DC: Alexander Graham Bell Association for the Deaf.

Swift, E., & Rosin, P. (1990). A remediation sequence to improve speech intelligibility for students with Down syndrome. *Language, Speech, and Hearing Services in Schools, 21*, 140–146.

Tavze, C. S. (1990). *Blooming Mother Goose.* East Moline, IL: LinguiSystems.

Thaut, M. H. (1985). The use of auditory rhythm and rhythmic speech to aid temporal muscular control in children with gross motor dysfunction. *Journal of Music Therapy, 22*, 108–128.

Tiffany, W. R., & Carrell, J. (1977). *Phonetics: Theory and application.* New York: McGraw-Hill.

Waling, S., & Harrison, W. (1987). *A speech guide for teachers and clinicians of hearing impaired children.* Tucson: Communication Skill Builders.

Walker, J. B. (1972). The use of music therapy as an aid in developing functional speech in the institutionalized mentally retarded. *Journal of Music Therapy, 9*, 1–12.

Warren, A. R., & McCloskey, L. A. (1993). Pragmatics: Language in social contexts. In J. Berko Gleason (Ed.), *The development of language* (3rd ed., pp. 196–237). New York: Macmillan.

Weismer, S. E., Digney, K., Krueger, W., & Ricke, C. (1990, November). *Linguistic input manipulations during lexical training.* Paper presented at the annual convention of the American Speech-Language-Hearing Association, Seattle, WA.

Wilson, D. K. (1972). *Voice problems of children.* Baltimore: Williams & Wilkins.

Wilson, D. K. (1979). *Voice problems of children* (2nd ed.). Baltimore: Williams & Wilkins.

Wingfield, A., Lombardi, L., & Sokol, S. (1984). Prosodic features and the intelligibility of accelerated speech: Syntactic versus prosodic segmentation. *Journal of Speech and Hearing Research, 27*, 128–134.

Witt, A. E., & Steele, A. L. (1984). Music therapy for infant and parent: A case example. *Music Therapy Perspectives, 1*(4), 17–19.

Wode, H. (1980). Grammatical intonation in child language. In L. R. Waugh & C. H. van Schooneveld (Eds.), *The melody of language: Intonation and prosody* (pp. 331–345). Baltimore: University Park Press.

Yorkston, K. M. (1988). Prosody in the adult. In D. E. Yoder & R. D. Kent (Eds.). *Decision making in speech-language pathology* (pp. 146–147). Toronto: Decker.

Yorkston, K., & Beukelman, D. (1981). Ataxic dysarthria: Treatment sequences based on intelligibility and prosodic considerations. *Journal of Speech and Hearing Disorders, 46*, 398–404.

Yorkston, K. M., Beukelman, D. R., & Bell, K. R (1988). *Clinical management of dysarthria speakers.* Boston: Little, Brown.

Yoss, K. A., & Darley, F. L. (1974). Therapy in developmental apraxia of speech. *Language, Speech, and Hearing Services in Schools, 5*, 23–31.

Zoller, M. B. (1991). Use of music activities in speech-language therapy. *Language, Speech, and Hearing Services in Schools, 22*, 272–276.

INDEX

Treatment Approaches

Please also see Clinical Notes for each prosodic feature or component for information on using treatment approaches.

DURATION TREATMENT APPROACHES

LOUDNESS TREATMENT APPROACHES

PAUSE TREATMENT APPROACHES

Purpose/Focus Combination	*Purpose/Focus Combination*

Direct/Intraturn
    Description, 115
    Sample program, 116–117
	Indirect/Intraturn
	    Description, 118–122
	    Sample program, 122–123

Direct/Interturn
    Description, 115, 118
    Sample program, 120
	Indirect/Interturn
	    Description, 122
	    Sample program. *See* Appendixes A, B, and C

PITCH TREATMENT APPROACHES

Purpose/Focus Combination	*Purpose/Focus Combination*

Direct/Pitch Height
    Description, 44–45
    Sample program, 46–47
	Indirect/Pitch Height
	    Description, 54
	    Sample program, 55–56

Direct/Pitch Slope or Declination
    Description, 45
    Sample program. *See* Appendixes A B, E, 57–59
	Indirect/Pitch Slope or Declination
	    Description, 56
	    Sample program, 57–59

Direct/Pitch Direction
    Description, 45
    Sample program, 51
	Indirect/Pitch Direction
	    Description, 56, 59, 62
	    Sample program, 60–62

Direct/Pitch Variation
    Description, 45, 47, 50
    Sample program, 52–53
	Indirect/Pitch Variation
	    Description, 62–63
	    Sample program, 64

PROSODIC COMPONENTS

Intonation Treatment Approaches

Purpose/Focus Combination	*Purpose/Focus Combination*

Direct/Onset
    Description, 162
    Sample programs. *See* Appendixes A, B, and E
	Indirect/Onset
	    Description, 169
	    Sample programs. *See* Appendixes A, B, and E

Rhythm Treatment Approaches

Stress Treatment Approaches

INDEX

Subject